Best of the Best

Recipe Hall of Fame Dessert Cookbook

Winning Recipes from Hometown America

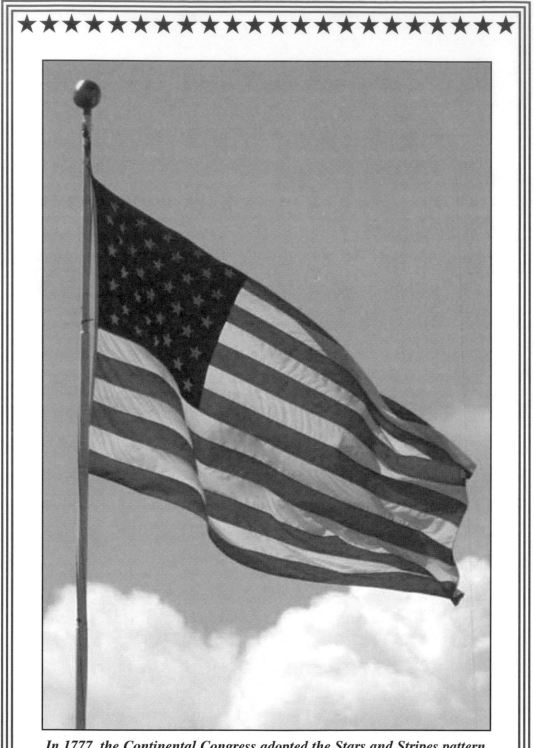

In 1777, the Continental Congress adopted the Stars and Stripes pattern for our national flag. Since then, the Star Spangled Banner has undergone a series of transformations, but has always remained a steadfast symbol of unity, freedom and justice.

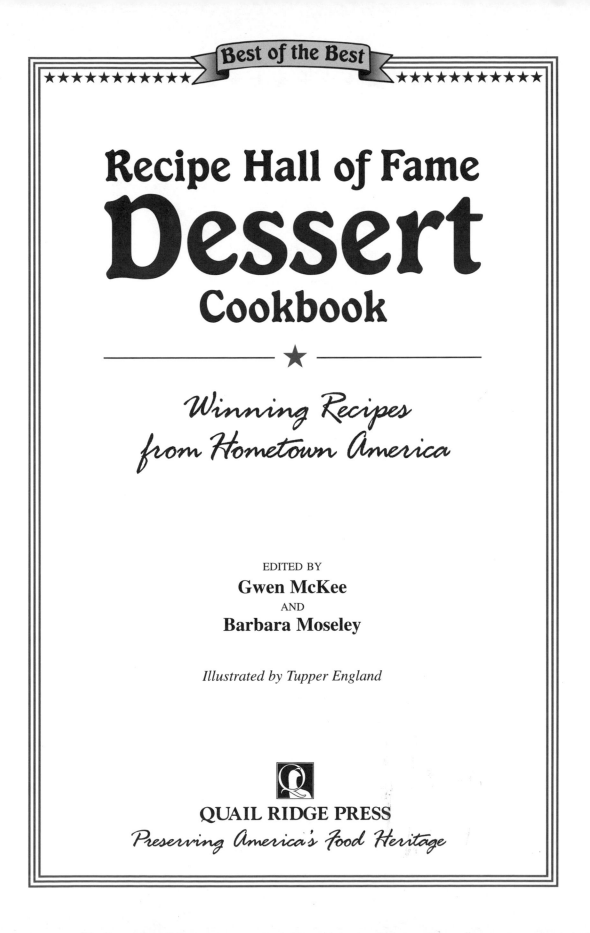

Best of the Best

Recipe Hall of Fame Dessert Cookbook

Winning Recipes from Hometown America

EDITED BY

Gwen McKee

AND

Barbara Moseley

Illustrated by Tupper England

QUAIL RIDGE PRESS

Preserving America's Food Heritage

Library of Congress Cataloging-in-Publication Data

Recipe hall of fame dessert cookbook: winning recipes from hometown America / edited by Gwen McKee and Barbara Moseley;
illustrated by Tupper England.
p. cm. — (Best of the best cookbook series)
Includes index.
ISBN 1-893062-19-8
1. Desserts. I. McKee, Gwen. II. Moseley, Barbara. III. Quail Ridge Press cookbook series.
TX773.R28 2000
641.8'6—dc21 00-042511
CIP

ISBN 1-893062-19-8

Book design by Cynthia Clark
Food styling by Bobbi Cappelli / Cover photo by Greg Campbell
Printed in Canada

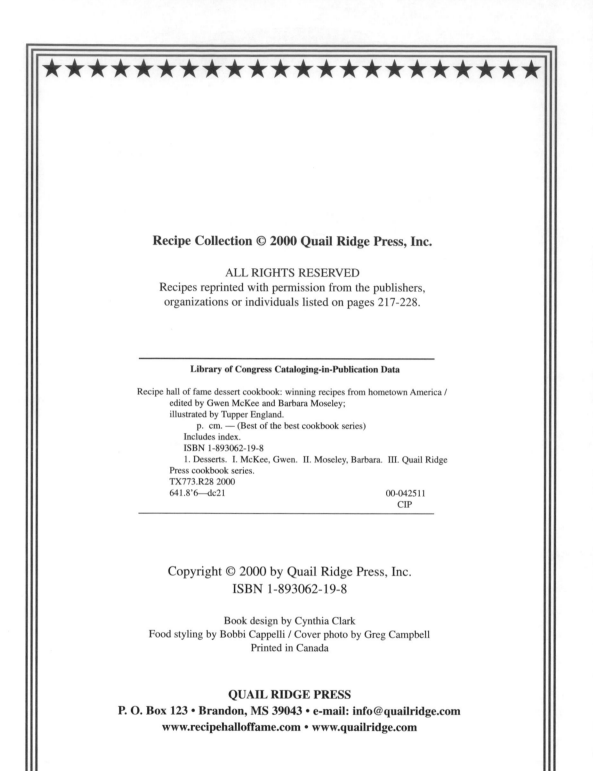

QUAIL RIDGE PRESS
P. O. Box 123 • Brandon, MS 39043 • e-mail: info@quailridge.com
www.recipehalloffame.com • www.quailridge.com

Contents

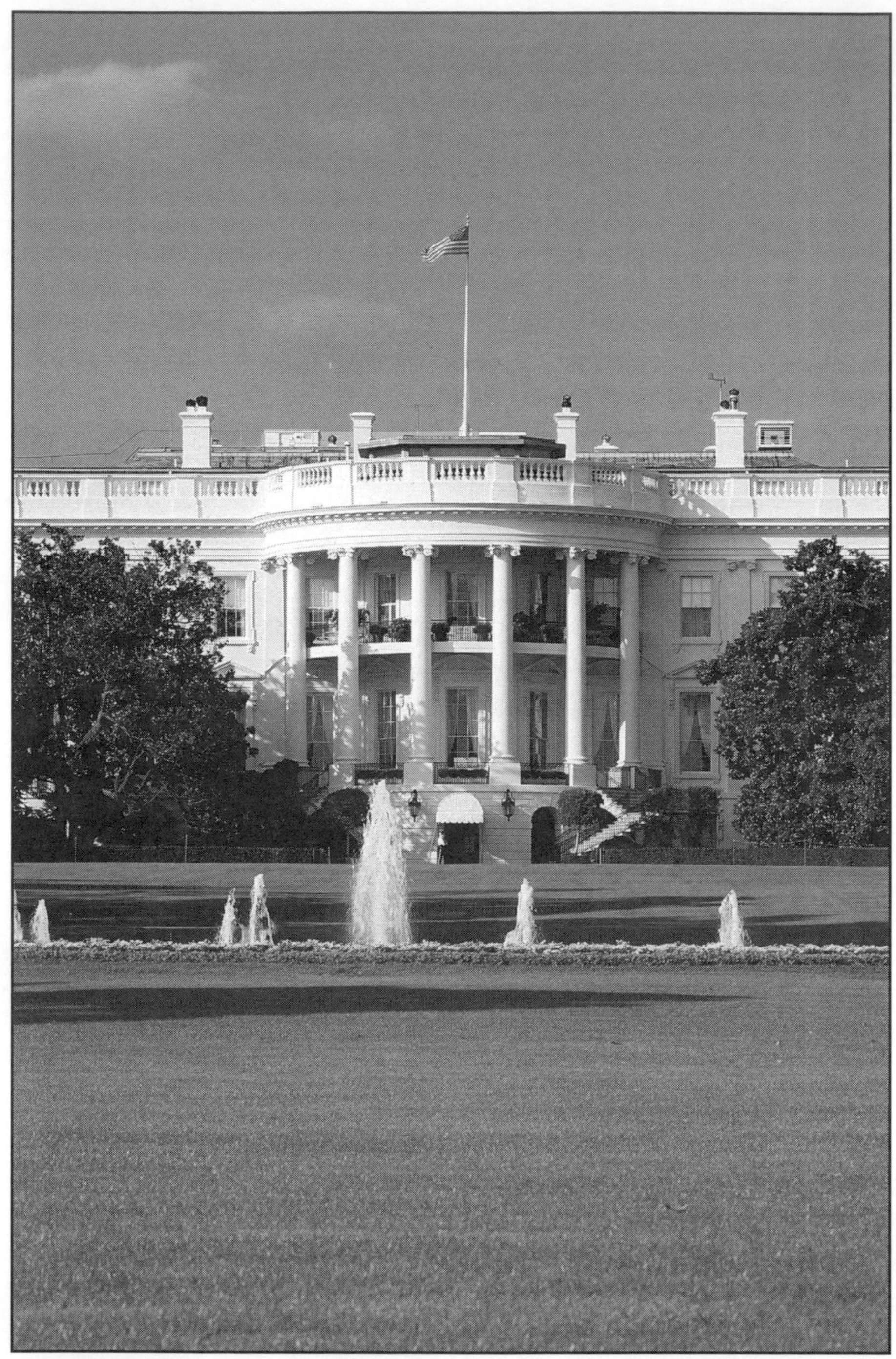

Every President but one has lived in the White House, the exception being George Washington, who directed the building of the house during his presidency.

Preface

What's for dessert? A strawberry shortcake? A flaky apple pastry? A light soufflé? How about cheesecake? Or let's just have some cookies and ice cream! No matter what dessert you choose, it is most often the highlight of the meal.

Because we have heard this over and over, and because we count ourselves among true dessert lovers, we have compiled the most popular, most requested, most memorable knock-your-socks-off desserts for the *Recipe Hall of Fame Dessert Cookbook.* WOW!

Where did these incredible recipes come from? Well, in one word, *America.* Its many cultures, many tastes, many cuisines, are all represented within the pages of this cookbook. America the beautiful is also America the delicious!

But more specifically, these recipes were chosen from the more than 4,000 dessert recipes in our BEST OF THE BEST STATE COOKBOOK SERIES, each of which was already a chosen favorite from their state. Some 2,000 cookbooks from around the country who are contributors to their state's individual BEST OF THE BEST COOKBOOK (see page 238 for a complete listing), sent us their selections: "These are our best recipes, and we are proud to share them." Below each recipe you can see which cookbook and state the recipe represents, then in a contributor section (beginning on page 217), you can find out more specifics about each cookbook. From large publisher's cookbooks to small community treasures, each of these cookbooks has added a delicious contribution.

As you may know, the predecessor to this cookbook is the very successful *Recipe Hall of Fame Cookbook,* for which there were so very many dessert recipes nominated that space would allow only a small percentage to be included. The natural solution was to create a book of desserts alone to showcase an exceptional array of fabulous cakes, pies, puddings, ice creams, soufflés, cookies, candies, trifles, and tortes that are deserving of their own recognition. Enter *The Recipe Hall of Fame Dessert Cookbook.*

And enter it does! This entirely new selection of over 300 winning dessert recipes has been selected and tested from outstanding cookbooks all over the country. From old standards like Red Velvet Cake and Black Bottom Pie, to new and exciting creations like Pastry Tulip Cups and Mocha Polka Nut Torte, to quick and easy favorites like Pecan Crunchies and Lonesome Cowboy Bars, these recipes are absolutely to die for! As in the original *Recipe Hall of Fame Cookbook,* the criteria for selection is the same:

1. Taste, 2. Taste, and 3. **Taste!**

You might be surprised to find out that most of these recipes are not at all difficult to prepare. What in the world are Easy Lemon Bars and Salted Nut Rolls doing in a Recipe Hall of Fame? The reason is quite plain: People vote for recipes that are easy to make, that are most often requested, and that they like making over and over again because they enjoy the compliments! We call these recipes "unpretentious," because they may use package mixes and any shortcuts possible to bring about the quickest, most delicious results. And besides, nobody needs to know how simple Lazy Betty and Margarita Pie are to make. Let them think you slaved for hours and hours. They'll think you are a terrific cook. And guess what? You are!

Many people deserve credit for helping to put this book together. We wish to thank the contributors for their wonderful recipes. Hooray for all these people who created, discovered, handed down, and shared these delicious desserts with us. We applaud you and we thank you. Thanks also to tourist bureaus, chambers of commerce, food editors, and other people-in-the-know, who enabled us to enhance this book with facts, figures, and photographs from their area of America. Our creative illustrator, Tupper England, waved her American flag proudly in capturing some of the places these recipes came from. Thanks, once again, Tup. Our staff deserves a big hug for all their dedication in making it just right. Without the help of all these people, this book would not be.

In our travels throughout the United States, we have followed cooking traditions and heritages that have taught us quite a bit about what people eat and what they like. Sometimes there is no way to improve on old standards, but often there is a new twist to an old favorite, the young cooks teaching the older cooks new tricks with modern ingredients and equipment. We have found and firmly believe that cooking should be fun. Perhaps within the pages of this cookbook, you will find a recipe that tastes just like your Grammy's Chocolate Pie, or Aunt Clara's Peach Ice Cream, or Gran Sally's Bread Pudding. We encourage you to invite your children, grandchildren or great-grandchildren into your kitchen to join in the cooking; you'll reap the rewards of seeing their smiling faces when they take their very own cookies out of the oven. Now you are creating a memory that will be passed on and enjoyed for many cooks to come.

We are extremely pleased to share these outstanding recipes. The proof is in the pudding, so we invite you to enjoy desserts that are truly THE BEST OF THE BEST OF **THE BEST!**

Gwen McKee and Barbara Moseley

Cakes

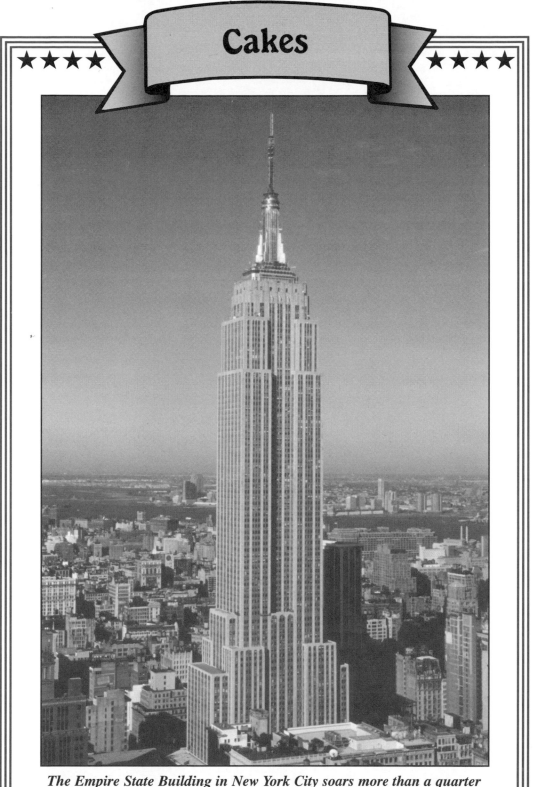

The Empire State Building in New York City soars more than a quarter mile into the Manhattan sky. On a clear day visitors can see up to 80 miles, viewing the states of Connecticut, New Jersey, Pennsylvania and Massachusetts, as well as New York.

Red Velvet Cake

2 (1-ounce) bottles red food coloring
3 tablespoons cocoa
½ cup shortening
1½ cups sugar
2 eggs
1 cup buttermilk
2¼ cups flour
¼ teaspoon salt
1 teaspoon vanilla
1 tablespoon vinegar
1 teaspoon baking soda

Mix together food coloring and cocoa into paste and let stand. Cream shortening and sugar. Add eggs and coloring paste and mix well. Add buttermilk by hand. Add flour, salt, and vanilla. Beat well by hand. Add vinegar and baking soda. Bake at 350° for 30 minutes if using a 9x13-inch pan, or for 25 minutes in 3 (8-inch) cake pans.

FROSTING:
4 tablespoons flour
1 cup milk
½ cup butter, softened
½ cup shortening
1 cup sugar
Dash of salt
2 teaspoons vanilla

Cook flour and milk until thick. Cool. Cream remaining ingredients, then add to milk mixture.

San Ramon's Secret Recipes (California)

Black Magic Cake

1¾ cups flour
2 cups sugar
¾ cup cocoa
2 teaspoons baking soda
1 teaspoon baking powder
1 teaspoon salt
2 eggs
1 cup strong black coffee
1 cup buttermilk
½ cup vegetable oil
1 teaspoon vanilla

Preheat oven to 350°. Grease and flour Bundt pan; combine dry ingredients; add eggs, coffee, buttermilk, oil, and vanilla. Beat at medium speed 2 minutes. Batter will be thin. Bake 30-40 minutes. Serve each slice with a dollop of Caramel Fluff.

CARAMEL FLUFF:
2 cups chilled whipping cream
¾ cup brown sugar
1 teaspoon vanilla
Shaved chocolate

In a chilled bowl, beat whipping cream, brown sugar, and vanilla until stiff. Can sprinkle with shaved chocolate for additional decoration.

Auburn Entertains (Alabama)

Luscious Chocolate Cake

4 ounces unsweetened chocolate
1/3 cup butter or margarine
1 3/4 cups unsifted all-purpose flour
1 1/2 cups sugar
1 1/2 teaspoons baking soda
1 teaspoon salt
1 1/2 cups dairy sour cream
2 eggs
1 teaspoon vanilla

Melt baking chocolate and butter in top of double boiler, or microwave 1 minute on HIGH. Stir to blend well; cool. Combine remaining ingredients in large bowl; blend in melted chocolate. Beat 3 minutes at medium speed. Pour batter into a 9x13-inch greased and floured pan. Bake at 350° for 25-30 minutes. Frost with Chocolate Caramel Frosting.

CHOCOLATE CARAMEL FROSTING:

1/3 cup butter
1 cup brown sugar, packed
1/3 cup light cream or evaporated milk
2 ounces semisweet chocolate
2 cups confectioners' sugar
1 teaspoon vanilla

Melt butter; add brown sugar and light cream. Bring to boil over low heat, stirring. Remove from heat. Add semisweet chocolate, blend until melted. Pour into bowl. Cool at room temperature. Beat in confectioners' sugar and vanilla. Beat until smooth. May add milk to thin. Be sure to cool cake and frosting completely before icing cake.

Foresters' Favorite Foods (Georgia)

Holiday Chocolate Cake

Absolutely delicious.

2 cups sugar
1¾ cups unsifted all-purpose flour
¾ cup cocoa
2 teaspoons baking soda
1 teaspoon baking powder
1 teaspoon salt
2 eggs
1 cup buttermilk
1 cup strong black coffee
½ cup vegetable oil
2 teaspoons vanilla

Combine sugar, flour, cocoa, baking soda, baking powder, and salt in large bowl. Add eggs, buttermilk, coffee, oil, and vanilla. Beat at medium speed for 2 minutes (batter will be thin). Pour into 2 greased and floured 9-inch round cake pans. Bake at 350° for 30-35 minutes. Cool 10 minutes. Remove from pans. Cool completely.

Slice cake layers in halves horizontally. Place bottom slice on serving plate; top with ⅓ of Ricotta Cheese Filling. Alternate cake layers and filling, ending with cake on top. Frost with Chocolate Whipped Cream.

RICOTTA CHEESE FILLING:

1¾ cups (15 ounces) ricotta cheese
¼ cup granulated sugar
3 tablespoons Grand Marnier or orange-flavored liqueur or orange juice concentrate
¼ cup candied red or green cherries, coarsely chopped
⅓ cup semisweet chocolate mini-chips

Combine ricotta cheese, sugar, and liqueur in small bowl. Beat until smooth. Fold in candied fruit and mini-chips. (If ricotta cheese is unavailable, use 1 cup heavy cream. Whip with sugar and liqueur until stiff.)

CHOCOLATE WHIPPED CREAM:

⅓ cup confectioners' sugar
2 tablespoons cocoa
1 cup heavy cream
1 teaspoon vanilla

Combine sugar and cocoa in small bowl. Add cream and vanilla; beat until stiff. Cover top of cake.

A Tasting Tour Through Washington County (Kentucky)

Kentucky is known as the "Bluegrass State" because of the abundant growth of bluegrass in its rich limestone soil. Bluegrass is not really blue—it's green. But in the spring, it produces bluish-purple buds that give a rich blue cast to a large field.

Chocolate Cookie Sheet Cake

2 cups flour
2 cups sugar
½ teaspoon salt
1 teaspoon cinnamon
1 cup margarine
1 cup water
3 tablespoons cocoa
2 eggs
1 teaspoon soda
½ cup buttermilk
1 teaspoon vanilla

Sift flour, measure, and resift with sugar, salt and cinnamon. Bring to boil the margarine, water and cocoa. Pour over the flour and sugar mixture. Mix eggs, soda, buttermilk and vanilla together. Add to above mixture. Bake in a greased and floured 10½ x 15½ x 1-inch pan for 20 minutes at 350°. (May use 9 x 13-inch pan.) Cook about 40 minutes.

ICING:
½ cup margarine
2 tablespoons cocoa
6 tablespoons milk
1 box confectioners' sugar
½ cup chopped pecans
1 teaspoon vanilla

Start cooking icing the last 5 minutes cake is baking. Mix margarine, cocoa and milk in saucepan over low heat. Remove from heat and add sugar, nuts and vanilla. Frost cake while hot. Makes 36 squares. The cinnamon makes the difference!

Cotton Country Cooking (Alabama)

Fudge Upside Down Cake

¾ cup sugar
2 tablespoons butter
½ cup milk
1 cup flour
2 teaspoons baking powder
¼ teaspoon salt
2 tablespoons cocoa
½ cup chopped walnuts
½ cup brown sugar
½ cup sugar
⅓ cup cocoa
1½ cups boiling water

Cream together ¾ cup sugar and butter. Stir in milk. Sift flour, baking powder, salt, and 2 tablespoons cocoa together. Add to creamed mixture and beat until smooth. Stir in walnuts. Spread batter into a 9-inch square pan. In a small bowl, combine brown sugar, ½ cup sugar, and ⅓ cup cocoa. Sprinkle over batter. Pour boiling water over top. Bake at 350° for 35-40 minutes. The cake will rise to the top and boiling water will combine with the sugar/cocoa mixture to make a rich chocolate syrup underneath. Serve with ice cream, whipped cream or plain in sherbet glasses or sauce dishes.

What's Cooking in Melon Country (Colorado)

Frozen Kahlua Cake

A Must!

¾ cup butter, softened
2 cups sugar
¾ cup cocoa
4 egg yolks
1 teaspoon baking soda
2 tablespoons cold water
½ cup cold coffee
½ cup Kahlua
1⅓ cups flour
2 tablespoons vanilla extract
4 egg whites, beaten

Preheat oven to 325°. Cream butter and sugar. Add cocoa and egg yolks. Dissolve soda in water and combine with coffee and Kahlua; add to batter, alternating with flour. Add vanilla and fold in stiffly beaten egg whites. Grease and flour Bundt pan. Pour in batter; remove air bubbles. Bake 1 hour.

GLAZE:
1 cup powdered sugar
½ cup Kahlua

Combine glaze ingredients and pour over warm cake; cover with foil and freeze.

TOPPING:
1 cup whipping cream, whipped

About 1 hour before serving, remove from freezer onto cake plate and ice with whipped cream. Serves 12.

The Dallas Symphony Cookbook (Texas)

Angel Food Cake

Never fails, even in the classroom.

1½ cups egg whites
¼ teaspoon salt
1 teaspoon cream of tartar
1 cup sifted granulated sugar
1 cup powdered sugar
1 cup sifted cake flour
1 teaspoon vanilla
½ teaspoon almond extract

Set oven at 425° and put 10-inch angel food pan in oven to preheat. Beat egg whites, salt, and cream of tartar until stiff. Fold in granulated sugar 2 tablespoons at a time until all is used. Sift together the powdered sugar and cake flour 5 times. Fold it into the egg white mixture 2 tablespoons at a time. Add flavorings. Put in the tube pan and bake 23 minutes. Cool inverted.

Goodies and Guess-Whats (Colorado)

Amaretto Cake

1 cup butter
2½ cups sugar
6 eggs
1 cup sour cream
1 teaspoon vanilla
1 teaspoon orange extract
1 teaspoon lemon extract
2 teaspoons almond extract
¼ teaspoon baking soda
½ teaspoon salt
3 cups sifted cake flour
½ cup Amaretto di Saronno

Preheat oven to 325°. Have all ingredients at room temperature. Beat butter and sugar until creamy. Add eggs one at a time, beating well after each egg has been added. Add sour cream, beat, then add extracts, baking soda, and salt. Gradually beat in flour that has been sifted three times and then measured. Add Amaretto and beat well. Pour into large greased Bundt cake pan. Bake 1 hour until done. Turn out on wire rack and cool.

GLAZE FOR CAKE:

1 (8-ounce) jar orange marmalade
½ jar (about 4 ounces) apricot preserves
¼ cup Amaretto di Saronno
1 cup chopped toasted almonds

Heat marmalade, preserves, and Amaretto until melted. Drizzle on cooled cake then sprinkle with chopped toasted almonds.

Giant Houseparty Cookbook (Mississippi)

★ **Editor's Extra:** We also like using just apricot preserves instead of orange marmalade. This cake is outstanding even without the glaze.

Milk Chocolate Candy Bar Cake

CAKE:

2½ cups flour
¼ teaspoon salt
2 sticks butter or margarine, softened
2 cups sugar
4 eggs
12 ounces milk chocolate chips
1 cup chocolate syrup
¼ teaspoon soda
1 cup buttermilk
2 teaspoons vanilla

Grease and flour tube pan. Sift together the flour and salt. In a mixer bowl, cream butter and sugar. Add 4 eggs one at a time, mixing between each addition. Melt chocolate chips; add chocolate syrup. Mix soda and buttermilk and add to butter, sugar and egg mixture. Blend in flour, then chocolate mixture, and add vanilla. Pour into prepared pan and bake 2 hours at 300°.

ICING:

1½ cups sugar
1 cup evaporated milk
¼ stick butter or margarine
6 ounces milk chocolate chips
1 teaspoon vanilla

Put sugar, evaporated milk and butter in a saucepan over medium heat and bring to a boil. Boil 10 minutes. Add chocolate chips and vanilla. Beat until smooth and well mixed. Spread or pour over cooled cake. Serves 24.

Cookin' in the Spa (Arkansas)

Mississippi Mud Cake

2 sticks oleo or margarine
2 cups sugar
4 eggs
2 tablespoons cocoa
1½ cups all-purpose flour
1 cup angel flake coconut
1 teaspoon vanilla
1½ cups chopped pecans

Cream oleo or margarine with sugar. Add remaining ingredients and beat well after each addition. Bake in 9x13-inch greased and floured pan for 30-40 minutes at 350°.

FROSTING:

1 jar marshmallow cream
½ cup canned milk
1 box powdered sugar
⅓ cup cocoa
1 teaspoon vanilla
1 stick margarine, softened

While cake is still warm, spread with marshmallow cream and ice with mixture of remaining ingredients.

The Mississippi Cookbook (Mississippi)

Fudgy Peanut Butter Cake

2 cups flour
2 cups sugar
1 teaspoon baking soda
1 cup water
1 cup butter
¼ cup cocoa
½ cup buttermilk
2 eggs
1 teaspoon vanilla

Combine flour, sugar, and soda; mix well and set aside. Combine water, butter, and cocoa in a heavy saucepan on low heat. Bring to a boil, stirring constantly. Gradually stir into flour mixture. Stir in buttermilk, eggs, and vanilla. Pour into a greased and floured 9x13x2-inch baking pan; bake at 350° for 30 minutes or until a wooden pick inserted in center comes out clean. Let cake cool.

ICING:
1 cup peanut butter
1 tablespoon vegetable oil
¼ cup + 1 tablespoon butter
3 tablespoons cocoa
1 teaspoon vanilla
3 - 5 tablespoons buttermilk
2½ cups sifted powdered sugar

Combine peanut butter and oil; mix well. Spread on cooled cake. Combine butter and cocoa in a small saucepan; cook over low heat, stirring constantly, until butter melts and mixture is smooth. Remove from heat; add remaining ingredients. Beat until spreading consistency; spread over peanut butter mixture.

Cooking with Morehouse Parish Sheriff Ladies' Auxiliary
(Louisiana II)

Burnt Caramel Cake

This was before oleo, so my mother always used fresh-churned butter. This recipe has been in our family since my childhood. I've used it many times and it's always been one of our favorites.

½ cup sugar, burnt until dark
½ cup boiling water
1½ cups sugar
⅔ cup butter or oleo, softened
2 eggs, beaten
1 cup water
Pinch of salt
1 teaspoon vanilla
2 cups flour
2 teaspoons baking powder

In heavy pot or skillet, burn ½ cup sugar until dark. Put ½ cup boiling water in burnt sugar; let boil to a syrup (takes about 7 minutes). Cool but keep warm. Cream sugar and butter or oleo; add the beaten eggs and beat to a creamy batter. Then add water, salt, vanilla, and burnt syrup, leaving 2 tablespoons in the skillet for Icing. Add the flour and baking powder; beat for 2 minutes. Bake in 2 (9-inch) greased and floured cake pans in preheated 350° oven 25-30 minutes.

ICING:
2 tablespoons burnt syrup (from above)
2 cups sugar
3 tablespoons butter
⅔ cup milk or cream
2 tablespoons white corn syrup

Put 2 cups sugar in skillet with burnt syrup; add butter the size of a small egg, milk or light cream, and white corn syrup. Boil until it forms a soft ball in cold water; then cool and beat. Spread on cake. If icing gets too thick to spread, add a little cream or milk.

Recipes and Remembrances (Oklahoma)

Swiss-born Louis Chevrolet came to America to sell a wine pump he invented. He went on to design the first cars for the company that bore his name, now a division of General Motors. The Dodge brothers started out as bicycle manufacturers. After working briefly for Henry Ford, they founded Dodge Brothers, then later sold it to Chrysler.

Peanut Butter Sheet Cake

2 cups flour
1 teaspoon soda
2 cups sugar
½ teaspoon salt
1½ sticks margarine
½ cup Crisco oil
½ cup chunky peanut butter
1 cup water
2 eggs, slightly beaten
1 teaspoon vanilla
½ cup buttermilk

Mix flour, soda, sugar, and salt in mixing bowl. Bring margarine, oil, peanut butter, and water to boil. Pour over dry ingredients and mix well. Add beaten eggs, vanilla, and buttermilk and mix well. Pour into 11x15x1-inch sheet pan; bake 15-18 minutes at 350°.

While cake is baking, make icing. Let cake cool 5 minutes before spreading on icing.

PEANUT BUTTER CAKE ICING:
½ cup Milnot or milk
1 cup sugar
2 tablespoons margarine
½ cup extra crunchy peanut butter
½ cup miniature marshmallows
1 teaspoon vanilla

While peanut butter cake is baking, prepare this icing. Bring Milnot (evaporated milk), sugar, and margarine to boil and cook 2 minutes, stirring gently to keep from scorching. Remove from heat and stir in peanut butter, marshmallows, and vanilla until melted. Wait 5 minutes for cake to cool, then pour over cake and spread to cover.

Thank Heaven for Home Made Cooks (Oklahoma)

Black Bottom Cupcakes

1 (8-ounce) package cream cheese
½ cup sugar
1 egg, beaten
⅛ teaspoon salt
1 (6-ounce) package chocolate chips
1½ cups flour
1 cup sugar
¼ cup cocoa
1 teaspoon soda
½ teaspoon salt
1 cup water
⅓ cup salad oil
1 tablespoon vinegar
1 teaspoon vanilla

Combine cream cheese, sugar, egg, and salt. Stir in chocolate chips and set aside. This is topping for batter. Sift flour, sugar, cocoa, soda, and salt. Add water, salad oil, vinegar, and vanilla. Fill muffin pans ⅓ full of cocoa batter. Top with 1 tablespoon of cream cheese mixture. Bake at 350° for 20-25 minutes. Yields 18 cupcakes.

Hospitality (Texas)

Italian Cream Cake

½ cup shortening
½ cup margarine
2 cups sugar
5 eggs, separated
2 cups flour
1 cup buttermilk
Dash of salt
1 teaspoon baking soda
1 teaspoon vanilla
1 cup pecans, chopped
½ cup coconut

Cream shortening, margarine, sugar, and egg yolks (save egg whites) until fluffy. Sct aside. Mix flour, buttermilk, salt, soda, and vanilla and set aside. Beat egg whites until stiff and fold into buttermilk/flour mixture. Combine the two and add pecans and coconut. Mix well. Pour into greased/floured 9 x 13-inch pan and bake 30-40 minutes at 350°. Top with icing recommended below.

ICING:
1 stick margarine, softened
8 ounces cream cheese, softened
1 box powdered sugar
1 teaspoon vanilla
1 cup pecans, chopped

Cream margarine and cheese; then add powdered sugar, vanilla, and pecans, mixing well after each addition.

Joyce's Favorite Recipes (Tennessee)

Apricot Almond Cake

1 cup butter, softened
2 cups sugar
2 eggs
1 cup sour cream
1 teaspoon almond extract
2 cups flour
1 teaspoon baking powder
1 teaspoon salt
1 cup slivered almonds
1 (12-ounce) jar apricot preserves

Preheat oven to 350°. Cream butter and sugar until light. Beat in eggs, one at a time. Fold in sour cream and extract. Sift flour, baking powder and salt, and fold in. Put a third of the mixture in a greased and floured tube pan. Spread half of the almonds and half of the apricot preserves over the batter. Spoon in rest of batter. Add remaining preserves and top with remaining almonds. Bake for 1 hour 10 minutes at 350°. Yields 16 servings.

Per Serving: Cal 379; Prot 4 g; Chol 71 mg; Fiber 1 g; Percent of Calories: Prot 4%; Carbo 52%; Fat 44%

Palmetto Evenings (South Carolina)

Almond Cake with Raspberry Sauce

. . . has the consistency of cheesecake.

¾ cup sugar
½ cup unsalted butter, room temperature
8 ounces almond paste
3 eggs
¼ teaspoon almond extract
1 tablespoon kirsch or triple sec
¼ cup all-purpose flour
⅓ teaspoon baking powder
Confectioners' sugar

Combine sugar, butter and almond paste, blending well; beat in eggs, almond extract and liqueur. Gently blend in flour and baking powder just until mixed. Do not overbeat! Pour batter into a buttered and floured 8-inch round pan. Bake at 350° for 40-50 minutes or until tester comes out clean. Invert on a cake plate and sprinkle with confectioners' sugar.

SAUCE:

1 pint fresh, or 1 (12-ounce) package frozen, red raspberries
2 tablespoons sugar (or less) to taste

Combine ingredients in a blender container and purée. Press through a sieve to remove seeds. Serve over thin slices of cake. Serves 10-12.

Bluegrass Winners (Kentucky)

Lemon Jelly Cake

1 cup butter
2 cups sugar
3 cups flour
3 teaspoons baking powder
½ teaspoon salt
¾ cup milk
1 teaspoon vanilla
6 egg whites, stiffly beaten

Cream butter and sugar, beating until light and fluffy. Add sifted dry ingredients alternately with milk. Add vanilla. Fold in stiffly beaten egg whites. Pour into 3 greased round 9-inch layer pans. Bake at 350° for 25-30 minutes, or until top springs back when touched. Cool on racks.

LEMON JELLY FILLING:
½ cup butter
1 cup sugar
6 egg yolks
Grated rind of 2 lemons
Juice of 2 lemons

Combine all ingredients in top of double boiler. Cook over hot water, stirring constantly until thick, about 20-25 minutes. Cool completely, then put in freezer for a few minutes to firm up a little more. Spread between layers of cake and ice top and sides with 7-minute icing. If you prefer, spread filling between layers and on top, and sprinkle with coconut. Ice sides with 7-minute icing.

Into the Second Century (Mississippi)

★ **Editor's Extra:** To make 7-minute icing, beat 2 egg whites, 2 cups of sugar, and ⅓ cup water over boiling water for 7 minutes, or until stiff. Beat in 1 teaspoon vanilla.

Sour Cream Lemon Pound Cake

1 cup butter, softened
3 cups sugar
6 eggs
¼ cup lemon juice
1 tablespoon grated lemon rind
3 cups flour
½ teaspoon soda
½ teaspoon salt
1 cup sour cream

Cream butter and sugar. Add eggs one at a time, beating well after each. Add lemon juice and rind. Mix flour, soda, and salt together and add alternately with sour cream to the creamed mixture. Pour into greased and floured 10-inch angel food pan (16-cup size). Bake at 325° for 1 hour and 30 minutes, or until it tests done. Cool 15 minutes before turning out on rack to cool. If desired, a Lemon Glaze can be poured over cake.

LEMON GLAZE:
2 cups powdered sugar
¼ cup melted butter
¼ cup lemon juice
2 tablespoons grated lemon rind

Mix all ingredients together and beat until of spreading consistency.

Variations: Orange juice and grated orange rind can be substituted for lemon; ¼ cup poppy seed or ½ cup finely chopped pecans or walnuts can be added.

German Recipes (Iowa)

C's Pound Cake

This is a really good cake.

1 stick margarine, softened
1 cup Crisco
3 cups sugar
6 eggs
3½ cups flour
½ teaspoon baking powder
½ teaspoon salt
1 cup milk
1 tablespoon butternut flavoring

Blend margarine, Crisco and sugar until creamy. Add eggs, one at a time. Sift dry ingredients. Add alternately with milk. Add in flavoring. Pour in a greased and floured tube pan. Bake at 325° for about 1 hour and 15 minutes or until done.

CHOCOLATE GLAZE:
1 cup semisweet chocolate pieces
¼ cup white corn syrup
2 tablespoons water

Melt chocolate pieces in double boiler. Stir in syrup and water. Stir until smooth. Drizzle over cake.

Have Fun Cooking with Me (North Carolina)

Case's Orange Pound Cake

First to sell at any bake sale.

CAKE:

1 cup butter, softened
2 cups sugar
6 eggs
2 cups all-purpose flour
½ teaspoon orange extract
3 tablespoons orange juice
1 tablespoon lemon juice
Zest of 2 oranges*

Preheat oven to 350°. Cream butter and sugar. Add eggs, one at a time, and beat well after each. Gently beat in remaining ingredients. Bake in a greased and floured tube pan 45 minutes or until tester comes out clean. Cool in pan 10 minutes, turn out, and place top side up. Pour glaze over warm cake, if desired.

ORANGE GLAZE:

2 cups confectioners' sugar
4 tablespoons orange juice
½ teaspoon orange extract

Combine all ingredients and pour over warm cake. As cake cools, occasionally spoon glaze over the top and sides. Serves 16.

*The term "zest" refers to finely grating the outer layer of a whole orange, lemon or lime.

Gulfshore Delights (Florida)

7-Up Pound Cake

½ cup shortening
1 cup margarine, softened
2½ cups sugar
5 eggs
3 cups flour
8 ounces 7-Up
1 teaspoon vanilla
1 teaspoon butter flavoring

Cream shortening, margarine, and sugar together. Add eggs. Alternate flour, 7-Up, and flavors while adding into cream mixture and blending. Bake in a greased Bundt pan at 325° for 1 hour and 30 minutes.

Home Cookin' (Colorado)

Four Corners Monument is the only point in the U.S. where four states touch: New Mexico, Arizona, Colorado and Utah.

Five-Flavor Pound Cake

1 cup margarine, softened
½ cup shortening
3 cups sugar
5 eggs
3 cups all-purpose flour
1 teaspoon baking powder
1 cup milk
1 teaspoon each coconut, butter, rum, lemon, and vanilla flavoring

Cream together margarine, shortening, and sugar. Add eggs 1 at a time, beating thoroughly after each addition. Sift together flour and baking powder; add alternately to batter with milk. Add flavorings last and beat well. Bake in a 10-inch tube pan at 325° for 1½ hours. Cool in pan 10 minutes. Add Glaze, if desired.

GLAZE:

½ teaspoon each coconut, butter, rum, lemon, and vanilla flavoring
½ cup sugar
¼ cup water

Combine in heavy saucepan. Bring to a boil and stir until sugar is melted. Spoon half of hot mixture over cake before removing from pan. Keep remaining Glaze on low heat while Glaze soaks into cake, then turn out cake and spoon remaining Glaze over cake. Stays moist and freezes well.

Cooking with Tradition (Georgia)

Brown Sugar Pound Cake

3 cups flour
½ teaspoon baking powder
¼ teaspoon salt
¾ cup butter, room temperature
¾ cup shortening
1 (1-pound) box light brown sugar
1 cup sugar
5 large eggs
1 cup milk
1½ teaspoons vanilla
1 cup pecans, chopped

Into a large bowl, sift together the flour, baking powder, and salt. In another large bowl, cream the butter and shortening until light and creamy. Gradually add the brown sugar and sugar, mixing until light and creamy. Add eggs one at a time to the sugar, beating well after each addition. Add the dry ingredients alternately with the milk, ending with the dry ingredients, beating each addition just until blended. Stir in vanilla and nuts. Pour batter into a greased and floured 10-inch tube pan. Bake at 325° for 1 - 2 hours. Cool the cake upright for 10 minutes on a wire rack and let cool. Serve unfrosted. Serves 12-14.

Natchez Notebook of Cooking (Mississippi)

Coconut Pound Cake

2 sticks butter or margarine, softened
½ cup vegetable shortening
3 cups sugar
6 eggs
3 cups flour
1 cup milk
Dash of salt
½ teaspoon almond flavoring
½ teaspoon coconut flavoring
1 (3½-ounce) can grated coconut

Cream butter, shortening, and sugar. Add eggs, one at a time, beating 2 minutes after each egg. Add flour and milk alternately. Add salt and flavorings. Fold in coconut; pour into tube pan lined on bottom with waxed paper. Bake at 350° for 1 hour and 15 minutes. Start in COLD oven.

TOPPING:
1 cup sugar
1 cup water
1 teaspoon coconut flavoring

Boil 1 minute and pour over cake while hot. Serves 16-20.

The Nashville Cookbook (Tennessee)

★ **Editor's Extra:** In reference to butter and margarine, softened and room temperature mean the same thing. Easy to micro—soften firm butter 1½ to 2 minutes at 10% power.

Cherry Cake with Sauce

¼ cup shortening
¾ cup sugar
1 egg
1½ cups flour
2 teaspoons baking powder
½ teaspoon salt
½ cup milk
¼ teaspoon almond extract
2 cups sour cherries (well drained, reserve juice)
½ cup chopped walnuts

Cream shortening, sugar, and egg. Sift dry ingredients together and add to shortening mixture, alternating with milk. Add flavoring. Fold in cherries and nuts. Bake in greased 9-inch baking dish for 30-35 minutes at 375°.

SAUCE:
Reserved cherry juice with enough water to make 1 cup
¾ cup sugar
2 tablespoons cornstarch
Sweetened whipped cream for garnish, if desired

Mix juice mixture with sugar and cornstarch. Cook slowly, stirring while cooking, until thickened and clear. Serve sauce over individual pieces of warm cake. Garnish with whipped cream, if desired.

The Bell Tower Cookbook (Michigan)

Carrot Cake

Pineapple and coconut make this an outstanding cake.

2 cups sifted flour
2 teaspoons baking powder
1½ teaspoons baking soda
1 teaspoon salt
2½ teaspoons cinnamon
2 cups sugar
4 eggs
1½ cups oil
2 cups finely grated carrots
⅓ cup chopped pecans
1 (8-ounce) can crushed pineapple, drained
1 (3½-ounce) can flaked coconut

Sift together first five ingredients. Add sugar, eggs, and oil; mix well. Stir in carrots, pecans, pineapple, and coconut; blend thoroughly. Pour into three greased and floured 9-inch cake pans. Bake at 350° for 35-40 minutes. Cool briefly in pans, then turn onto racks. Cool completely.

CREAM CHEESE FROSTING:

¼ pound butter or margarine, softened
1 (8-ounce) package cream cheese, softened
1¼ teaspoons vanilla
1 (1-pound) box confectioners' sugar

Combine frosting ingredients. If frosting is too thick, add small amount of milk. Spread frosting between layers and on top of cake. Serves 10.

Sunny Side Up (Florida)

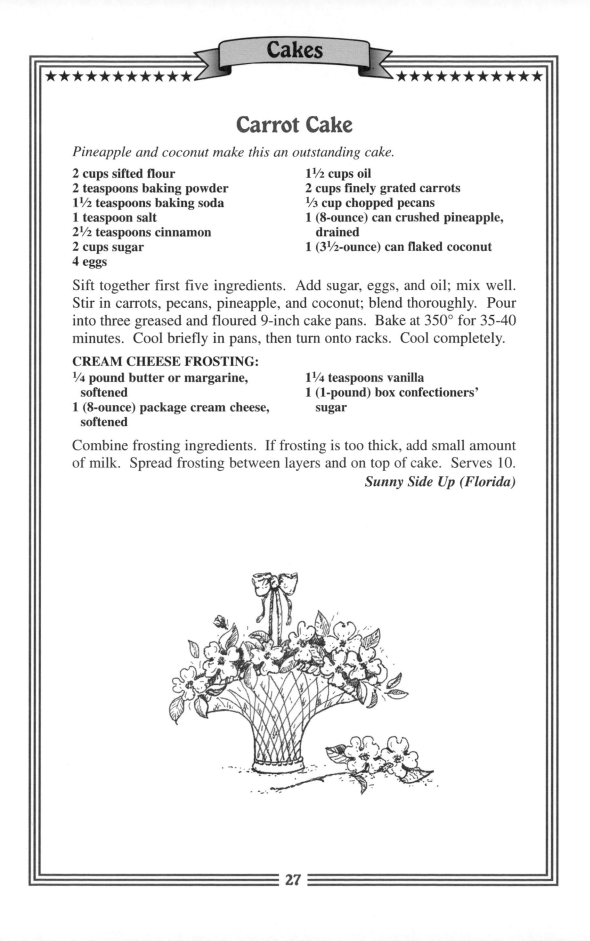

Caramel Apple Cake

The best!

CAKE:

3 eggs
2 cups sugar
1½ cups vegetable oil
2 teaspoons vanilla extract
3 cups flour
1 teaspoon salt
1 teaspoon baking soda
3 cups chopped, peeled apples
1 cup chopped pecans

In mixing bowl, beat eggs until foamy; gradually add sugar. Blend in oil and vanilla. Combine flour, salt, and baking soda; add to egg mixture. Stir in apples and pecans. Pour into a greased 10-inch tube pan. Bake at 350° for 1 hour 15 minutes. Cool in pan 10 minutes. Remove to serving plate.

TOPPING:

½ cup butter
¼ cup milk
1 cup packed brown sugar
Pinch salt

Combine all ingredients in saucepan; boil 3 minutes, stirring constantly. Slowly pour over warm cake. (Some topping will run down sides onto serving plate. Keep spooning back onto cake a few more times.)

Cooking with Grace (Wisconsin)

Mammy's Strawberry Shortcake

This recipe has been a family specialty for seven Southern generations.

1½ tablespoons butter
½ cup sugar
1 egg
3 tablespoons water
1 heaping cup flour
¼ teaspoon soda
¼ teaspoon baking powder
2 quarts strawberries
Whipped cream (optional)

Melt butter; add sugar, egg and water. Mix well. Sift flour, soda, and baking powder. Add to mixture to make batter the consistency of soft biscuit dough. Bake at 375° in 8-inch-square pan greased with butter for 20 minutes. This recipe may be doubled. To serve, split cake when cool, through the middle. Crush 2 quarts of strawberries and put part between the layers, the remainder on top. Serve with whipped cream, if desired.

Dixie Cookbook IV (Arkansas)

Classic Cranberry Cake with Sauce Topping

2 eggs
1 cup sugar
1 cup sour cream
1¾ cups flour
¼ teaspoon baking soda
1½ teaspoons baking powder
1 teaspoon vanilla
2 cups fresh cranberries, cut in half

Cream eggs and sugar; add sour cream. Reserve 2 tablespoons flour. Mix together the remaining flour, soda, and baking powder. Mix into batter. Add vanilla and mix again. Sprinkle the reserved flour over the halved cranberries and stir them into the batter with spoon. Pour the batter into greased and floured 9x13-inch pan. Bake 30 minutes at 350°.

SAUCE TOPPING:
1½ cups granulated sugar
1 cup whipping cream
2 tablespoons butter
1 teaspoon vanilla

Mix sugar, cream, and butter in medium saucepan; boil 2 minutes, stirring constantly. Remove from heat. Add vanilla. Serve warm sauce over cake. Sauce may be reheated as used.

Blessed Be the Cook (Wisconsin)

Threshers' Spice Cake

1½ cups sugar
½ cup butter
1 or 2 eggs
1 cup sour milk
1 teaspoon baking soda
2 cups flour
2 teaspoons cinnamon
¼ teaspoon cloves
¼ teaspoon allspice
¼ teaspoon nutmeg
1 cup raisins
1 cup chopped nuts

Preheat oven to 375°. Grease and flour a 9x13x2-inch pan. Cream sugar and butter. Add eggs. Stir soda into milk and add to mixture. Stir in remaining ingredients. Bake for 25 minutes, or until a toothpick inserted in center comes out clean. Yields 24 servings.

An Apple from the Teacher (Illinois)

★ **Editor's Extra:** To sour milk, use 1 tablespoon lemon juice or vinegar plus milk to make 1 cup. Let stand 5 minutes.

Do-Nothing-Cake
(Pineapple Goody Cake)

So easy.

2 cups flour
2 cups sugar
2 eggs
1 teaspoon soda
½ teaspoon salt
1 teaspoon vanilla
1 (20-ounce) can crushed pineapple, undrained

Put all ingredients in large bowl and mix with spoon (not mixer). Pour into 9x13x2-inch pan. Bake at 350° for 30-40 minutes or until center is done.

TOPPING:
1 stick butter or margarine
1 cup sugar
1 (5½-ounce) can evaporated milk
1 cup chopped nuts
1 cup coconut

Combine butter, sugar, and milk in small saucepan. Cook 5 minutes. Add nuts and coconut. Spoon on cake while hot. Yummy!

Granny's Kitchen (Virginia)

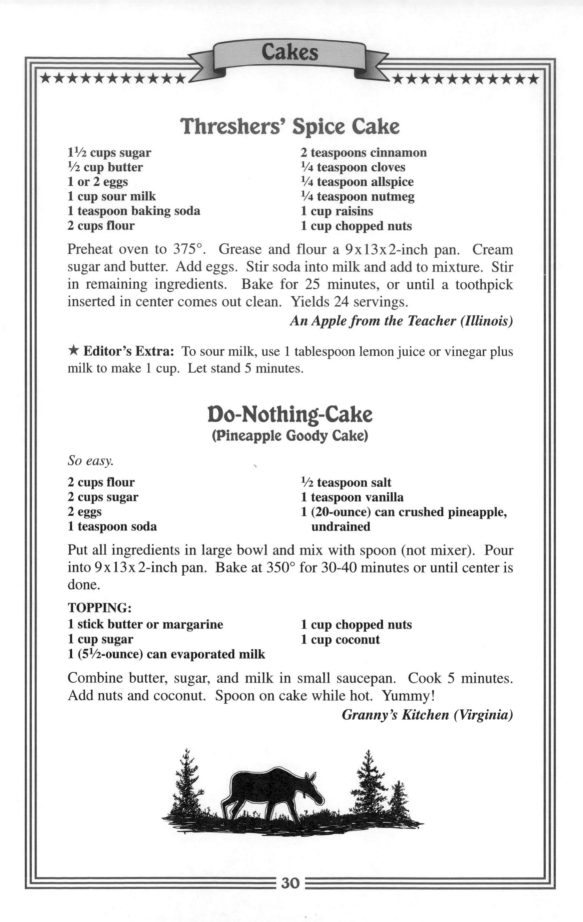

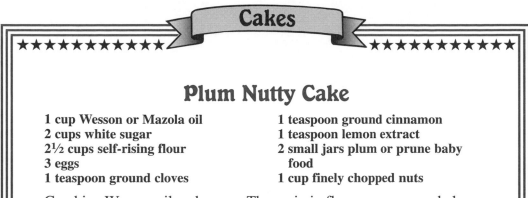

Plum Nutty Cake

1 cup Wesson or Mazola oil
2 cups white sugar
2½ cups self-rising flour
3 eggs
1 teaspoon ground cloves
1 teaspoon ground cinnamon
1 teaspoon lemon extract
2 small jars plum or prune baby food
1 cup finely chopped nuts

Combine Wesson oil and sugar. Then mix in flour, eggs, ground cloves, ground cinnamon, lemon extract and plum or prune baby food. After this is mixed well, add nuts. Grease Bundt pan. Pour in mixture. Bake at 325° for 55 minutes. (Start in cold oven.)

Feeding the Faithful (South Carolina)

Pumpkin Cake in a Jar

This dessert treat is baked and presented in a wide-mouth canning jar. Because the jar is sealed, the cake keeps indefinitely. It can be made well ahead of time. Great for small servings and to take as a gift.

⅔ cup shortening
2⅔ cups sugar
4 eggs
2 cups fresh or canned pumpkin
⅔ cup water
3½ cups flour
½ teaspoon baking powder
1½ teaspoons salt
1 teaspoon ground cloves
½ teaspoon allspice
1 teaspoon cinnamon
2 teaspoons soda
1 cup chopped walnuts

Cream shortening and sugar, adding sugar slowly. Beat in eggs, pumpkin and water. Sift together flour, baking powder, salt, cloves, allspice, cinnamon, and soda. Add to pumpkin mixture and stir well. Add nuts. Pour batter into 8 greased pint-size, wide-mouth jars (with lids and rings for sealing), filling half full. Place jars on cookie sheet.

Bake upright uncovered in preheated 325° oven about 45 minutes. Cake will rise and pull away from sides of jar. When done, remove one jar at a time. While still warm, place 8 wax paper circles cut to fit inside canning jars on top end of cake. Wipe sealing edge of jar. Place lid on jar and close tightly with ring. Turn jar upside down until sealed (lid will remain flat when pressed in center.)

To serve: Open jar, slide a knife around inside of jar to loosen cake, and remove from jar. Warm cake in oven, if desired. Slice and serve with whipped cream.

Duluth Woman's Club 70th Anniversary Cookbook (Minnesota)

★ **Editor's Extra**: This is also good substituting applesauce for pumpkin and pecans for walnuts.

Mother's Fruitcake

3 cups plain flour
1/4 teaspoon soda
1 teaspoon salt
1 teaspoon baking powder
1/2 teaspoon cinnamon
1/2 teaspoon nutmeg
1/2 teaspoon cloves or allspice
2 cups sugar
1 cup Crisco
4 large eggs
1 1/2 cups applesauce (or pear or pumpkin)
1 1/2 cups preserves (fig, pear, or peach)
2 cups blanched, steamed raisins (1 cup each light/dark)
1/2 cup cherries, cut in fourths
1 1/2 cups shredded coconut (optional)
2 cups chopped pecans
Cherry and pecan halves for decoration

Sift together first 7 ingredients and set aside. Cream sugar and Crisco. Add remaining ingredients, mixing after each addition. Add flour mixture. Cream well. Put in greased and floured tube pan. Decorate top with cherries and pecan halves. Bake at 300° for 2 1/2 - 3 hours.

Feast of Goodness (Louisiana II)

Tutti-Frutti Cake

1/4 cup orange juice
1 tablespoon lemon juice
1 1/4 cups sugar, divided
1/2 cup butter, softened
3 tablespoons finely grated orange peel
1 tablespoon finely grated lemon peel
1/2 cup seedless raisins, chopped
1 egg, beaten
1 1/3 cups sifted cake flour
1/2 teaspoon baking powder
1 teaspoon baking soda
1/2 teaspoon salt
1 cup buttermilk
Whipped cream

Combine fruit juices and 1/2 cup sugar. Stir until sugar dissolves. Let stand. Cream butter to consistency of mayonnaise. Add remaining sugar gradually while creaming. Beat in grated peels and raisins. Add egg; beat well. Mix and sift flour, baking powder, baking soda, and salt. Sift into butter mixture alternately with buttermilk.

Bake in a 9-inch well-greased-and-floured square cake pan at 350° for about 40 minutes or until cake tests done. Remove from oven, spoon juice/sugar mixture evenly over top. Cool in pan. Cut in squares to serve with whipped cream. Yields 9 servings.

Ferndale Friends Cook Book (Michigan)

Blackberry Jam Cake with Caramel Icing

Mother's recipe for blackberry jam cake has always been particularly popular with the men.

1 cup butter, softened
1 cup sugar
4 eggs
2½ cups flour
1 teaspoon baking soda
1 teaspoon nutmeg
¼ cup buttermilk
1½ cups blackberry jam

Cream butter and sugar. Add eggs one at a time, beating well after each addition. Sift flour, soda and nutmeg together and add to the batter, alternating with buttermilk and jam, beginning and ending with flour mixture. Pour into 3 greased and lined 8- or 9-inch layer pans and bake at 375° for about 25 minutes or until done. When cool, spread with Caramel Icing.

CARAMEL ICING:
2 cups dark brown sugar
2 tablespoons butter
½ cup rich milk
1 teaspoon vanilla
¼ teaspoon cream of tartar
Pinch of salt

Mix sugar, butter and milk in a saucepan. Cook over medium heat, stirring constantly until mixture is dissolved. Cook 10 minutes more or until the soft ball stage is reached. Remove from heat, add vanilla, cream of tartar and salt, and beat until the icing begins to thicken. Spread on cake.

The Smithfield Cookbook (Virginia)

Aunt Eileen's Peach Cake

Easy, can prepare ahead.

4 eggs
2 cups sugar
1 cup vegetable oil
3 cups all-purpose flour
1 teaspoon salt
1 tablespoon baking powder
¼ cup orange juice
2½ teaspoons vanilla
2 cups sliced fresh peaches
¼ cup sugar
2 teaspoons cinnamon
Confectioners' sugar

Preheat oven to 350°. Beat eggs, and add sugar and oil, mixing well. Combine flour, salt, and baking powder; add to egg mixture alternately with orange juice. Add vanilla extract. In a separate bowl, toss peaches with sugar and cinnamon. Pour one-third batter into a greased, lightly floured tube pan. Layer one-half peach mixture over it. Cover with one-third batter and the remaining peach mixture. Spread remaining batter over all. Bake 1 hour. Cool cake 10 minutes before turning out onto a wire rack. Sprinkle with confectioners' sugar. Serves 10.

Note: Two cups fresh blueberries or 2 - 3 large apples, peeled, cored, and thinly sliced, may be substituted for peaches.

Atlanta Cooknotes (Georgia)

Pineapple Upside-Down Cake

⅓ cup butter
½ cup chopped nuts
1 cup light brown sugar
1 large can sliced pineapple
½ cup butter, softened
1 cup sugar
2 eggs
1½ cups flour
½ cup milk
½ teaspoon vanilla
1 teaspoon baking powder

Melt ⅓ cup butter in iron skillet (or 9x13-inch pan). Mix nuts with brown sugar and spread over butter. Lay pineapple slices evenly over mixture. Cream ½ cup butter and 1 cup sugar. Add eggs, beating well after each. Add flour and milk, a little at a time. Then add vanilla and baking powder. Pour over pineapple and bake at 350° for 30 minutes. Let stand about 5 minutes; then invert. Serves 10-12.

Nell Graydon's Cook Book (South Carolina)

Upside-Down Apple Cake

4 or 5 tart cooking apples
Lemon juice
2 tablespoons butter
1 cup (packed) light brown sugar, sifted
1 egg
1 cup sugar
1 cup whipping cream
1 teaspoon vanilla extract
2 cups all-purpose flour
2 teaspoons baking powder
Confectioners' sugar

Peel apples and remove cores. Slice apples paper-thin, then sprinkle lightly with lemon juice to keep from discoloring. Place butter in a 9-inch round, shallow baking dish. Place in a preheated 325° oven until melted, then remove from oven. Do not turn off heat. Sprinkle brown sugar over butter. Overlap apple slices in baking dish, working from center to edges, until bottom is covered.

Place egg in a medium-size mixing bowl and beat well with an electric mixer. Add sugar gradually and beat until mixed. Mix cream and vanilla. Sift flour with baking powder, then add to egg mixture alternately with cream mixture, beating well after each addition. Pour over apples. Bake for about 35 minutes or until a cake tester inserted comes out clean. Let cool 10 minutes, then turn onto a rack and cool. Place on a cake plate and cut into servings. Sprinkle with confectioners' sugar. Yields 8 servings.

Dining Under the Magnolia (Alabama)

Eggnog Cakes

¾ cup butter, softened
1¼ cups sugar
8 egg yolks
2½ cups sifted flour
3 teaspoons baking powder
¼ teaspoon salt
¾ cup milk
1 teaspoon vanilla
½ cup chopped nuts
½ box vanilla wafers, crushed

Cream butter and sugar well. Add egg yolks and blend well. Sift dry ingredients 3 times; add to sugar mixture alternately with milk and vanilla. Beat until smooth. Pour into 3 square pans lined with waxed paper. Bake 20 minutes at 350°. After cake cools, cut into small squares.

Dip squares of cakes on all sides with Whiskey Sauce and roll in mixture of chopped nuts and crushed vanilla wafers. Store in airtight container. Improves with age. Do not taste for 3 days. Freezes well.

WHISKEY SAUCE:
1 stick butter, softened
1 (1-pound) box confectioners' sugar, sifted
1 cup bourbon

Cream butter and sugar. Add bourbon and mix well.

The Pick of the Crop (Mississippi)

Polynesian Cake

This is a special cake.

1 cup oil
1¼ cups sugar
3 eggs
2 teaspoons vanilla
2 small jars strained carrots*
2 cups flour
2 teaspoons cinnamon
2 teaspoons baking powder
1 small can crushed pineapple, drained
½ pound coconut
1 cup chopped nuts

Beat oil, sugar, eggs, vanilla, and carrots in mixer. Add dry ingredients that have been sifted together 2 times. Add pineapple, coconut, and nuts. Bake in greased Bundt pan 350° for 50-55 minutes. Frost with Cream Cheese Frosting.

CREAM CHEESE FROSTING:
1 (3-ounce) package cream cheese, softened
2 tablespoons butter, softened
1 teaspoon vanilla
2 - 3 cups powdered sugar

Combine; thin with a little cream to make it spread nicely.

*Can use 1 cup cooked mashed carrots or grated carrots.

Oma's (Grandma's) Family Secrets (Iowa)

Perfect Cake

A beautiful heirloom cake . . . and delicious!

1 cup butter
2 cups sugar
5 eggs
1 teaspoon vanilla extract
3½ cups cake flour
2½ teaspoons baking powder
¼ teaspoon salt
1 cup milk

Cream butter and sugar until light and fluffly. Add eggs, one at a time, beating well after each addition. Blend in vanilla. Sift the flour, baking powder and salt together and then add alternately with the milk, blending thoroughly. Pour batter into 3 or 4 (9-inch) round greased and floured cake pans. Bake at 350° for 25-30 minutes or until cake tests done. Frost top, sides and layers with Perfect Cake Icing.

PERFECT CAKE ICING:

2 cups sugar
1 cup water
¼ cup white Karo Syrup
3 egg whites, stiffly beaten
1 teaspoon vanilla extract

Boil sugar, water and syrup together until it spins a thread. Pour slowly and in a very thin stream over stiffly beaten, but not dry, egg whites, beating constantly. Beat until stiff enough to hold its shape. Blend in the vanilla extract and then add the following:

1 fresh coconut, grated
1 small can pineapple, crushed and drained
1 cup chopped pecans
1 small bottle maraschino cherries, chopped in small pieces

After blending, spread immediately on cake. You may also use a Seven Minute Frosting instead of the cooked frosting; however, I prefer the cooked frosting since the frosting will hold its shape on the cake until it is all eaten.

Bevelyn Blaire's Everyday Cakes (Georgia)

Fresh Coconut Cake with Rum and Orange Filling

A coconut cake is a traditional holiday dessert in the South. This cake's delicious flavor comes from including grated orange rind in the batter, orange juice and rum on the layers, and an orange filling between the layers. It may be made well in advance and frozen.

¾ cup butter, softened
1½ cups sugar
2 eggs, separated
2 cups flour
2 teaspoons baking powder
¼ teaspoon salt
¾ cup milk
1 orange rind, grated

Preheat oven to 350°. Grease the bottom of two 9-inch cake pans. Cut wax paper to fit the bottoms, and grease and flour the wax paper. Cream the butter and sugar until light and fluffy. Beat in egg yolks one at a time. Sift the flour, baking powder, and salt together. Add alternately with milk, beginning and ending with dry ingredients. Whip egg whites until stiff but not dry. Fold into the cake batter along with the grated orange rind. Pour the batter into the pans and bake at 350° for about 25 minutes or until a toothpick inserted in the middle comes out clean. Let the cakes cool in the pans for a few minutes, invert onto rack, and peel off wax paper.

¼ cup orange juice
½ cup rum

Slice the layers in half to get 4 thin layers, prick with a fork, and drizzle with the mixture of orange juice and rum. Set aside.

1 cup sugar
¼ teaspoon salt
4 tablespoons cornstarch
1 cup orange juice
2 tablespoons butter
1 orange rind, grated
2 tablespoons lemon juice

In saucepan, blend sugar with salt and cornstarch until mixture is smooth. Gradually add orange juice and bring to a boil on top of stove. Boil 1 - 2 minutes, remove from heat, and stir in butter, orange rind, and lemon juice. Cool. Spread ⅓ of mixture on first layer; stack second and third layers, repeating process. Add fourth layer.

8 ounces heavy cream
2 teaspoons rum
⅓ cup sugar
Grated meat of 1 fresh coconut

Whip cream until soft peaks form and add rum and sugar. Continue to whip until stiff. Spread over cake and pat shredded coconut onto sides and top. Yields one 4-layer 9-inch cake.

Fearrington House Cookbook (North Carolina)

Myrtle's Famous Banana Cake

1¾ cups sugar
½ cup butter, softened
2 eggs, beaten
1 teaspoon baking soda
½ cup buttermilk
1 cup mashed bananas
2¼ cups sifted cake flour
1 teaspoon vanilla flavoring

Cream together sugar and butter. (High-grade margarine can be substituted for the butter, if you prefer, but that is something Myrtle would never do.) When mixture is light and fluffy, add eggs and continue beating until smooth. Dissolve baking soda in buttermilk and stir into batter. Add bananas, cake flour, and flavoring. Mix well and pour into 2 greased and floured (8-inch) pans or one (9x13-inch) baking pan. Bake at 350° for 30-45 minutes. Can make 4 - 6 cupcakes as well as the flat cake, for this makes a generous amount of batter. The cupcakes take about 20 minutes to bake. Can frost with Brown Sugar Frosting. Makes about 20 servings.

BROWN SUGAR FROSTING:

3 tablespoons brown sugar, packed
3 tablespoons butter
3 tablespoons cream
1½ cups powdered sugar
1 teaspoon vanilla flavoring
Dash of salt

Heat brown sugar, butter, and cream together over low heat, stirring until well blended and sugar is dissolved. Remove from fire and stir in remaining ingredients, using enough powdered sugar to make of spreading consistency. When smooth and creamy, frost the cake.

Up a Country Lane Cookbook (Iowa)

King Cake

1 stick plus 1 tablespoon butter
⅔ cup fat-free evaporated milk
⅓ cup plus 2 tablespoons sugar
2 teaspoons salt
2 packages dry yeast
⅓ cup warm water
4 eggs
1 tablespoon grated lemon rind
2 tablespoons grated orange rind
5 cups plus 1 cup flour

In a saucepan, melt 1 stick butter, milk, ⅓ cup sugar, and salt. Cool to lukewarm. In a large mixing bowl, combine 2 tablespoons sugar, yeast, and water. Let stand until foaming, about 5 - 10 minutes. Beat eggs into yeast; then add milk mixture and rinds. Stir in flour, ½ cup at a time, reserving 1 cup to flour kneading surface. Knead dough until smooth, about 5 - 10 minutes. Place in large mixing bowl greased with 1 tablespoon butter, turning dough once to grease top; cover and let rise in a warm place until doubled, about 1½ - 2 hours.

1 stick butter, melted
¾ cup granulated sugar
½ cup dark brown sugar, packed
1 tablespoon cinnamon

Mix sugars and cinnamon; set aside.

When dough has doubled, punch down and divide in half. On a floured surface, roll half into a rectangle 30x15. Brush with half of melted butter and cut into 3 lengthwise strips. Sprinkle half of sugar mixture on strips, leaving a 1-inch lengthwise strip free for sealing. Fold each strip lengthwise toward the center, sealing the seam. You will now have three 30-inch strips with sugar mixture enclosed in each. Braid the 3 strips and make a circle by joining ends. Repeat with other half of dough. Place each cake on a 10x15-inch baking sheet, cover with a damp cloth, and let rise until doubled, about 1 hour.

1 cup sugar, colored (⅓ cup each of yellow, purple, and green)
1 egg, beaten
2 (¾-inch) plastic babies or 2 beans

Tint sugar by mixing food coloring until desired color is reached. For purple, use equal amounts of blue and red. A food processor aids in mixing, and keeps the sugar from being too moist.

Brush each cake with beaten egg and sprinkle with colored sugars, alternating colors. Preheat oven to 350°. Bake 20 minutes. Remove from pan immediately so sugar will not harden; while still warm, place 1 plastic baby in each from underneath. Makes two 9x12-inch cakes. Freezes well.

To freeze: Wrap cooled cake tightly in plastic. Before serving, remove plastic and thaw.

Jambalaya (Louisiana)

Pumpkin Jellyroll

3 eggs
⅔ cup pumpkin
1 cup sugar
¾ cup flour
1 teaspoon lemon juice
1 teaspoon baking powder
2 teaspoons cinnamon
1 teaspoon ginger
½ teaspoon nutmeg
Chopped nuts (optional)

FILLING:
1 cup powdered sugar
2 (3-ounce) packages cream cheese
4 tablespoons soft oleo (or butter)
½ teaspoon vanilla

Line a 10x15-inch jellyroll pan with foil and spray with cooking spray. Beat eggs for 5 minutes and add rest of ingredients. Pour mixture in foil-lined pan and bake at 375° for 15 minutes. Turn onto a kitchen towel that has been sprinkled with powdered sugar. Pull foil off and roll in towel to cool, starting at narrow end. When cool, unroll, spread with filling mixture and roll up jellyroll again.

125 Years–Walking in Faith (Iowa)

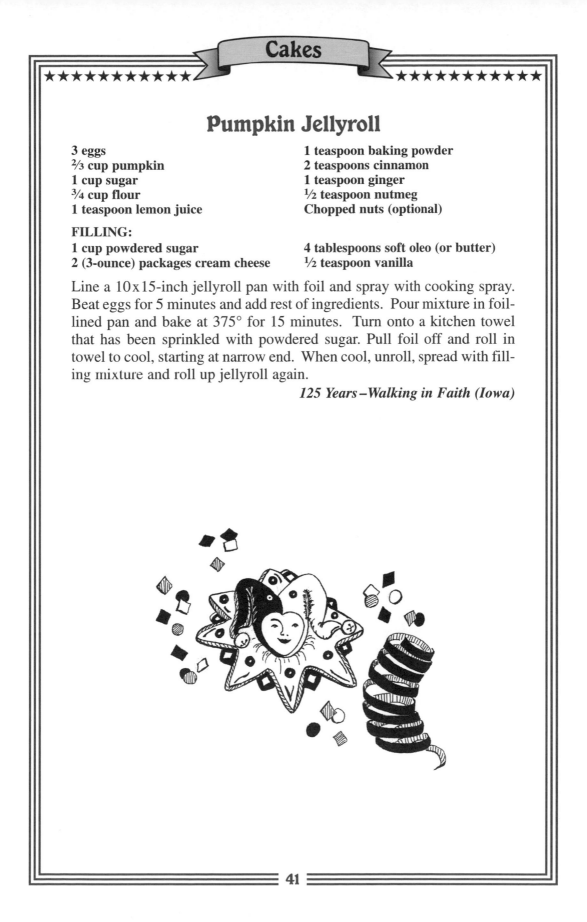

Angel Food Charlotte Russe Cake

1 cup sifted cake flour
1½ cups sugar, divided
1¼ cups egg whites
¼ teaspoon salt
1¼ teaspoons cream of tartar
1 teaspoon vanilla extract
¼ teaspoon almond extract

Sift flour before measuring, then sift four times with ½ cup of the sugar. Sift remaining cup of sugar. Add salt to egg whites and beat until foamy. Add cream of tartar; beat until they hold in peaks. Add sifted sugar a few tablespoons at a time, beating after each addition. Fold in vanilla and almond extracts. Fold in flour and sugar mixture ½ cup at a time. Pour into angel food cake pan and bake in moderate 375° oven for 35 minutes. Turn pan upside down and let cake cool for an hour before removing.

FILLING:

1 envelope gelatin
¼ cup cool water
¾ cup sherry
1 cup whipping cream
½ cup sugar

Dissolve gelatin in water. Heat sherry to boiling point; stir into gelatin mixture. Let cool. Whip cream, add sugar and fold into cooled gelatin mixture. Let congeal in refrigerator. Cut cake into two layers and place filling between layers and in hole. Ice with the following icing.

ICING:

4 egg whites
1 cup sugar
1 tablespoon corn syrup (white)
⅛ teaspoon cream of tartar

Place all ingredients in top of double-boiler and heat, stirring occasionally, until very hot. Pour into small bowl of electric mixer and beat at high speed 10 minutes or until it holds in peaks. Let cake stand overnight in refrigerator before serving. Serves 8-10.

This cake can be frozen very successfully if wrapped in heavy paper. Remove paper before starting to thaw cake to keep icing intact.

Charleston Receipts (South Carolina)

Cake Mix Creations

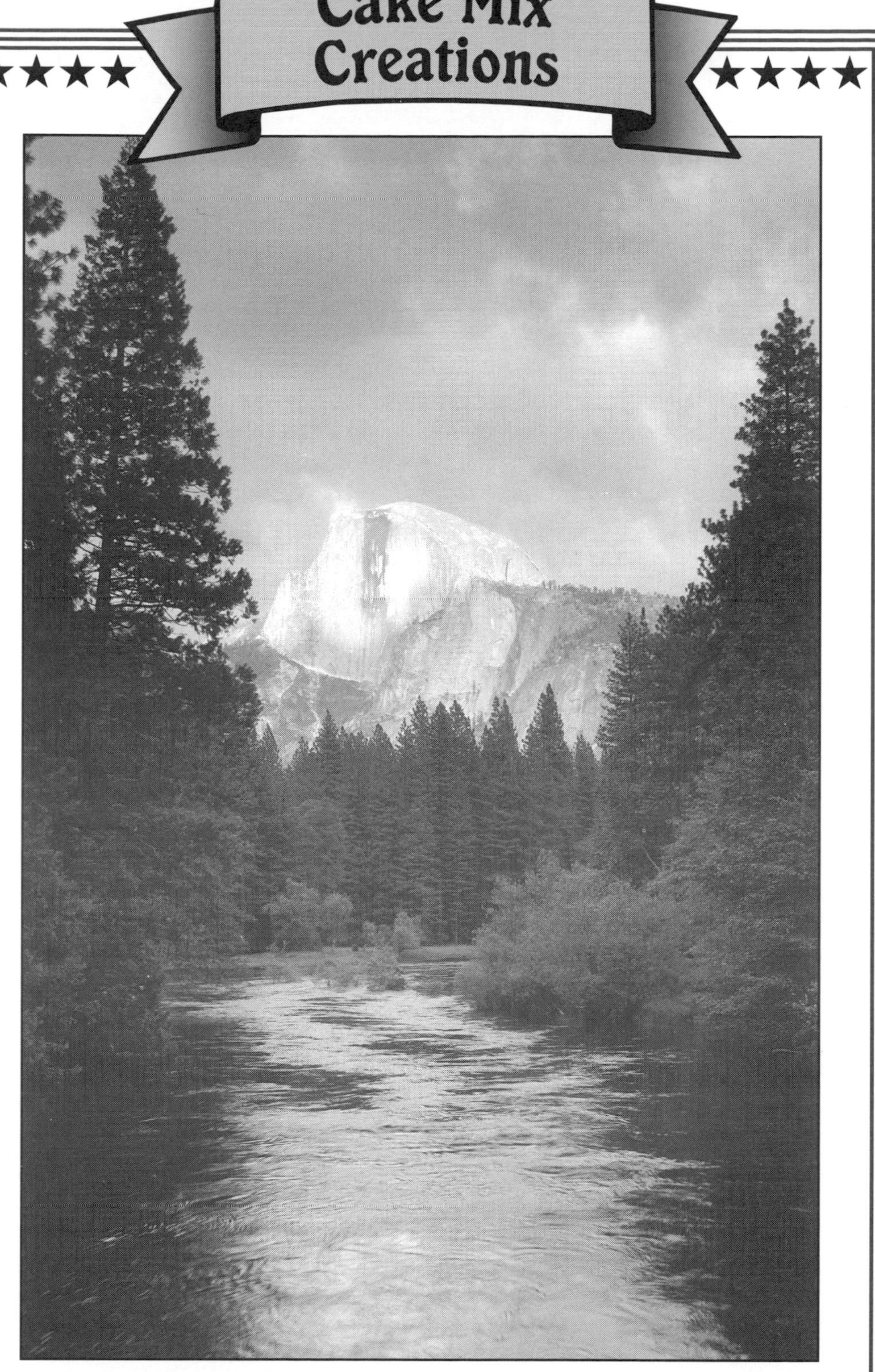

Yosemite National Park's most distinctive monument, Half Dome, dominates valley views. Yosemite was the first territory ever set aside by Congress for public use and protection in 1864.

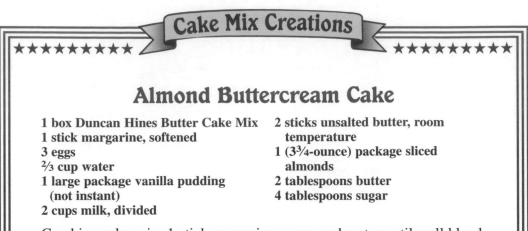

Almond Buttercream Cake

1 box Duncan Hines Butter Cake Mix
1 stick margarine, softened
3 eggs
⅔ cup water
1 large package vanilla pudding (not instant)
2 cups milk, divided
2 sticks unsalted butter, room temperature
1 (3¾-ounce) package sliced almonds
2 tablespoons butter
4 tablespoons sugar

Combine cake mix, 1 stick margarine, eggs, and water until well blended. Bake in a greased and floured angel cake tube pan according to directions on cake box. Let stand at least 4 hours.

Combine pudding mix and ⅓ cup milk. Mix until smooth. Bring remaining 1⅔ cups milk to boil in a medium saucepan. Take off heat and combine with pudding mixture. Return to heat and bring to a full boil, stirring constantly. Cool 3 - 4 hours. Place a sheet of wax paper over top of pudding during cooling to prevent formation of a skin.

To make buttercream, blend unsalted butter with electric mixer until creamy. Gradually add vanilla pudding mixture by the tablespoonful until all is used. It is very important that the pudding and the butter are at room temperature or the buttercream will curdle.

To prepare toasted almonds, melt 2 tablespoons of butter over medium heat in a large frying pan. Stir in almonds and cook until they start to become golden. Add sugar and continue stirring until the sugar is melted and the almonds are golden brown. Cool on wax paper.

To assemble cake: Cut into 3 layers using a sharp knife. Fill each layer with buttercream. Reassemble and frost top and sides with the buttercream. Cover completely with almonds. Serves 12.

Symphony of Flavors (California)

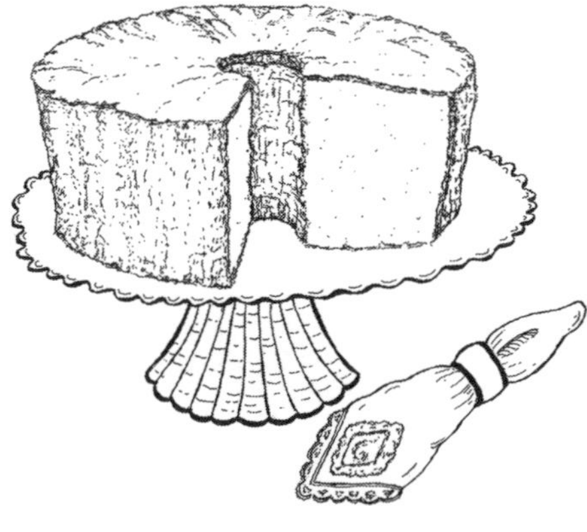

Easy Almond Rum Cake

Makes a nice holiday gift.

1 package yellow cake mix (not pudding)
¼ teaspoon nutmeg
1½ cups eggnog (commercial)
2 eggs
¼ cup butter, melted
2 tablespoons rum or 1 teaspoon rum extract
2 tablespoons margarine, softened
½ cup sliced almonds, toasted
5 cherries and mint leaves

Beat first 6 ingredients together for 4 minutes. Grease a springform or angel food cake pan with softened margarine, and pat toasted almonds against side of pan, lining sides and also bottom. Put pan into refrigerator to help almonds stay in place.

Carefully pour or spoon the cake batter into pan and bake at 350° for 40 minutes, or until a toothpick comes out clean. Remove from pan carefully. Cake may be garnished with 5 red cherries and mint leaves, or holly leaves. Serves 8 - 10.

Cook Book (California)

Rouge Rum Cake

½ cup chopped nuts (walnuts or pecans)
1 package yellow cake mix
1 package Jell-O instant butter pecan pudding and pie filling
4 eggs
½ cup water
½ cup Wesson oil
½ cup cheap dark 80-proof rum

Preheat oven to 325°. Grease and flour 10-inch tube pan and sprinkle nuts over bottom. Mix all ingredients together. Pour batter over nuts and bake for 1 hour. Cool and invert to serving plate. Prick top.

GLAZE:
½ stick margarine
2 tablespoons water
½ cup granulated sugar
¼ cup dark rum

Melt margarine in saucepan. Stir in water and sugar. Boil 5 minutes, stirring constantly. Remove from heat and stir in rum. Spoon or brush evenly over top and sides of cake. Allow cake to absorb Glaze and repeat until Glaze is used up.

Note: Cake holds up very well if wrapped in foil and stored tightly. Good up to about 4 months stored this way.

How to Make A Steamship Float (Michigan)

Heavenly Coconut Cream Cake

1 white cake, baked as directed
1 can Eagle Brand Condensed Milk
1 (15-ounce) can Coco Lopez Cream of Coconut
1 (8-ounce) container Cool Whip
7 ounces shredded coconut

Bake white cake in 9x13-inch pan as directed. Mix 1 can condensed milk with cream of coconut. Pour over warm cake which has been pierced with fork. Cool in refrigerator. Frost with Cool Whip and coconut. Keep refrigerated.

Seasoned With Love (Oklahoma)

Patrick's "A Bit O' Green Cake"

1 package white cake mix
1 small box instant pistachio pudding mix
3 eggs
1 cup vegetable oil
1 cup ginger ale
1 teaspoon vanilla
½ cup chopped almonds or walnuts, if desired

In large mixing bowl combine cake mix, pudding, eggs, oil, ginger ale, vanilla, and nuts, if desired. Beat at medium speed 2 minutes. Pour into greased Bundt pan and bake in 350° oven for about 50 minutes or until top springs back when touched with fingertip. Let cool in pan 10 minutes. Invert onto cake platter. Let cool completely.

FROSTING:

1 package instant pistachio pudding mix
1¼ cups milk
1 (8-ounce) container whipped topping or 1½ cups whipped cream

In mixing bowl combine pudding mix and milk. Beat until smooth and thick. Fold in whipped topping or whipped cream. Frost cool cake.

Simply Sensational (Michigan)

Quickie Italian Cream Cake

Outstanding! This is too good and too easy to be true.

1 (18¼-ounce) package reduced fat white cake mix
1 cup low-fat buttermilk
2 large egg whites
1 large egg
¼ cup canola oil
3 tablespoons light brown sugar
¼ cup flaked coconut
2 tablespoons chopped pecans
Cream Cheese Frosting

Preheat oven to 350°. Coat a 9x13x2-inch pan with nonstick cooking spray and dust with flour. In a large mixing bowl, combine cake mix, buttermilk, egg whites, egg, and oil, beating until well mixed. In a small mixing bowl, combine brown sugar, coconut, and pecans together; set aside. Spread half the batter in the bottom of the pan, sprinkle with brown sugar mixture, and carefully top with remaining batter, spreading it out. Bake for 30 minutes, or until a toothpick inserted into center comes out clean. Let cool and spread with Cream Cheese Frosting. Makes 28 servings.

CREAM CHEESE FROSTING:

1 (8-ounce) package fat-free cream cheese, softened
2 tablespoons light stick margarine
1 (16-ounce) box confectioners' sugar
1 teaspoon vanilla extract

In a mixing bowl, beat cream cheese and margarine together. Blend in sugar, mixing well. Add the vanilla, mixing well again.

Cal 185; Fat 4.4g; Cal from Fat 21.5%; Sat Fat 1g; Prot 2.8g; Carbo 34g; Sod 190g; Chol 9mg

Trim and Terrific One-Dish Favorites (Louisiana II)

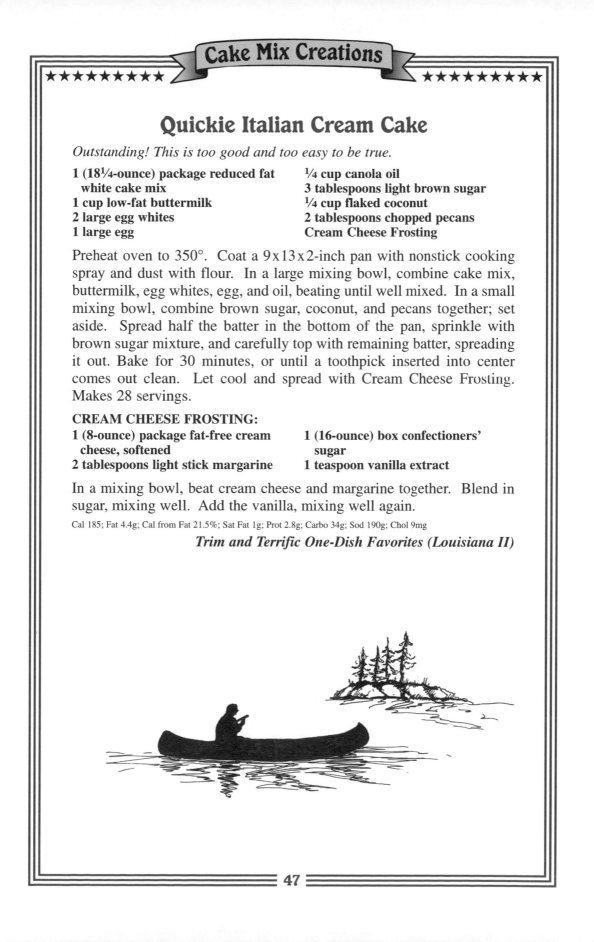

Pound Cake Squares

1 (16-ounce) box pound cake mix
1 stick butter, softened
4 eggs, divided
1 (8-ounce) package cream cheese
1 (16-ounce) package confectioners' sugar
1 teaspoon vanilla extract
1 cup chopped pecans
Whipped cream for topping (optional)

Combine cake mix, butter, and 2 eggs; mix until well blended. Spread in a greased (9x13x2-inch) pan. Reserve 3 tablespoons confectioners' sugar and combine remainder with the softened cream cheese. Beat in 2 eggs and vanilla. Spread over cake mixture and sprinkle pecans over top. Cook at 350° for 45 minutes. While cake is warm, sift reserved sugar on top.

Serve like brownies or cut into larger squares and top with whipped cream for a luscious dessert! Yields 2 - 3 dozen.

Family Secrets (Alabama)

Strawberry Cake

1 box yellow cake mix
4 eggs
1 cup cooking oil
½ cup boiling water
1 regular box strawberry gelatin
1 (5-ounce) package frozen strawberries

Combine cake mix, eggs, one at a time, and oil. Add boiling water with strawberry gelatin. Mix well and add the strawberries. Bake in a stem pan at 325° for one hour.

Carolina Cuisine (South Carolina)

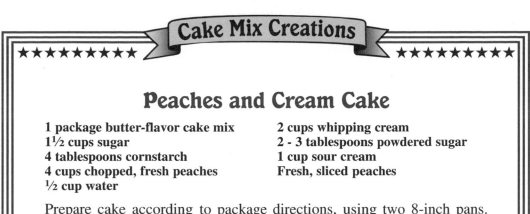

Peaches and Cream Cake

1 package butter-flavor cake mix
1½ cups sugar
4 tablespoons cornstarch
4 cups chopped, fresh peaches
½ cup water
2 cups whipping cream
2 - 3 tablespoons powdered sugar
1 cup sour cream
Fresh, sliced peaches

Prepare cake according to package directions, using two 8-inch pans. Cool and split each layer.

Combine sugar and cornstarch in a saucepan; add peaches and water. Cook over medium heat, stirring constantly, until smooth and thickened. Cool mixture completely.

Combine whipping cream and powdered sugar in a medium mixing bowl; beat until stiff peaks form. Spoon ⅓ of peach filling over split layer cake and spread ⅓ cup sour cream over filling. Repeat procedure with remaining layers, peach filling, sour cream, ending with remaining cake layer. Frost with sweetened whipped cream and garnish with fresh peach slices.

Festival (Mississippi)

Mamie's Pineapple Orange Cake

Very moist and rich.

1 box lite yellow cake mix
1 large can lite mandarin oranges, undrained
½ cup unsweetened applesauce
½ cup Kraft Free Mayonnaise
1 cup Egg Beaters
1 large can unsweetened crushed pineapple, undrained
1 (3-ounce) package instant vanilla pudding mix
1 box Betty Crocker Fluffy White Frosting Mix, prepared

Mix together the first 5 ingredients. Spray 3 (9-inch round) cake pans with Pam and flour each. Divide batter into pans and bake at 325° for 20 minutes. Cool.

Mix pineapple with pudding mix. Refrigerate. When pudding is semi-set, mix in 1 cup prepared frosting. Chill until firm. Ice cake and serve. Serves 16.

The Lite Switch (Texas II)

Key Lime Cake

1 package Duncan Hines Lemon Supreme Cake Mix
½ cup water
½ cup Key lime juice
1 (3-ounce) package lime Jell-O
½ cup Crisco or Puritan oil
4 eggs

ICING:
2 cups sifted confectioners' sugar
¼ cup lime juice

With an electric mixer, blend all ingredients together on medium speed for about 2 minutes. Pour into greased tube pan or 9x13x2-inch baking pan and bake at 325° for 45 minutes (test by inserting toothpick in center). After removing from oven, use an ice pick and stick through cake, top to bottom, many times. Drizzle with icing while warm.

Margaritaville Cookbook (Florida)

Lemon Apricot Cake

3 eggs
⅓ cup canola oil
1 can apricot nectar
1 package yellow cake mix (pudding in mix)

Heat oven to 350°. Combine all ingredients in large bowl and beat at medium speed for 2 minutes. Bake in greased and floured 10-inch tube pan for 40-45 minutes. Cool right side up for 20-25 minutes before removing from pan. Spread icing while still warm.

ICING:
¼ cup butter or margarine
2½ cups sifted confectioners' sugar
¼ cup lemon juice
⅛ teaspoon grated lemon rind (optional)

Blend until smooth and spread over cooled cake.

L' Heritage Du Bayou Lafourche (Louisiana II)

There are only four states designated as commonwealths: Virginia, Kentucky, Massachusetts, and Pennsylvania. They chose to be called commonwealths after independence from Great Britain. Only one state does not have counties; Louisiana calls its "counties" parishes.

Piña Colada Cake

1 (18½-ounce) box white cake mix
1 small (3-ounce) package vanilla instant pudding
¼ cup oil
½ cup water
⅓ cup rum (Puerto Rican light is best)
4 eggs
1 small (8¼-ounce) can crushed pineapple, undrained
1 cup coconut

Mix cake mix, pudding, oil, water, and rum. Add eggs, one at a time, and beat well after each addition. Mix in pineapple. Then fold in coconut. Bake in a 350° oven for 30 minutes. Makes sheet or layer cake (bake layers 25 minutes).

PIÑA COLADA FROSTING:
1 small can crushed pineapple, undrained
⅓ cup rum
1 small package vanilla instant pudding mix
1 (8-ounce) container Cool Whip
Coconut to taste

Mix crushed pineapple, rum, and vanilla instant pudding. Beat until it thickens. Fold in 1 container of Cool Whip. Frost cake and top with coconut.

The Country Gourmet (Mississippi)

Grand Marnier Cake

1 package butter recipe golden cake mix
1 (3-ounce) package instant vanilla pudding mix
1 stick butter, softened
4 eggs
¾ cup milk
⅓ cup Grand Marnier liqueur
½ cup chopped pecans
Confectioners' sugar

Mix cake mix and pudding. Add other ingredients and beat 4 minutes until smooth. Bake in greased Bundt pan at 325° for 60 minutes or until done. When cake is cool, sprinkle with confectioners' sugar.

Talk About Good II (Louisiana)

Seduction Cake

1 (6-ounce) package semisweet chocolate chips
¾ cup chopped pecans
1 (18.5-ounce) box chocolate butter cake mix
4 eggs
½ cup oil
¼ cup water
1 teaspoon vanilla extract
1 (3½-ounce) box instant chocolate pudding
1 (8-ounce) carton sour cream

Coat chocolate chips and pecans in a spoon or two of dry cake mix. Mix remaining ingredients together and fold in chocolate chips and pecans. Pour into a greased and floured Bundt or tube pan. Bake at 350° for 50 minutes. Serves 16.

Lone Star Legacy II (Texas II)

Snicker Cake

1 German chocolate cake mix
1 package caramels
⅓ cup milk
½ cup oleo
1 cup chocolate chips
1 cup chopped nuts

Mix cake mix according to directions. Pour ½ of cake batter into a greased 9x13-inch pan and bake at 350° for 20 minutes. Melt caramels, milk, and oleo together until smooth and creamy. Pour over hot cake and add chocolate chips and nuts. Add the other half of cake batter and bake at 275° for 20 minutes and then 350° for 10 minutes.

Four Square Meals a Day (Colorado)

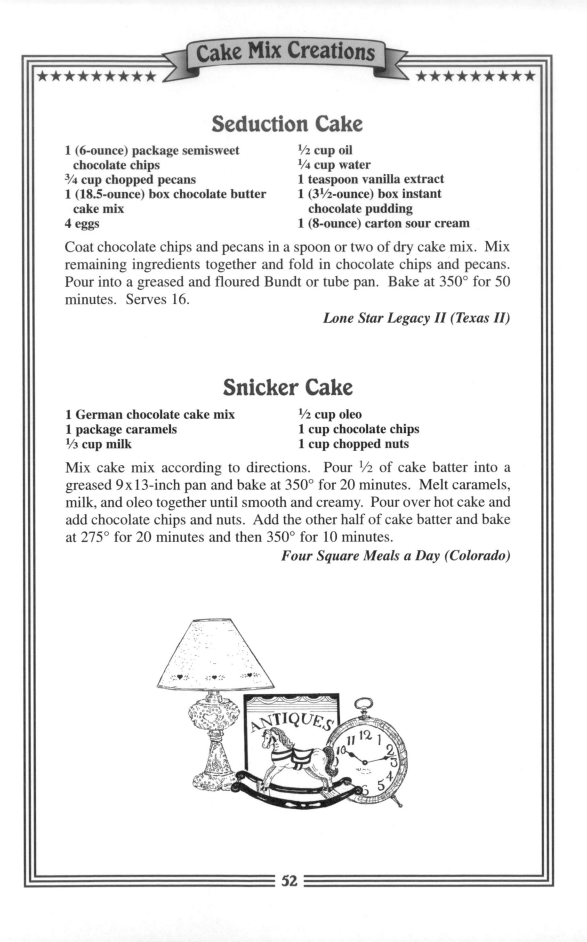

Chocolate Cherry Cake

1 package devil's food cake mix
1 (21-ounce) can cherry pie filling
1 teaspoon almond extract
2 eggs, beaten

Preheat oven to 350°. Grease and flour 9x13x2-inch pan. In large bowl, combine all ingredients and mix well. Bake 25-30 minutes and frost while warm.

FROSTING:
1 cup sugar
5 tablespoons margarine
⅓ cup milk
1 (6-ounce) package semisweet chocolate chips

In small saucepan, combine first 3 ingredients. Cook until it comes to a boil, stirring constantly. Stir 1 minute longer. Remove from heat. Add chips. Stir until smooth.

Dixie Delights (Tennessee)

Chocolate Amaretto Cake

Delicious and moist! A real winner!

BATTER:
1 (18½-ounce) box chocolate cake mix
1 (3¾-ounce) box instant chocolate pudding mix
2 (7-ounce) rolls or cans almond paste
4 eggs
½ cup vegetable oil
½ cup amaretto liqueur
½ cup water

Blend cake and pudding mix with almond paste. Add eggs, oil, amaretto, and water. Mix well. Pour into a greased and floured Bundt pan. Bake at 350° for 45-50 minutes. Cool and glaze.

GLAZE:
½ cup butter or margarine
½ cup sugar
½ cup amaretto liqueur
¼ cup water

Mix Glaze ingredients and bring to a boil. Boil 1 minute. Pour over the cake while Glaze is still hot. Be ready for rave reviews! Yields 20 slices.

Cook 'em Horns: The Quickbook (Texas II)

Hawaiian Dump Cake

And you don't even have to wear a lei to enjoy it.

1 (21-ounce) can cherry pie filling (apple is good, too)
1 (20-ounce) can crushed pineapple, undrained
1 (18½-ounce) box yellow cake mix
2 sticks margarine or butter, melted
1 (8-ounce) package shredded coconut
1 cup chopped pecans

In a 9x13-inch baking dish, layer the following ingredients, spreading each over the one it covers: pie filling, crushed pineapple, dry cake mix, margarine, coconut, and chopped pecans. Bake 1 hour in 350° oven. So good and so easy.

Cook 'em Horns: The Quickbook (Texas II)

Almost Better Than Harrison Ford Cake

1 package German chocolate cake mix
1 can sweetened condensed milk
1 jar caramel topping
1 (8-ounce) carton Cool Whip
Heath bar crumbles

Make and bake cake according to package directions and pour into a greased and floured 9x13-inch pan. Remove from oven and poke holes in cake with the handle of a wooden spoon. Pour condensed milk over all the holes. Pour caramel topping over all. Frost with Cool Whip and sprinkle with crumbles. Refrigerate.

Recipes from the Heart (Great Plains)

Miracle Butter Cake

1 Duncan Hines Yellow Cake Mix
2 eggs
1 stick butter, melted

Mix and spread in bottom of 9x13-inch pan.

TOPPING:
1 (8-ounce) bar cream cheese, softened
2 eggs
1 box powdered sugar

Mix all ingredients and pour over cake mixture. Bake at 350° for 35-40 minutes only.

Asbury United Methodist Church Cook Book (Arkansas)

Pumpkin Pudding Cake

Very rich, and so easy!

3 eggs, beaten
1 cup sugar
1 teaspoon cinnamon
1 (32-ounce) can pumpkin
½ teaspoon ginger (optional)
¼ teaspoon cloves
1 (14-ounce) can evaporated milk
1 (2-layer) white or yellow cake mix
1 stick butter, melted
1 cup walnuts or pecans, chopped
Whipped cream or ice cream

Mix eggs, sugar, cinnamon, pumpkin, ginger, cloves, and milk. Whisk until blended and pour into a greased or sprayed 9x13-inch pan. Sprinkle 1 package cake mix over top. Drizzle melted butter over top. Sprinkle with chopped nuts. Bake at 350° for 1 hour. Serve with whipped cream or ice cream.

Taking Culinary Liberties (Colorado)

Mexico City Earthquake Cake

The finished cake will have cracks and crevices.

1 cup coconut
1 cup chopped pecans
1 box German chocolate cake mix
½ cup soft margarine
1 (8-ounce) package cream cheese
1 teaspoon vanilla
1 (16-ounce) package powdered sugar

Spray a 9x13-inch baking pan. Layer coconut and pecans. Prepare cake mix according to package directions; pour over coconut and nut mixture. Mix margarine, cream cheese, vanilla, and powdered sugar. Spoon over cake batter. Bake in preheated 350° oven for 40-50 minutes.

Good Sam Celebrates 15 Years of Love (New Mexico)

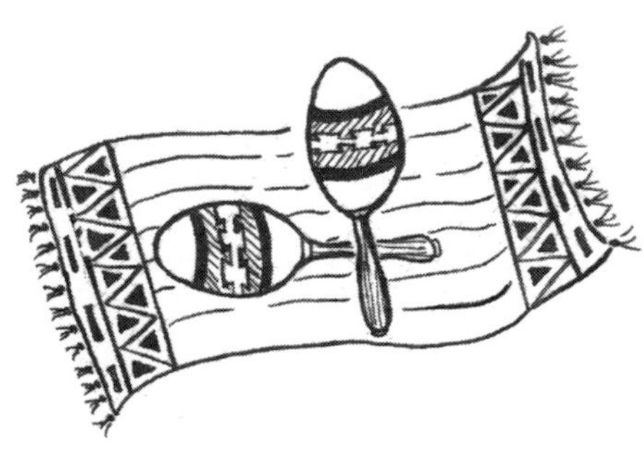

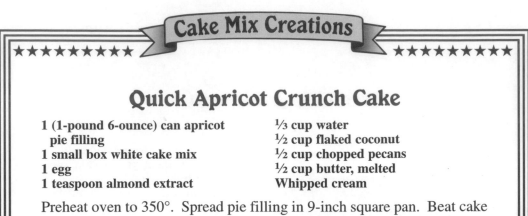

Quick Apricot Crunch Cake

1 (1-pound 6-ounce) can apricot pie filling
1 small box white cake mix
1 egg
1 teaspoon almond extract
⅓ cup water
½ cup flaked coconut
½ cup chopped pecans
½ cup butter, melted
Whipped cream

Preheat oven to 350°. Spread pie filling in 9-inch square pan. Beat cake mix, egg, extract and ⅓ cup water for 4 minutes. Pour over filling. Sprinkle with coconut and pecans; drizzle with butter. Bake for 40 minutes. Serve warm. Top with whipped cream.

Miss Daisy Entertains (Tennessee)

White Turtle Cake

1 (2-layer) package yellow cake mix
1 cup water
1 (14-ounce) can sweetened condensed milk, divided
1 cup vegetable oil
3 eggs
1 (14-ounce) package caramels
1 cup chopped pecans

Preheat oven to 350°. Combine cake mix, water, ½ of condensed milk, oil, and eggs; beat well. Spread ½ the batter into greased 9x13-inch pan. Bake 30 minutes. Melt caramels with remaining condensed milk, stirring often. Stir in pecans. Pour over hot cake. Spread remaining batter over caramel layer. Bake for 20 minutes. Spread White Turtle Frosting over warm cake.

WHITE TURTLE FROSTING:

½ cup melted margarine
1 pound powdered sugar
6 tablespoons milk
1 teaspoon vanilla extract

Combine margarine, sugar, and milk; beat well. Add vanilla; mix well.

Seasoned with Love (Illinois)

The legend of the Chicago Fire: After three months without rain, Chicago was as dry as a tinderbox. On the night of October 8, 1871, Mrs. O'Leary, a boardinghouse keeper, went to the barn to milk her cow. She left her lighted lantern in the barn and the cow kicked it over, igniting straw in the stall. Destroying 65 acres per hour, in 27 hours the fire killed 250 people and destroyed much of the North Side of Chicago, leaving only the pumping station and the Old Water Tower of the Chicago Water Company remaining. They stand today as reminders of the past.

Easy Lemon Bars

1 package 1-step angel food cake mix
1 (21-ounce) can lemon pie filling
2 cups powdered sugar
Milk for thinning
Lemon extract flavoring

With a spoon, stir together cake mix and pie filling (do not use electric mixer). Pour into ungreased jellyroll pan (11x15) and bake in 350° oven for 20-25 minutes. When baked, frost with a powdered sugar frosting (powdered sugar thinned with a little milk) flavored with lemon extract.

Note: For diabetics, replace lemon pie filling with sugar-free yogurt—I use lemon, but you can use your choice of flavors—and then I do not frost the bars.

125 Years of Cookin' with the Lord (Great Plains)

Goofy Bars

"These are my absolute favorite bars," says 3rd grader Ian Laessig.

2 eggs plus water
1 white or yellow cake mix
1 cup brown sugar
1 cup miniature marshmallows
1 cup chocolate chips

Put eggs in a measuring cup and mix well; add enough water to make ⅔ cup. Mix well with cake mix and brown sugar and place in a greased 9x13-inch cake pan. Sprinkle with marshmallows and chocolate chips. Bake in a 350° oven for 25-30 minutes. Cool before cutting into bars.

A Collection of Recipes (Wisconsin)

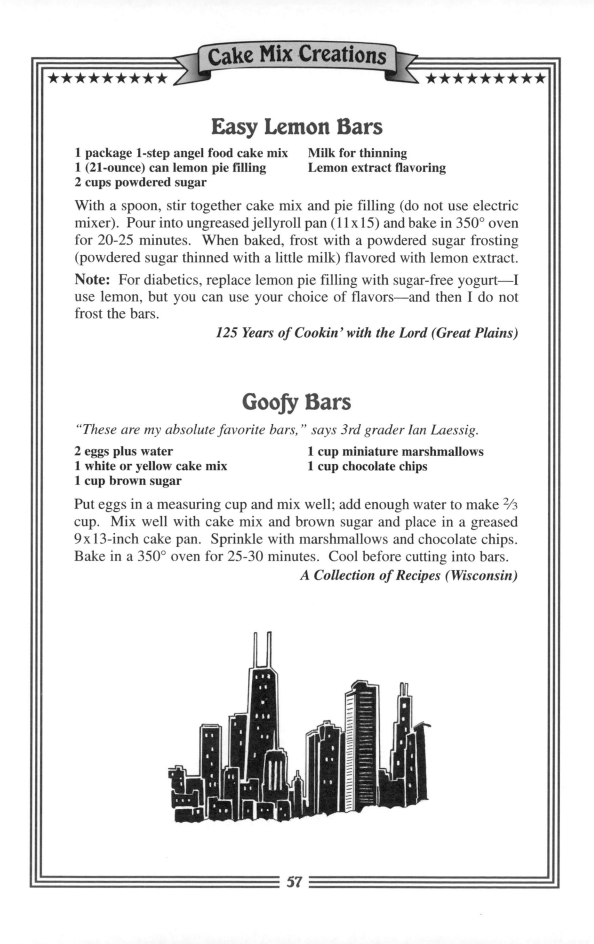

Lazy Betty

2 cans pie filling mix (your choice)
1 package yellow cake mix
1 cup chopped nuts
½ pound margarine
Cool Whip

Pour pie filling mix into ungreased 9x13x2-inch baking dish. Smooth filling, sprinkle with cake mix, then with the chopped nuts. Melt margarine and drizzle over entire top. Bake at 375° for about 40 minutes. Serve topped with Cool Whip.

Cooking with Mr. "G" and Friends (Louisiana II)

Easy Cheesy Lemon Bars

No question about it, these superior Lemon Bars will be the first to disappear when served at any gathering.

1 (18-ounce) package lemon cake mix
½ cup butter or margarine, melted
1 egg
1 (7.2-ounce) package powdered white frosting mix
2 teaspoons lemon extract
1 (8-ounce) package cream cheese, softened
1 cup powdered sugar
1 tablespoon butter or margarine
2 - 3 tablespoons milk

Combine cake mix, butter or margarine, and egg; mix well. Press into 9x13-inch pan. With electric mixer, blend frosting mix, lemon extract, and softened cream cheese. Beat well. Pour over bottom layer. Bake at 350° for 30-40 minutes. Cool. To prepare frosting, combine powdered sugar, butter or margarine, and milk. Beat well; spread or drizzle on bars.

Marketplace Recipes Volume II (Wisconsin)

Wisconsin is known as the "Mother of Circuses" because around 100 circuses have been based in the state, more than any other state in the union. Baraboo is home to Circus World Museum, located at the birthplace of the Ringling Brothers Circus along the banks of the Baraboo River. Delavan, where the Clown Hall of Fame is located, boasts that between 1847 and 1894, no fewer than 26 circuses had their winter quarters there.

Pumpkin Cheesecake Bars

1 (16-ounce) package pound cake mix
3 eggs, divided
2 tablespoons margarine or butter, melted
4 teaspoons pumpkin pie spice, divided
1 (8-ounce) bar cream cheese, softened
1 (14-ounce) can sweetened condensed milk
1 (16-ounce) can pumpkin
½ teaspoon salt
1 cup chopped nuts

Preheat oven to 350°. In a large mixer bowl, on low speed, combine cake mix, 1 egg, margarine, and 2 teaspoons pie spice until it is crumbly. Press into bottom of 10x15-inch jellyroll pan. In a large mixer bowl, beat cheese until fluffy. Gradually beat in sweetened condensed milk, then remaining 2 eggs, pumpkin, remaining pie spice, and salt. Mix well. Pour over crust, sprinkle with nuts. Bake 30-35 minutes or until set. Cool, chill, and cut into bars. Store in refrigerator. Yields 48 bars.

Cookin' in the Spa (Arkansas)

Chess Cake

1 yellow cake mix
1 stick margarine, melted
1 egg
2½ cups powdered sugar
1 (8-ounce) package cream cheese, softened
2 eggs

Mix together cake mix, margarine, and 1 egg; pat in 9x13-inch pan. Beat remaining ingredients, and pour on crust mixture. Bake at 325° for 40 minutes. (Do not open oven door while baking).

Our Favorite Recipes II (Indiana)

Without Rival Chocolate Fudge Kahlua Cake

This unbelievably easy-to-make cake is sinfully delicious. It is wonderful topped with whipped cream, vanilla ice cream, or kahlua ice cream for a sublime chocolate repast!!!

1 (18.25-ounce) chocolate fudge,* with pudding in the mix, cake mix
16 ounces sour cream
¼ cup cooking oil
1 (12-ounce) package real semisweet chocolate morsels
2 eggs
½ cup Kahlua

Preheat oven to 350°. Grease and flour a 12-cup Bundt pan. Combine ingredients with electric mixer; beat 4 minutes. Pour into Bundt pan; bake for 50 minutes or until cake tester (or toothpick) inserted comes out clean. Cool in pan 10-15 minutes; turn onto cake plate.

CHOCOLATE KAHLUA GLAZE:

1 cup powdered sugar
2 tablespoons unsweetened cocoa
1 tablespoon margarine, softened
1 tablespoon kahlua
1 tablespoon water

Away from burner but in small saucepan, combine glaze ingredients; stir until smooth and creamy; over low heat, warm glaze 3 - 5 minutes; stir often. Drizzle over warm cake. Allow glaze to cool before serving. Yields 12-16 servings.

*You may also use a chocolate butter, with pudding in the mix, cake mix. Just as delicious!

Southern Flavors' Little Chocolate Book (Arkansas)

Chocolate Chess Bars

You will get requests for this bar cookie.

1 (18.25-ounce) package lite devil's food cake mix
1 egg
½ cup light margarine, melted
1 tablespoon water
1 (8-ounce) package light cream cheese
1 (16-ounce) box powdered sugar
3 egg whites
1 teaspoon vanilla

In large mixing bowl, combine cake mix, 1 egg, melted margarine, and water. Beat by hand until well blended. Pat batter into bottom of a 9x13x2-inch baking pan coated with nonstick cooking spray. In mixing bowl, beat cream cheese, powdered sugar, and 3 egg whites until mixture is smooth and creamy. Add vanilla. Pour over batter in pan. Bake at 350° for 45 minutes or until top is golden brown. Cool and cut into squares. Yields 48 squares.

A Trim & Terrific Louisiana Kitchen (Louisiana II)

Microwave Pineapple and Apple Dump Cake

1 (20-ounce) can crushed pineapple, drained
1 (20-ounce) can apple pie filling
1 (18.5-ounce) box yellow pudding cake mix
1 cup chopped nuts
2 sticks melted margarine

Grease 9x13-inch dish. Spread pineapple in bottom and top with apple filling. Sprinkle with cake mix and level. Sprinkle with nuts. Pour melted margarine over all. Microwave uncovered on HIGH 15-16 minutes.

Oven method: Bake at 350° for 40-45 minutes. A lemon cake mix also tastes good in this recipe.

Appletizers (Ohio)

Speedy Little Devils

1 stick margarine, melted
1 Duncan Hines Deluxe II Devil's Food Cake Mix
¾ cup creamy peanut butter
1 (7½-ounce) jar marshmallow creme

Combine melted margarine and dry cake mix. Reserve 1½ cups for top crust. Pat remaining crumb mixture into ungreased 9x13x2-inch pan. Top that layer with combined peanut butter and marshmallow creme and spread evenly. Crumble remaining mixture over that. Bake 20 minutes at 350°. Cool. Cut into 3 dozen bars.

Colorado Cookie Collection (Colorado)

German Chocolate Upside-Down Cake

Easy and delicious—indulge and bulge!

1 cup flaked coconut
1 cup chopped pecans
1 package German chocolate cake mix
1 stick butter or margarine
1 (8-ounce) package cream cheese, softened
1 (1-pound) box confectioners' sugar

Combine coconut and pecans; spread evenly on bottom of a greased 9x13x2-inch pan. Mix cake mix according to directions on package; pour over coconut-pecan mixture. Put butter and cream cheese into a saucepan; heat until mixture is warm enough to stir in confectioners' sugar. Spoon mixture over top of cake batter. (As cake bakes, the cream cheese mixture will settle to bottom with coconut and pecans, making a delicious "frosting.") Bake at 350° for 50-60 minutes, or until done. Serve from pan; do not cut until cake is cooled.

Holiday Treats (Virginia)

Cheesecakes

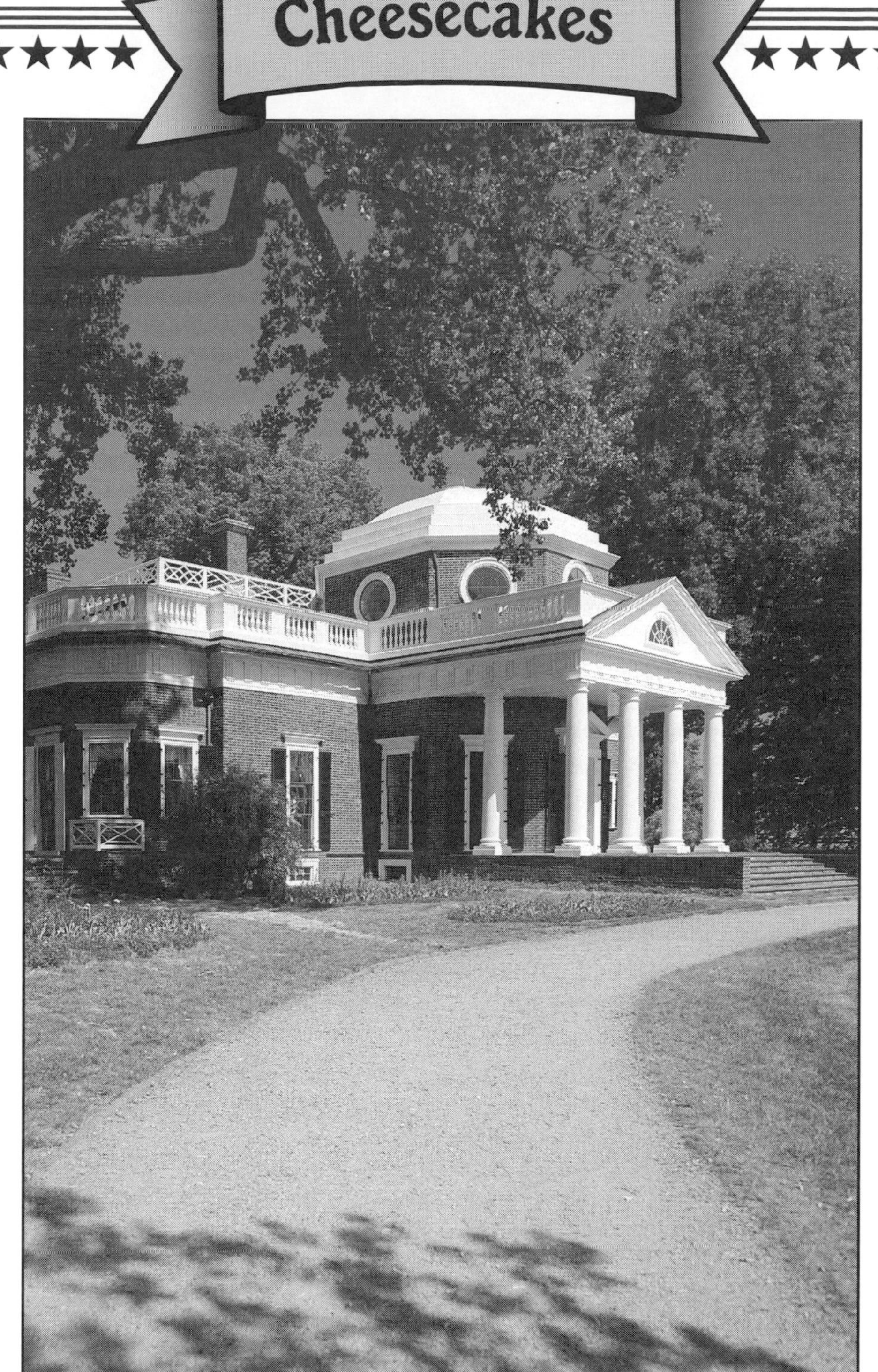

Thomas Jefferson, author of the Declaration of Independence and our third president, built this elaborate 43-room home near Charlottesville, Virginia, which took more than 40 years to complete. Monticello is the only house in America on the United Nation's World Heritage List of Sites.

Black Forest Cheesecake

This recipe won a Grand Prize at a local contest. The judges' comment unanimously was, "You must try it to believe it!"

1 (20-ounce) package Oreo cookies
1 tablespoon soft butter
1 pint small curd cottage cheese
2 (8-ounce) packages cream cheese
1½ cups sugar
4 eggs
⅓ cup cornstarch
2 tablespoons lemon juice
1 teaspoon vanilla
½ cup butter or margarine, melted
1 pint sour cream
1 (16-ounce) can cherry pie filling

Process cookies (including filling) into fine crumbs. Butter sides and bottom of springform pan. Dust sides with cookie crumbs, then put 1 cup crumbs in bottom and spread for base.

Process cottage cheese and cream cheese until smooth. Mix sugar and eggs in large mixer bowl; add cheese mixture, blending well. With mixer on low, add rest of ingredients except cherry pie filling, mixing until smooth. Pour half the batter into prepared pan; sprinkle with 1 cup crumbs. Using a spoon, dip out about half cherries out of pie filling and carefully place at random on top of crumbs. Carefully pour rest of batter on top; sprinkle remaining crumbs over all. Bake at 325° for 70 minutes. Leave in turned-off oven to cool for 2 hours. Do not disturb! Before serving, decorate top with remaining cherry pie filling. Serves 12-15.

Didyaeverhavaday? (California)

Oreo Cheesecake

½ (16-ounce) package Oreo cookies
¼ cup melted butter
24 ounces cream cheese, softened
1 cup sugar
3 eggs
1 teaspoon almond extract
½ cup chocolate chips
½ cup whipping cream

Pulverize cookies in food processor or blender. Reserve ½ cup crumbs for topping. Add melted butter to cookies in blender container. Process until moistened. Press into 9-inch springform pan. Beat cream cheese, sugar, eggs, and almond flavoring in mixer bowl until smooth. Pour into prepared pan. Bake at 350° for 45 minutes. Chill completely. Remove cheesecake from pan. Melt chocolate chips in whipping cream in saucepan over low heat, stirring constantly. Drizzle over cheesecake. Sprinkle with reserved cookie crumbs. Yields 8 servings.

Approx Per Serving: Cal 718; Fat 52g; Cal from Fat 64%; Prot 11g; Carbo 55g; Fiber 1g; Chol 209mg; Sod 467mg.

The Pioneer Chef (Oklahoma)

Raspberry Topped Cheesecake

1 package yellow cake mix, divided
4 eggs, divided
2 tablespoons oil
2 (8-ounce) packages cream cheese
½ cup sugar
1½ cups milk
3 tablespoons lemon juice
3 tablespoons vanilla
Fresh raspberries, frozen if necessary

Preheat oven to 300°. Reserve 1 cup dry cake mix. In large bowl, combine remaining cake mix, 1 egg, and oil. Blend thoroughly and press this crust into bottom and sides of a springform cake pan. Blend cream cheese and sugar. Add 3 eggs and 1 cup cake mix. Beat 1 minute at medium speed. At low speed, add milk and flavorings. Pour into crust. Bake 55-60 minutes. Chill before serving. Top with fresh raspberries. Serves 10-12.

The VIP Cookbook: A Potpourri of Virginia Cooking (Virginia)

★ **Editor's Extra:** Try substituting cherry pie filling for raspberries.

God's Country White Chocolate Cheesecake

We endure plenty of ribbing when it comes to the prairie—people unfamiliar with its beauty think this must be "God's country, because no one else would want to live there." Maybe He knows something they don't and plans to visit when a sliver of this cake will be waiting at His place—it's truly a little slice of heaven.

1 - 3 tablespoons butter or margarine, softened
1 cup finely chopped, lightly toasted macadamia nuts
24 ounces white chocolate, chopped or broken
¾ cup heavy cream, scalded
3 (8-ounce) packages cream cheese
1 cup sugar
¼ cup flour
4 eggs, room temperature (let sit out 30 minutes)
1 tablespoon vanilla or ¼ cup white crème de cacao
Sweetened whipped cream
12-14 macadamia nuts and/or 12-14 fresh raspberries dipped in 1 ounce melted white chocolate

Coat sides and bottom of 8- or 9-inch springform pan with butter. Sprinkle macadamia nuts over buttered surface, turning pan and shaking to distribute evenly. Chill in freezer 15 minutes.

Partially melt chocolate in double boiler or microwave. Add scalded cream, whisking until chocolate is melted and mixture is smooth. Set aside.

Beat the cream cheese, sugar, and flour. Add the chocolate mixture, then eggs, one at a time. Stir in vanilla and pour into prepared pan. Bake 20 minutes at 425°; reduce heat to 300° and bake 45-55 minutes more until cheesecake is nearly set. Turn off oven. Cool in oven 30 minutes. Cool 1 hour on rack, then refrigerate 6 - 24 hours.

At least 2 hours before serving, prepare Raspberry Sauce. Chill. Line baking sheet with wax paper. Partially melt 1 ounce white chocolate, then stir until smooth. Dip macadamia nuts and raspberries halfway into melted chocolate. Invert onto waxed paper. Chill. Serve thin wedges of cheesecake with a small spoonful of Raspberry Sauce; garnish with whipped cream and top with a dipped macadamia nut and/or raspberry. Serves 12-14.

RASPBERRY SAUCE:

2 cups fresh or frozen raspberries
½ cup sugar
2 tablespoons framboise or raspberry schnapps (optional)

Combine berries and sugar in processor (reserve some berries for garnish). Purée sauce, strain, add liqueur, chill. Makes 1½ cups.

Presentations (Great Plains)

Lime Cheesecake

"The most luscious, creamy cheesecake you've ever had! Yes, it's totally fattening. But some things you've just got to do," says chef Stephen Daoust.

1 (9-ounce) package chocolate wafers, finely crushed
4 tablespoons butter, melted
3 extra-large eggs
1 cup sugar
½ cup fresh lime juice
1 tablespoon vanilla
24 ounces cream cheese
16 ounces sour cream
¼ cup sugar

Preheat the oven to 300°. Mix the crushed chocolate wafers with the melted butter and press the mixture into the bottom and 1 inch up the sides of a 9-inch springform pan. Chill.

Mix the eggs and 1 cup sugar with a blender for several minutes until pale yellow. Add the lime juice and vanilla and combine.

In a bowl, cream the cream cheese until soft, and slowly add the egg-and-sugar mixture. Fill the prepared pan and bake at 300° for 50 minutes or until the top is set. Allow to cool.

In a separate bowl, mix the sour cream with the ¼ cup sugar and spoon over the top of the cooled cake. Bake for 10 minutes more. Chill overnight.

Run a sharp knife between the crust and the pan before you unmold the cake. Serves 8-12.

The Williamsville Inn, West Stockbridge, MA.
Best Recipes of Berkshire Chefs (New England)

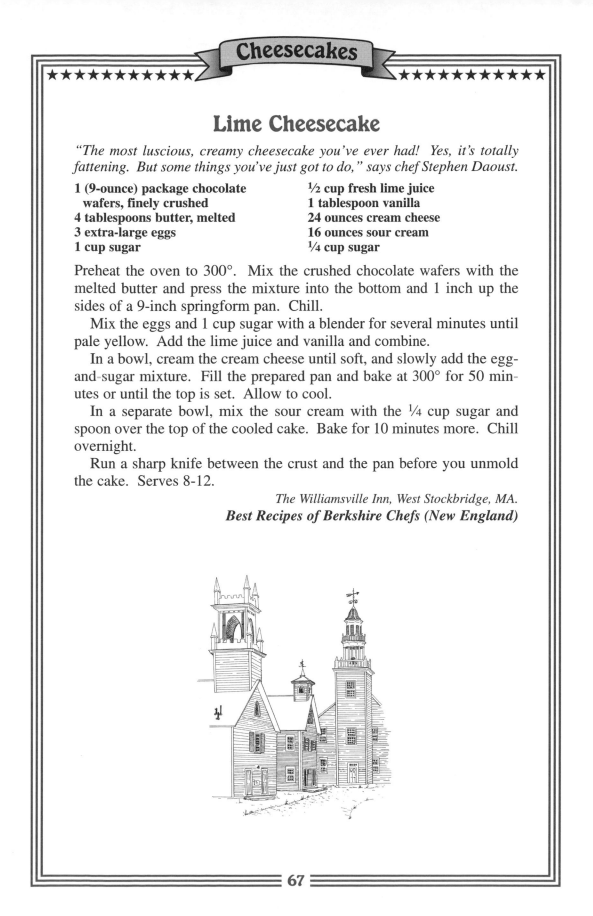

German Chocolate Cheesecake

Another delicious choice for cheesecake fanatics!

CRUST:

1 package German chocolate cake mix
½ cup shredded coconut
⅓ cup butter or margarine, softened
1 egg

FILLING:

16 ounces cream cheese
2 eggs
¾ cup sugar
2 teaspoons vanilla

TOPPING:

2 cups sour cream
1 teaspoon vanilla
¼ cup sugar

Mix crust ingredients until crumbly. Press into ungreased 9x13-inch pan. Beat filling ingredients together until smooth and fluffy. Spread over crust. Bake at 350° for 25-30 minutes. Cool. Combine topping ingredients and spread over cooled filling. Refrigerate for several hours before serving. Serves 8-10.

Kitchen Keepsakes by Request (Colorado)

Praline Cheesecake

24 ounces cream cheese
2 cups brown sugar
3 eggs
2 tablespoons flour
2 teaspoons vanilla
½ cup pecans

CRUST:

1 cup graham cracker crumbs
3 tablespoons sugar
3 tablespoons butter

Combine cream cheese and brown sugar in mixer; when thoroughly mixed, add everything else. Mix crust ingredients and press into 10-inch springform pan. Pour filling into crust. Bake at 350° 35-40 minutes. Serves 12.

Sample West Kentucky (Kentucky)

★ **Editor's Extra:** Most cheesecake recipes halve quite nicely. There's a small (6½-inch) springform pan available, but a round cake pan works just as well—bake it for a shorter period of time.

Amaretto Cheesecake

We have sold the book for this recipe alone!

CRUST:

1½ cups graham cracker crumbs
2 tablespoons sugar
1 teaspoon cinnamon
1 stick plus 2 tablespoons butter, melted

FILLING:

3 (8-ounce) packages cream cheese, softened
1 cup sugar
4 eggs
⅓ cup amaretto

TOPPING:

1 cup sour cream
1 tablespoon amaretto
2 tablespoons sugar

GARNISH:

½ cup roasted almonds, optional
1 tablespoon grated chocolate, optional

Mix all the ingredients together for the crust and press into bottom of 8- or 9-inch springform pan and up the sides ½ inch.

For the filling, beat the cream cheese until it is fluffy. Gradually add sugar. Add eggs one at a time, beating well after each. Stir in ⅓ cup amaretto and pour into pan. Bake at 375° for 45-50 minutes. Remove from oven and turn oven to 500°.

For the topping, mix ingredients and pour over the cheesecake and put in the oven for 5 minutes at 500°. Let the cake cool to room temperature and then refrigerate for 24-48 hours to ripen. Decorate with roasted almonds and grated chocolate. Yields 16 slices. Make a day or two ahead.

Cal 420.75, Prot 49.97gm, Fat 30.80gm, Carbo 29.81gm, Fiber 0.17gm, Chol 150.70mg, Sat Fats 15.63gm, Iron 0.79mg, Calcium 66.52mg, Sod 289.85mg, Pot 149.47mg, Vit A 1236.86 I.U., Vit C 0.14mg, Thiam 0.06mg, Ribo 0.23mg, Nia 0.39mg

The Enlightened Gourmet (South Carolina)

South Carolinians led the resistance to the Stamp Act. More revolutionary battles were fought in this state than in any other.

Apple Cheesecake

Easy to prepare and tastes fabulous; this is a nice fall dessert.

CRUST:

½ cup butter or margarine, melted
⅓ cup sugar
1 cup flour
¼ teaspoon vanilla extract

Mix all ingredients in a bowl. Press mixture over the bottom and 1 inch up side of a 9-inch springform pan.

FILLING:

1 (8-ounce) package cream cheese, softened
¼ cup sugar
1 egg
½ teaspoon vanilla extract

Mix all Filling ingredients in a bowl. Pour mixture over prepared layer.

APPLE MIXTURE:

3 cups thinly sliced apples
⅓ cup sugar
1 teaspoon cinnamon
Sliced almonds to taste (optional)

Toss apples with sugar and cinnamon in a bowl. Spoon Apple Mixture over Filling. Sprinkle with almonds. Bake at 450° for 10 minutes. Reduce oven temperature to 400°. Bake for 25 minutes longer. Cool in the pan. Yields 16 servings.

Dawn to Dusk (Michigan)

Blueberry Cheesecake Macadamia

Superb dessert—guests will call it divine!

CRUST:

1 (3½-ounce) jar macadamia nut pieces, crushed in blender
1 cup all-purpose flour
¼ cup brown sugar, firmly packed
½ cup sweet butter, softened

Combine all ingredients. Mix well; press onto bottom of a 10-inch springform pan. Bake in preheated oven at 400° for 10-15 minutes. Reduce oven to 350°.

FIRST LAYER:

3 (8-ounce) packages cream cheese, softened
1 teaspoon vanilla extract
1 cup sugar
4 eggs, room temperature

Crumble cheese in large bowl. Add remaining ingredients; beat at high speed with electric mixer until blended and smooth, approximately 5 minutes. (Food processor may be used.) Pour over crust. Bake at 350° for 40 minutes until set (not completely firm). Remove from oven; cool for 10 minutes.

SECOND LAYER:

1 cup sour cream
2 tablespoons sugar
½ teaspoon vanilla extract

Combine sour cream, sugar and vanilla. Spread over top of cheesecake. Bake at 350° for 5 minutes. Cool; spread blueberry topping over. Refrigerate before serving.

TOPPING:

1 tablespoon cornstarch
2 to 3 tablespoons cold water
2 cups fresh or frozen blueberries

In a saucepan, mix cornstarch with cold water to form a smooth paste. Stir in blueberries; cook until thickened. Let cool; spread on cake. Cool 1 hour, then refrigerate. Serves 12.

Suncoast Seasons (Florida)

★ **Editor's Extra:** This is superb even without the blueberry topping.

Eden Shale's Cheesecake

Gorgeous! Delicious! A well-guarded secret until now!

CRUST:

6 tablespoons butter
8 double graham crackers, crushed
3 tablespoons sugar

Melt butter. Add crushed graham crackers and sugar. Press into bottom and sides of a 10-inch springform pan. Set aside.

CHOCOLATE FILLING:

1 cup butter
3 ounces unsweetened chocolate
2 cups light brown sugar
1 cup granulated sugar
2 tablespoons flour
4 eggs
4 teaspoons milk
2 teaspoons vanilla

Melt butter with chocolate. Remove from heat. Add brown sugar, granulated sugar and flour. Beat in eggs, one at a time. Add milk and vanilla. Pour into prepared crust.

CREAM CHEESE FILLING:

3 (8-ounce) packages cream cheese
1¼ cups granulated sugar
⅛ teaspoon salt
3 eggs
1 teaspoon vanilla

Cream cream cheese with granulated sugar and salt until fluffy. Add eggs separately. Add vanilla. Layer over chocolate mixture; do not stir or mix layers. Bake at 350° for 1 hour. Check every 5 minutes thereafter until center is soft set. Allow to rest for 15 minutes.

TOPPING:

2 cups sour cream
¼ cup granulated sugar
1 teaspoon vanilla

Combine sour cream, granulated sugar and vanilla. Spread over top of cake. Return to oven for 10 minutes. Allow to cool for 1 hour, then refrigerate for at least 4 hours. Freezes well. Simply divine! Serves 16-20.

Fillies Flavours (Kentucky)

Strawberry Marbled Cheesecake

A culinary masterpiece!

SAUCE:

1 (10-ounce) package frozen strawberries in syrup, thawed
1½ teaspoons cornstarch
Red food coloring, optional

In blender container, combine strawberries and cornstarch; blend until smooth. In heavy saucepan, over medium heat, cook and stir until thickened. Add food coloring, if desired. Reserve ⅓ cup sauce; cool. Chill remaining sauce.

CRUST:

1¼ cups graham cracker crumbs
¼ cup sugar
⅓ cup margarine or butter, melted

Preheat oven to 300°. Combine crumbs, sugar, and margarine; press on bottom of 9-inch springform pan.

FILLING:

3 (8-ounce) packages cream cheese
1 (14-ounce) can sweetened condensed milk (not evaporated)
3 eggs
¼ cup lemon juice

In mixer bowl, beat cheese until fluffy. Gradually beat in sweetened condensed milk until smooth. Add eggs and lemon juice; mix well. Spoon half the batter into prepared pan. Spoon half the reserved strawberry sauce in small amounts over batter. Repeat, ending with sauce. With knife, cut through batter to marble. Bake 50 minutes or until center is set. Cool. Chill. Remove side of springform pan. Serve with chilled strawberry sauce. Refrigerate leftovers.

Watonga Cheese Festival Cookbook 17th Edition (Oklahoma)

On April 22, 1889, men, women, and children raced across the plains to stake a homestead claim on the newly opened Indian territory. The University of Oklahoma adopted the nickname that became associated with the settlers who arrived "sooner" than the others.

Pumpkin Cheesecake with Bourbon Sour Cream Topping

A beautiful presentation for your holiday table.

CRUMB CRUST:

¾ cup graham cracker crumbs
½ cup finely chopped pecans
¼ cup sugar
¼ cup packed light brown sugar
¼ cup butter, melted, cooled

Butter 9-inch springform pan. Combine crumbs, pecans, sugar, and brown sugar in bowl. Stir in melted butter. Press mixture over bottom and ½ inch up side of pan. Chill, covered, in the refrigerator for 1 hour.

PUMPKIN FILLING:

1 (15-ounce) can solid-pack pumpkin
3 eggs
2 teaspoons ground cinnamon
¾ teaspoon ground nutmeg
½ teaspoon ground ginger
½ teaspoon salt
½ cup packed light brown sugar
24 ounces cream cheese, softened
½ cup sugar
2 tablespoons whipping cream
1 tablespoon cornstarch
1 tablespoon vanilla extract
1 tablespoon bourbon

Preheat oven to 350°. Whisk pumpkin, eggs, cinnamon, nutmeg, ginger, salt, and brown sugar in a large bowl. Cut cream cheese into chunks and cream together with sugar in large bowl of an electric mixer. Beat in cream, cornstarch, vanilla, bourbon, and pumpkin mixture until smooth. Pour into crust. Bake on the middle rack of oven for 50-55 minutes or until the center is set. Let cool in the pan on a wire rack for 5 minutes.

BOURBON SOUR CREAM TOPPING:

2 cups sour cream
2 tablespoons sugar
1 tablespoon bourbon
16 pecan halves

Whisk the sour cream, sugar, and bourbon in a bowl. Spread over cheesecake. Bake for 5 minutes. Let cool in pan on wire rack. Chill, covered, for 12 hours. Remove sides; decorate with pecans. Yields 10-12 servings.

Dining by Design (California)

★ **Editor's Extra:** To prevent cheesecake from "cracking," do not whip the filling, but rather cream it at medium speed.

Cream Cheese Cupcakes

2 (8-ounce) packages cream cheese
¾ cup sugar
2 eggs
1 teaspoon vanilla
24 vanilla wafers
1 can cherry pie filling

Mix cream cheese and sugar until creamy. Add eggs and vanilla. Put 1 vanilla wafer in each cupcake liner. Put 2 tablespoons of mix on top. Bake at 375° for 15-20 minutes. Let cool; put 1 tablespoon pie filling on top. Yields 24.

Best Made Better Recipes, Volume II (Kentucky)

Fudge Truffle Cheesecake

CRUST:

1½ cups vanilla wafer crumbs
½ cup powdered sugar
¼ cup cocoa
⅓ cup margarine, melted

Combine all crust ingredients and press into bottom and 2 inches up sides of a 9-inch springform pan; chill.

FILLING:

3 (8-ounce) packages cream cheese, softened
1 (14-ounce) can sweetened condensed milk
2 cups semisweet chocolate chips, melted
3 eggs
2 teaspoons vanilla

Beat cream cheese in a large mixing bowl until fluffy. Gradually add milk; beat until smooth. Add melted chips, eggs, and vanilla; mix well. Pour into crust. Bake at 300° for 65 minutes. (Center will still jiggle slightly.) Cool for 15 minutes. Carefully run a knife between crust and sides of pan. Cool for 3 hours at room temperature. Chill overnight. May garnish with chocolate curls or whipped cream.

Country Classics II (Colorado)

The Continental Divide works its way 3,000 miles through the mountains, forest, grasslands and desserts of five Rocky Mountain states: Montana, Idaho, Wyoming, Colorado and New Mexico. All waters that fall to the east eventually flow into the Atlantic Ocean and all to the west, into the Pacific Ocean.

Apricot Cheesecake

CRUST:

¼ cup butter or margarine
2 tablespoons sugar
½ teaspoon vanilla
½ cup flour

Preheat oven to 325°. In large bowl, beat margarine until soft. Gradually add sugar and beat until light and fluffy. Add vanilla. Stir in flour. Flour fingers and press dough on bottom of 9-inch ungreased springform pan. Bake until golden brown (about 8 -10 minutes). Cool.

APRICOT FILLING:

¾ cup dried apricots
2 tablespoons sugar
½ cup water
2 tablespoons amaretto
1 teaspoon lemon juice

Bring to boil and cook for 5 minutes. Purée in blender. Cool to room temperature.

CREAM CHEESE FILLING:

⅔ cup sugar
2 tablespoons flour
⅛ teaspoon salt
3 (8-ounce) packages cream cheese, room temperature
2 eggs, room temperature
¼ cup amaretto
1 tablespoon vanilla
1 cup whipping cream, unwhipped

Combine sugar, flour, and salt. Mix well. Add cream cheese with mixer at medium speed. Mix until smooth and well blended. Add eggs, amaretto, and vanilla. Mix until blended. Stir in cream. Pour all on crust. Drop Apricot Filling by teaspoonfuls into cream cheese mixture and press down until covered. Bake 1 hour. Run spatula around edges and cool for 1 hour. Remove rim. Refrigerate 4 - 5 hours before cutting. Can top with hot apricot preserves.

Feast of Goodness (Texas II)

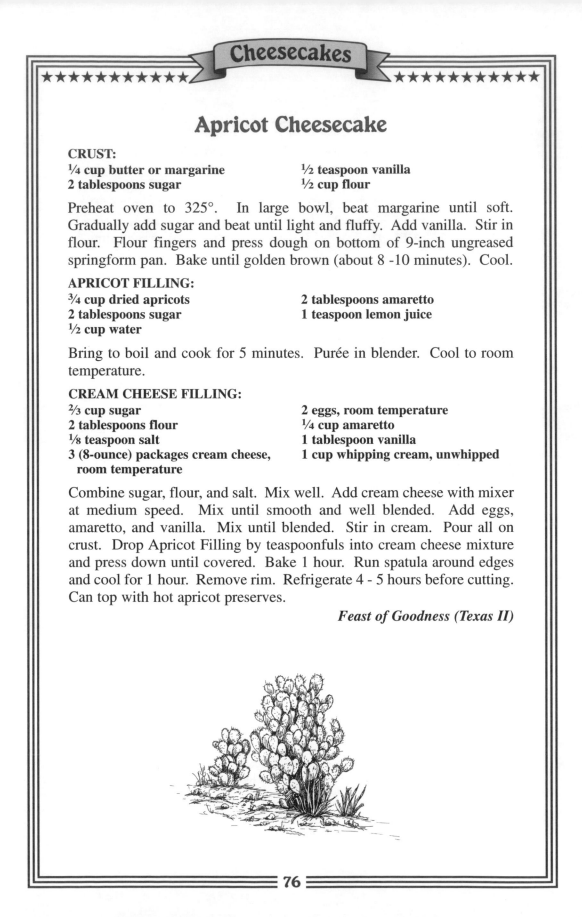

Strawberry Glazed Cream Cheesecake

CRUST:

¾ cup (3 ounces) coarsely ground walnuts
¾ cup finely ground graham crackers
3 tablespoons melted unsalted butter

Preheat oven to 350°. Place rack in center of oven. Lightly butter 9- or 10-inch springform pan. Combine above ingredients and press onto bottom of springform pan.

FILLING:

4 (8-ounce) packages cream cheese, softened
4 eggs
1¼ cups sugar
1 tablespoon lemon juice
2 teaspoons vanilla

Beat cream cheese by electric mixer or processor until smooth. Add eggs, sugar, lemon juice and vanilla. Beat thoroughly. Spoon over crust. Set pan on baking sheet to catch any butter that may drip out. Bake 10-inch cake 40-45 minutes or 9-inch cake 50-55 minutes. Remove from oven. Let stand at room temperature 15 minutes.

TOPPING:

2 cups sour cream
¼ cup sugar
1 teaspoon vanilla

Combine above ingredients and blend well. Cover and refrigerate. When cake finishes baking, spoon topping over, return to oven and bake 5 minutes longer. Let cool and refrigerate cake at least 24 hours or preferably 2 - 3 days.

GLAZE:

1 quart strawberries
1 (12-ounce) jar raspberry jelly
1 tablespoon cornstarch
¼ cup orange liqueur
¼ cup water

Wash and dry strawberries. Combine a little jelly with cornstarch in saucepan and mix well. Add remaining jelly, orange liqueur and water, and cook over medium heat, stirring until thickened and clear, about 5 minutes. Cool to lukewarm. Loosen cake from pan. Remove springform. Arrange berries on top, pointed end up. Spoon glaze over. Return to refrigerator until glaze is set. Yields 10-12 servings.

Seaboard to Sideboard (North Carolina)

★ **Editor's Extra:** Seedless raspberry preserves can be substituted for the jelly. This is a spectacular dessert!

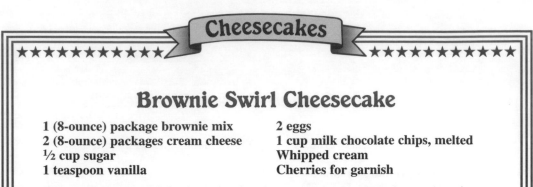

Brownie Swirl Cheesecake

1 (8-ounce) package brownie mix
2 (8-ounce) packages cream cheese
½ cup sugar
1 teaspoon vanilla
2 eggs
1 cup milk chocolate chips, melted
Whipped cream
Cherries for garnish

Grease bottom of 9-inch springform pan. Prepare basic brownie mix as directed on package; pour batter evenly into springform pan. Bake at 350° for 15 minutes.

Combine cream cheese, sugar, and vanilla, mixing at medium speed on electric mixer until well blended. Add eggs one at a time, mixing well after each addition. Pour over brownie mix layer. Spoon melted chocolate over cream cheese mixture; cut through batter with knife several times for marble effect. Bake at 350° for 35 minutes. Loosen cake from rim of pan; cool before removing rim of pan. Garnish with whipped cream and cherries.

A Collection of Recipes (Wisconsin)

Pies & Pastries

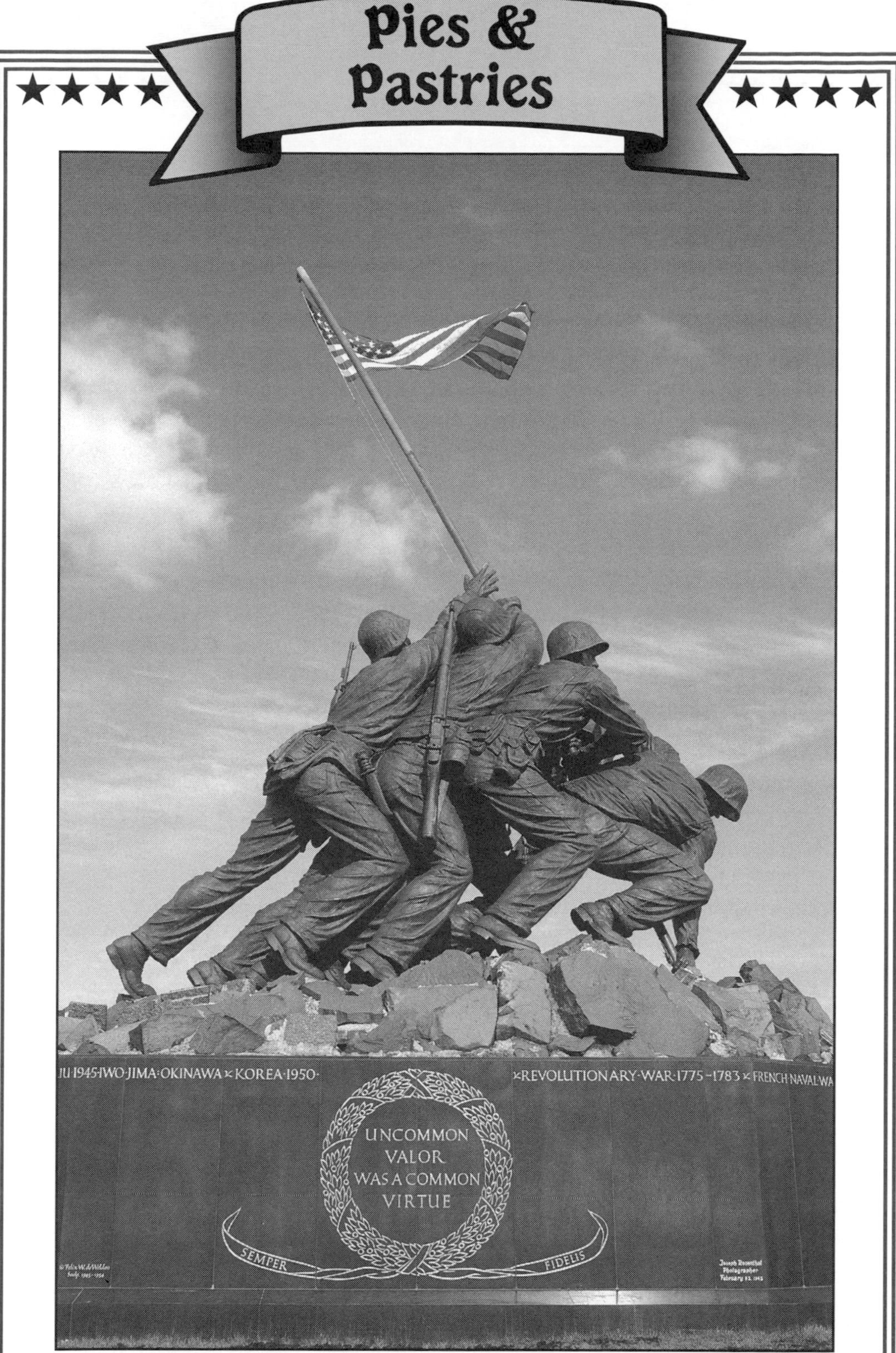

The Marine Corps War Memorial in Washington, D.C., depicts one of the most famous incidents in World War II, the capturing of Iwo Jima. The memorial is dedicated to all who have given their lives defending our nation.

Old-Fashioned Lemon Meringue Pie

1½ cups sugar
½ teaspoon salt
1½ cups water, divided
4 tablespoons butter
⅓ cup cornstarch
4 eggs, separated
¼ cup lemon juice
2 tablespoons lemon rind
1 (9-inch) baked pie shell

Combine sugar, salt, 1 cup of water and butter. Heat until sugar is dissolved. Blend cornstarch with ½ cup of cold water and add slowly to the hot mixture. Cook on low heat until clear, about 8 minutes. Beat egg yolks and add slowly; cook 3 minutes, stirring continually. Remove from heat and add lemon juice and rind. Cool. Pour in a baked pie shell. Set aside.

MERINGUE:
⅔ cup egg whites
¼ teaspoon salt
¼ teaspoon cream of tartar
⅔ cup sugar

Beat egg whites until foamy; add salt and cream of tartar. Continue beating and add sugar gradually until stiff peaks form. Pile on the lemon filling, sealing edges. Brown in a 375° oven for 10-15 minutes.

Taste the Good Life! Nebraska Cookbook (Great Plains)

Millionaire Pie

1 cup chopped pecans
1 can sweetened condensed milk
½ cup lemon juice
1 cup coconut
1 small can crushed pineapple, drained
1 (8-ounce) container Cool Whip
1 graham cracker pie shell

Mix all ingredients together and pour into pie shell. Chill and serve.

Fiftieth Anniversary Cookbook (Louisiana II)

Scintillating Lemon Pie

Customers always ask if this is Lemon Meringue, the only lemon pie most people know. This is not like any other lemon pie. They also wonder what "scintillating" means. You'll know after you taste it. It's one of our all-time favorite desserts.

Pastry for a 2-crust (9-inch) pie, divided
1½ tablespoons sugar
1 teaspoon nutmeg
3 lemons
1½ cups sugar
⅓ cup butter, softened
3 tablespoons flour
3 eggs
½ cup water

Preheat oven to 400°. Roll out ½ of the dough into 9-inch circle. Cut into 6 wedges. Place wedges on cookie sheet. Mix 1½ tablespoons sugar and nutmeg together in small bowl. Sprinkle over pastry wedges. Bake at 400° for no longer than 5 minutes, or until set. Remove from cookie sheet and set aside.

Grate yellow part of 1 lemon rind. Peel and slice lemons very thinly. Set aside.

Cream 1½ cups sugar, butter, and flour in mixer bowl. Beat in eggs. Beat in water. Stir in reserved lemon slices and grated rind. Roll out remaining pastry to form 9-inch pie shell. Pour lemon mixture into prepared pie shell. Bake at 400° for 25 minutes. Arrange baked pastry wedges on top of filling and bake for an additional 5 minutes, or until filling is firm. Makes 1 (9-inch) pie.

The Elsah Landing Restaurant Cookbook (Illinois)

Grasshopper Pie

Brookside Golf and Country Club's traditional house recipe. Elegant.

1⅓ cups fine crumbs of chocolate wafer cookies
¼ cup softened butter or margarine
1 cup whipping cream
1 envelope unflavored gelatin
¼ cup sugar
⅛ teaspoon salt
½ cup cold water
3 egg yolks, slightly beaten, reserve whites
¼ cup crème de menthe
¼ cup crème de cacao
¼ cup sugar
Whipped cream and chocolate curls for garnish

Thoroughly blend crumbs and butter. Press firmly with back of spoon over bottom and sides of 9-inch pie pan. Bake at 375° for 8 minutes. Allow to cool before filling.

In small mixing bowl, whip cream. Set aside. In small bowl, combine gelatin, sugar, and salt. Add cold water and egg yolks and blend thoroughly. Place mixture in top of double boiler. Cook over boiling water, stirring constantly until gelatin dissolves and mixture thickens slightly. Remove from heat. Stir in crème de menthe and crème de cacao. Chill thoroughly.

Beat egg whites until stiff but not dry. Gradually add sugar and continue beating until very stiff. Fold in gelatin mixture. Fold in whipped cream. Pour into chocolate crumb crust. Garnish with additional whipped cream and chocolate curls.

Note: Chocolate curls can be made from a block of unsweetened chocolate by making long thin strokes with a vegetable peeler.

A Taste of Columbus Vol IV (Ohio)

Perfect Custard Pie

Daddy's favorite pie, this is the recipe I used when I was doing a cooking program on WFHL-TV in the 1950s. I cut the pie while it was still warm and custard pie spilled across Channel 11's viewing area that day! But it is an excellent recipe if you chill it before serving.

1 (9-inch) unbaked pie shell
4 eggs, slightly beaten
½ cup sugar
¼ teaspoon salt
½ teaspoon vanilla
½ teaspoon almond
2½ cups scalded milk
Nutmeg

Let pie shell chill while you make the filling. Blend eggs, sugar, salt, vanilla and almond. Stir in scalded milk—that is the secret to this pie. Put your prepared crust into oven, which has been preheated to 400°, and let it bake for about 5 minutes. Leave pie pan on oven rack, pour filling into the pastry, then gently move rack into oven. Bake pie at 400° for 25-30 minutes. Test for doneness by inserting a silver knife into center of pie; if it comes out clean, the pie is done. Sprinkle top generously with nutmeg. Set pie on cooling rack for 30 minutes. Chill thoroughly in refrigerator before serving.

To scald milk: heat until milk reaches boiling point, but do not let it boil. When tiny bubbles form around edge of pan, remove from heat. To scald milk in microwave, use temperature probe and heat to 180°.

. . . and Garnish with Memories (Tennessee)

Grammy's Chocolate Pie

1½ cups sugar
¼ cup flour
½ cup cocoa
Dash of salt
3 egg yolks (save whites)
2 cups milk
1 tablespoon vanilla
1 (9-inch) pie crust, baked and cooled

Mix dry ingredients. Add egg yolks and milk. Cook over medium-high heat, stirring constantly, until thick and bubbly. Take off heat and add vanilla. Stir. Pour into the baked pie crust.

MERINGUE:
3 egg whites
6 tablespoons sugar

Beat egg whites until stiff. Fold in sugar. Put meringue on pie filling and brown in 375° oven. Serves 6 - 8.

Central Texas Style (Texas II)

Black Bottom Pie

½ cup sugar
2 teaspoons flour
1 tablespoon cornstarch
2 cups milk, scalded
4 beaten egg yolks
1 teaspoon vanilla
1 (6-ounce) package semisweet chocolate pieces, melted
1 (9-inch) pie shell, baked
1 tablespoon unflavored gelatin
¼ cup cold water
4 egg whites
½ cup sugar
Bourbon to taste (½ cup)
1 cup heavy cream, whipped
Chocolate pieces, grated for garnish

Combine sugar, flour, and cornstarch. Slowly add scalded milk to beaten egg yolks. Stir in sugar mixture. Cook and stir in top of double boiler until the custard coats a spoon. Add vanilla. To 1 cup of the custard add the melted chocolate. Pour in bottom of cooled pie shell. Chill.

Soften gelatin in cold water and add to remaining hot custard. Stir until dissolved. Chill until slightly thickened. Beat egg whites, adding sugar gradually until mixture stands in peaks. Fold in custard-gelatin mixture to which bourbon has been added. Pour over chocolate layer and chill until set. Garnish with whipped cream and chocolate pieces grated on top.

The Gulf Gourmet (Mississippi)

Hershey® Kiss Pie

Try serving in parfait glasses.

1 (12 to 13-ounce) package Hershey's Kisses
2 ounces milk
1 (8-ounce) package cream cheese
1 (12-ounce) carton Cool Whip
1 chocolate ready-made pie crust

Melt Kisses over medium heat in the milk. When melted, add cream cheese and stir until completely melted. Rapidly stir in Cool Whip with the heat off. (Be careful it doesn't burn.) Pour into crust. Refrigerate until set. Serves 6 - 8.

More Firehouse Favorites (California)

The town of Hershey, Pennsylvania, is a chocolate kingdom called "The Sweetest Place on Earth." Even the streetlights are shaped like Hershey's Kisses.

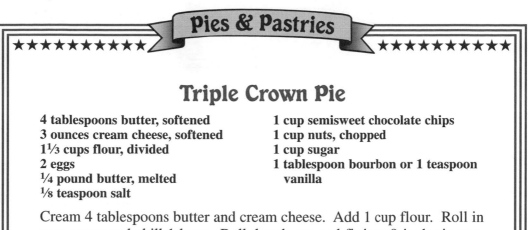

Triple Crown Pie

4 tablespoons butter, softened
3 ounces cream cheese, softened
1⅓ cups flour, divided
2 eggs
¼ pound butter, melted
⅛ teaspoon salt
1 cup semisweet chocolate chips
1 cup nuts, chopped
1 cup sugar
1 tablespoon bourbon or 1 teaspoon vanilla

Cream 4 tablespoons butter and cream cheese. Add 1 cup flour. Roll in wax paper and chill 1 hour. Roll dough out and fit into 9-inch pie pan. Beat eggs until frothy in food processor or blender. Add melted butter and ⅓ cup flour, then add remaining ingredients. Process until chocolate is very coarsely chopped. (Do not over process). Pour into pie shell and bake at 325° for 45-60 minutes, or until the center rises and the pastry is tan. Serve topped with whipped cream.

Note: For miniature tarts, cream ¼ pound butter with 6 ounces cream cheese, then blend in 2 cups flour. Chill in wax paper for 1 hour. Press 1-inch balls of dough into tiny muffin tins. Trim excess dough. Using the same filling as for the pie, fill tins ⅔ full. Bake at 325° for 25-35 minutes. Yields 48 tarts.

The Cooking Book (Kentucky)

French Silk Chocolate Pie

MERINGUE PIE CRUST:

2 egg whites
⅛ teaspoon salt
⅛ teaspoon cream of tartar
½ cup sugar
½ cup chopped pecans
1 teaspoon vanilla

Beat egg whites, salt and cream of tartar until foamy. Add sugar gradually and beat until stiff. Fold in pecans and vanilla. Place in greased 9-inch pie plate, building up sides ½ inch. Bake 1 hour at 300°. Cool.

FILLING:

1 stick butter, softened
¾ cup sugar
2 squares unsweetened chocolate, melted
1½ teaspoons vanilla
2 whole eggs
2 egg yolks
1 cup heavy cream, whipped

Cream butter and sugar. Blend in chocolate and vanilla. Add eggs and yolks, one at a time, beating 5 minutes between each one. Do not underbeat! Pour into cooled crust and refrigerate. Top with whipped cream and decorate with shaved chocolate, if desired. Serves 8.

Well Seasoned (Tennessee)

Peach Cream Pie

4 peeled, sliced fresh peaches
1 (9-inch) unbaked pie shell
⅔ cup sugar
4 tablespoons flour
⅛ teaspoon salt
½ teaspoon mace
1 cup half-and-half

Arrange peaches in shell. Combine dry ingredients. Stir into cream. Pour over peaches. Bake at 400° for 45 minutes; cover the edges of the pie crust for the first 30 minutes. Let cool. If it is not to be served for several hours and it is a hot summer day, it is wise to refrigerate this. However, it tastes best after cooling naturally. Serves 6 - 8.

Return Engagement (Iowa)

Gourmet Peach Pie

½ pint whipping cream
1 cup powdered sugar, divided
6 ounces cream cheese
1 (9-inch) baked pie shell
Sliced peaches

Whip cream with ½ cup of powdered sugar. Beat cream cheese with rest of powdered sugar. Fold together the whipped cream mixture and the cream cheese mixture. Spread in the cooled pie shell. Cool in refrigerator for at least 2 hours. Cover cream mixture with sliced fresh peaches.

GLAZE:
1 cup sugar
2 tablespoons cornstarch
1 cup mashed peaches
1 cup water
Yellow food color

Make a glaze by mixing together the sugar, cornstarch, mashed peaches, water and about 2 drops of food coloring. Boil until clear, stirring constantly. When cool, pour over pie. Canned cherry pie filling may be substituted for the fresh peaches when they are out of season.

Trading Secrets (Texas)

Mile-High Raspberry Pie

ALMOND PASTRY:

¼ cup butter
¼ teaspoon salt
2 tablespoons sugar
1 egg yolk
¾ cup sifted flour
¼ cup finely chopped almonds

Cream butter, salt, and sugar until light and fluffy. Add egg yolk; beat well. Stir in flour and almonds to make a stiff dough. Press into a 9-inch pie pan. Refrigerate 30 minutes, then bake for 10 minutes at 400°, until golden.

FILLING:

1 (10- to 12-ounce) package frozen raspberries; or 2½ cups fresh raspberries
1 cup sugar for frozen or 1⅓ cups for fresh
1 tablespoon lemon juice
Dash of salt
2 egg whites, room temperature
1 cup heavy cream, whipped
½ teaspoon almond extract

Thaw raspberries if frozen. Place raspberries in large bowl of mixer. Add sugar, lemon juice, salt, and egg whites. Beat 15 minutes, or until stiff. Fold in whipped cream and almond extract. Mound in baked pastry shell. Freeze until firm. Makes 8 servings.

The Very Special Raspberry Cookbook (New Mexico)

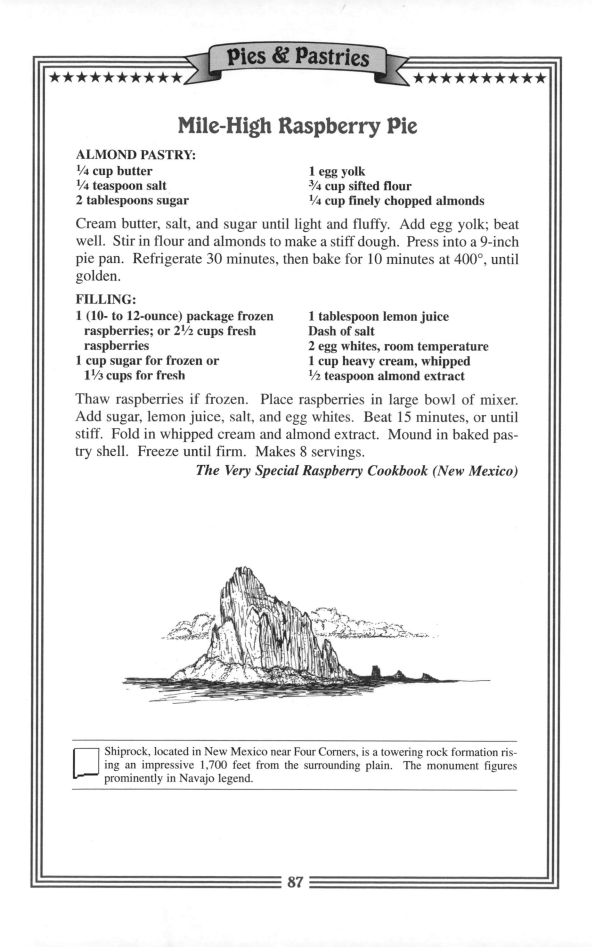

Shiprock, located in New Mexico near Four Corners, is a towering rock formation rising an impressive 1,700 feet from the surrounding plain. The monument figures prominently in Navajo legend.

Banana Split Pie

Mary's favorite!

3 egg yolks
½ cup granulated sugar
3½ tablespoons cornstarch
¼ teaspoon salt
2½ cups milk
½ cup crushed pineapple, well drained
1 teaspoon vanilla
1 large banana
8 -10 maraschino cherries
1 (9-inch) pie crust, baked

TOPPING:
Whipped cream
Maraschino cherries
Pecan pieces
¼ cup semisweet chocolate pieces, melted

Beat yolks and set aside. Combine sugar, cornstarch, and salt in saucepan. Add milk gradually, stirring as you do. Cook over medium heat until pudding begins to thicken. Add pineapple. Add egg yolks (to which some of hot filling has been added). Cook until pudding has thickened. Add vanilla. Remove from heat. Cool to room temperature.

Add banana, sliced or chopped, and chopped cherries. Pour into prebaked, cooled pie crust. Top with whipped cream. Garnish with maraschino cherries, chopped pecans, and drizzle melted semisweet chocolate over pie. Refrigerate leftovers—if any! Serves 6.

Luncheon Favorites (Missouri)

★ **Editor's Extra:** Make it Hawaiian by substituting ½ cup coconut in pie for the cherries and eliminating the chocolate.

Royal Hawaiian Pie with Blueberries

1 (15-ounce) can crushed pineapple
3 tablespoons cornstarch
½ cup sugar
1⅓ cups coconut
½ cup pecan pieces
2 bananas
1 (9-inch) baked pie shell
1 cup blueberries
Whipped cream or whipped topping
2 tablespoons chopped pecans

Drain pineapple, reserving juice; add enough water to drained juice to make 1 cup. Dissolve cornstarch in ½ cup juice. Stir into remaining juice and combine with sugar, pineapple, coconut, and pecan pieces. Cook, stirring, over medium heat until thickened. Cool. Slice bananas evenly into bottom of pie shell; cover with blueberries. Pour pineapple filling over top. Top with whipped cream and sprinkle with chopped pecans. Chill thoroughly before serving. Makes 8 servings.

The Blueberry Lover's Cookbook (Texas II)

Glazed Strawberry Pie

1½ quarts fresh strawberries
1 (9-inch) pie crust, baked, or graham cracker pie crust
1 cup sugar
2½ tablespoons cornstarch
Pinch of salt
½ cup water
1 tablespoon butter
Few drops of red food coloring
Whipped cream

Wash and hull berries. Put 1 quart of berries into prepared pie crust. Combine sugar, cornstarch and salt in saucepan. Crush remaining ½ quart berries and place in saucepan with sugar mixture and water. Bring mixture to a boil, stirring constantly, and cook until thick and clear. Remove from heat; add butter and enough food coloring to make the color pronounced but not too red. Strain glaze and pour carefully over the berries in the pie shell. Cool before serving. Pipe edges around pie with whipped cream.

A Cookbook of Pinehurst Courses (North Carolina)

Lemon-Crusted Fresh Blueberry Pie

LEMON PASTRY:

2 cups sifted flour
1 teaspoon salt
½ teaspoon grated lemon peel
⅔ cup shortening
4 - 6 tablespoons cold water
1 tablespoon lemon juice

Sift together flour and salt; stir in lemon peel. Cut in shortening with pastry blender until pieces are the size of small peas. Mix together water and lemon juice. Sprinkle 1 tablespoon liquid over part of flour mixture. Gently toss with fork; push to side of bowl. Sprinkle next tablespoon liquid over dry portion; mix lightly; push to moistened part at side of bowl. Repeat with remaining liquid until all flour mixture is moistened. Divide dough into 2 portions and form each portion into a ball. Flatten pastry balls 1 at a time, on lightly floured surface. Roll from center to edge until dough is ⅛ inch thick.

PIE:

4 cups fresh blueberries
¾ to 1 cup sugar
3 tablespoons flour
½ teaspoon grated lemon peel
Dash of salt
1 - 2 teaspoons lemon juice
1 tablespoon butter or margarine

In mixing bowl, combine blueberries, sugar, flour, lemon peel, and salt. Line a 9-inch pie plate with Lemon Pastry; pour in filling. Drizzle with lemon juice and dot with butter or margarine. Adjust top crust, cutting slits or decorations for escape of steam. Seal and flute edges. If desired, sprinkle top crust with additional sugar. Bake at 400° for 35-40 minutes. Yields 8 servings.

Vintage Vicksburg (Mississippi)

Blueberry Sour Cream Pie

1 ready-made pie crust

Follow one-crust pie directions on package. Place in 9-inch glass pie plate. Fold edge under, crimp, freeze 10 minutes. Prick with fork. Bake until sides are set, about 12 minutes.

1 cup sour cream
¾ cup sugar
2½ tablespoons flour
1 egg, beaten to blend
¾ teaspoon almond extract
¼ teaspoon salt
2½ cups fresh blueberries

Mix first 6 ingredients in medium bowl to blend. Mix in blueberries. Spoon into crust. Bake at 350° until filling is just set, about 25 minutes.

TOPPING:
6 tablespoons flour
¼ cup (½ stick) chilled unsalted butter, cut into pieces
⅓ cup chopped pecans
2 tablespoons sugar

Using fingertips, mix flour and butter in medium bowl until small clumps form. Mix in pecans and sugar. Spoon topping over pie. Bake until topping browns lightly, about 12 minutes. Cool pie at room temperature.

Blissfield Preschool Cookbook (Michigan)

Blueberry Cream Pie

1 can blueberries (reserve juice)
¼ cup sugar
2 tablespoons flour
1½ tablespoons lemon juice
¼ teaspoon cinnamon
1 (3-ounce) package cream cheese
½ cup powdered sugar
1 teaspoon vanilla
½ pint whipping cream
1 (9-inch) baked pie shell

Drain blueberries. Combine juice with sugar, flour, lemon juice, and cinnamon. Boil until thick, stirring constantly. Cool and add blueberries. Cream cream cheese, powdered sugar, and vanilla. Whip whipping cream until stiff. Stir together whipped cream and cream cheese combination. Spread into pie shell. Spoon blueberry mixture over top and chill overnight.

Madison County Cookery (Mississippi)

Deep-Dish Cherry Pie

A deep-dish cherry pie with a new way with the crust and a meringue-type cake topping.

1 cup flour
1 tablespoon powdered sugar
½ cup margarine or butter
1 can cherry pie mix

Sift flour and powdered sugar together; cut in butter. Pat evenly over bottom and sides of 10-inch deep-dish pie pan. Bake in moderate oven (350°) for 15 minutes until lightly browned. Spread cherry pie mix over partially baked crust; top with Meringue Cake Topping.

MERINGUE CAKE TOPPING:
2 egg whites
1 cup sugar
¾ cup flour
½ teaspoon baking powder
3 tablespoons coffee cream or half-and-half
1 teaspoon vanilla
¾ cup coarsely chopped pecans
½ cup coconut

Beat egg whites until very frothy; gradually add sugar a little at a time; beat until stiff peaks form. Sift flour and baking powder together; fold in meringue mixture alternately with cream. Fold in vanilla, nuts, and coconut; do not beat. Turn out over top of cherries. If desired, arrange a crown of candied cherries and chopped pecans over meringue. Bake in moderate oven (350°) for 30 minutes; do not overbake.

Great Lakes Cookery (Michigan)

Pineapple-Rhubarb Pie

3 cups rhubarb, cut up
1 cup crushed, drained pineapple
1 cup sugar
3 tablespoons tapioca
2 tablespoons lemon juice
½ teaspoon grated lemon rind
Pastry for 2-crust, 9-inch pie

Blend rhubarb, pineapple, sugar, tapioca, lemon juice and rind. Put in unbaked pie shell. Top with vented crust. Bake in 375° oven for 40-50 minutes. Cover with foil last 10 minutes to prevent over-browning.

Ritzy Rhubarb Secrets Cookbook (Great Plains)

Impossible Buttermilk Pie

1½ cups sugar
1 cup buttermilk (or 1 cup milk and 1 tablespoon vinegar)
½ cup Bisquick mix
½ cup margarine
1 teaspoon vanilla
3 eggs

Combine all ingredients in blender and beat for 30 seconds. Pour into a greased 9-inch pie plate. Bake at 350° for 30 minutes, or until knife blade inserted in center of pie comes out clean. Cool and serve.

A Shower of Roses (Louisiana II)

Raleigh House Buttermilk Pie

This pie was a popular dessert at Raleigh House. Many of my customers bought several for their freezers. They freeze well.

1 stick margarine, melted
2 cups sugar
3 eggs
3 rounded tablespoons flour
1 cup buttermilk
Dash nutmeg
1 teaspoon vanilla
1 (9- or 10-inch) unbaked pie shell

Mix melted margarine and sugar in mixer; beat well. Add eggs, one at a time, alternating with flour, beating after each addition. Add buttermilk, nutmeg, and vanilla. Mix again and pour into pie shell. Bake on the lower rack of a 375° oven for 30-35 minutes or until edges are firm but center is still a little trembly. This pie is good hot or cold. We always heated it in the microwave before serving. Yields 6 - 8 servings.

Raleigh House Cookbook (Texas II)

Cranberry-Glazed Cheese Pie

Cranberry-juiced, apply-delicious!

CRUST:

1½ cups graham cracker or cookie crumbs
3 tablespoons sugar
⅓ cup butter, melted

Combine crumbs, sugar, and butter; mix well. Press into a 9-inch pie plate. Bake at 350° for 10 minutes. Cool.

FILLING:

1 (3-ounce) package lemon gelatin
1¼ cups boiling water
1 (8-ounce) package cream cheese, softened
1½ cups grated apple
1 tablespoon sugar

Dissolve gelatin in boiling water; add cream cheese and blend until well mixed. Refrigerate until slightly jelled. Beat again. Mix grated apple with sugar; add to gelatin mixture, blend, and pour into prepared crust. Chill.

TOPPING:

2 teaspoons cornstarch
1 tablespoon sugar
½ cup cranberry or cranapple juice
1 apple, thinly sliced

Mix cornstarch and sugar; add juice and heat, stirring until thickened. Add apple slices and cook until soft. Arrange slices on top of pie, pouring any remaining juice mixture over. Chill.

Apple Orchard Cookbook (New England)

Sour Cream Apple Pie

This has to be the best apple pie ever.

1½ cups sugar, divided
7 tablespoons flour, divided
1 egg, slightly beaten
1 cup sour cream
1 teaspoon vanilla
¼ teaspoon salt
5 cups pared, cored, diced apples
1 (9-inch) unbaked pie shell
¼ cup butter

Mix 1 cup sugar and 2 tablespoons flour. Add egg, sour cream, vanilla, and salt. Beat until smooth. Add diced apples and pour into pie shell. Bake at 350° for 30 minutes. Mix remaining ½ cup sugar, 5 tablespoons flour, and butter to resemble crumbs. Cover the pie with crumbs and bake for 15 minutes longer. Serves 6 happy apple pie lovers. Can top with cheese or ice cream, your choice . . . I like mine plain.

Collectibles III (Texas II)

★ **Editor's Extra:** 2½ cups fresh blueberries can be substituted; use almond extract instead of vanilla.

Country Apple Pie with Lemon Glaze

Pastry for 2-crust pie
5 - 7 apples
¾ cup sugar
1 teaspoon cinnamon
2 tablespoons flour
1 tablespoon butter or margarine

Line 9-inch pie pan with bottom crust. Pare, core and slice apples. Combine with mixture of sugar, cinnamon, and flour. Place in pastry-lined pan. Dot with butter. Place top crust over filling. Trim and seal. Prick or cut slots to allow steam to escape. Bake at 400° for 30-40 minutes or until apples are cooked and crust is lightly browned. If crust begins browning too much before pie is done, place a sheet of foil over pie and continue baking.

LEMON GLAZE:

1 tablespoon butter, melted
1 tablespoon lemon juice
Powdered sugar (enough to thicken)

Wait about 10 minutes after pie is out of oven. Mix above ingredients in small bowl. Spread over pie.

A Matter of Taste (Ohio)

Sweet Potato Pie

My granddaughter, Denise, loves this pie, and she doesn't even like sweet potatoes very much. It's delicious with a scoop of homemade vanilla ice cream on top.

FILLING:

2 cups mashed, cooked sweet potatoes
6 tablespoons unsalted butter, softened
2 eggs, beaten
⅓ cup granulated sugar
1 teaspoon vanilla extract
½ teaspoon cinnamon
½ teaspoon freshly grated nutmeg
¼ cup evaporated milk
1 (9-inch) deep-dish pie shell, partially baked

Preheat oven to 350°. In a bowl mash together sweet potatoes and softened butter. Add eggs, sugar, vanilla, cinnamon, nutmeg, and evaporated milk, and stir well until smooth. Pour into pie shell; smooth the top.

TOPPING:

3 tablespoons unsalted butter, melted
½ cup tightly packed light brown sugar
⅓ cup all-purpose flour
⅔ cup finely chopped pecans

In a small bowl, combine melted butter, brown sugar, flour, and pecans. Stir to blend; the mixture will be crumbly. Sprinkle topping over pie. Bake on a cookie sheet 25-35 minutes.

Aunt Freddie's Pantry (Mississippi)

Raisin Cream Pie

1 cup raisins
1 cup water
1 cup sugar
½ cup brown sugar
4 tablespoons flour
2 eggs
½ cup water
2 tablespoons margarine
3 tablespoons lemon juice
1 tablespoon vanilla
Baked pie shell
Cool Whip

Bring to a boil raisins and 1 cup water. Beat sugars, flour, eggs, and ½ cup water together. Mix with hot raisins. Cook until thick. Remove from heat. Add margarine, lemon juice, and vanilla. Cool. Pour into baked shell. Top with Cool Whip.

25th Anniversary Cookbook (Ohio)

Blackberry Pie

Pastry (for single crust pie)
1 (4-ounce) container whipped cream cheese
⅛ cup sugar
⅛ cup sour cream
5 cups fresh blackberries, divided
1 cup sugar (more or less, depending on sweetness of berries)
3 tablespoons cornstarch
1 tablespoon lemon juice
Whipped cream

Cook pie shell and cool. Combine next 3 ingredients and spread in bottom of cooked pie shell. Arrange 1 cup of blackberries on the cream cheese mixture. Combine remaining berries and sugar in saucepan and mash and cook. Add the cornstarch and lemon juice. Cook until very thick. Pour into pie shell. Chill to set. Top with whipped cream.

A Taste of Salt Air & Island Kitchens (New England)

Elegant Pumpkin Pie

This pie is delicious plain or may be covered with meringue or sweetened whipped cream.

1 (9-inch) pastry shell
3 eggs, well beaten
½ cup dark brown sugar, firmly packed
1 teaspoon salt
½ teaspoon cinnamon
½ teaspoon nutmeg
½ teaspoon ginger
¼ teaspoon cloves
1½ cups milk, scalded
½ cup thick cream
2 cups strained, cooked pumpkin

Line 9-inch pie pan with pastry and make fluted standing rim. Combine eggs, sugar, salt and spices; gradually stir in milk, cream and pumpkin (the canned variety of strained pumpkin is ideal). Turn into uncooked pastry-lined pie plate and bake in hot oven 450° 10 minutes. Reduce heat to moderate 350°, and bake 20-25 minutes longer, or until knife comes out clean when carefully inserted in custard.

Gourmet of the Delta (Mississippi)

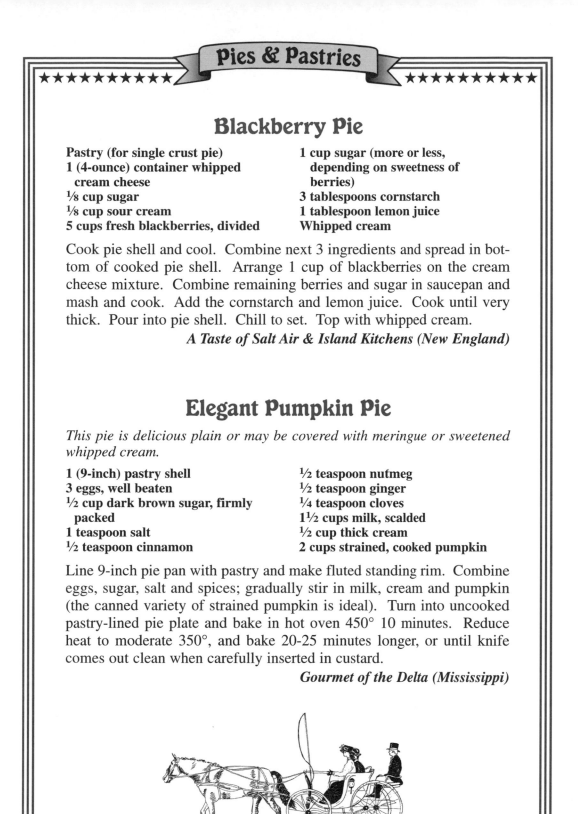

Kahlua Pecan Pie

¼ cup butter
¾ cup sugar
1 teaspoon vanilla
2 teaspoons flour
3 eggs
½ cup Kahlua
½ cup corn syrup
¾ cup evaporated milk
1 cup chopped pecans
1 (9-inch) unbaked pie shell

Set oven to 400°. Mix butter, sugar, vanilla and flour. Beat in eggs one at a time. Stir in Kahlua, corn syrup, evaporated milk and pecans, mix well. Pour into pie shell. Bake for 10 minutes then reduce heat to 325°. Continue cooking until firm, approximately 25 minutes.

From the Player's Club
Island Events Cookbook (South Carolina)

Mystery Pecan Pie

1 (8-ounce) package cream cheese, softened
⅓ cup sugar
¼ teaspoon salt
1 teaspoon vanilla
1 egg
9-inch baked pie shell
1¼ cups chopped pecans
3 eggs
¼ cup sugar
1 teaspoon vanilla
1 cup light corn syrup (Karo)

In medium bowl, combine cream cheese, ⅓ cup sugar, salt, vanilla and egg. Pour into pie shell. Sprinkle with pecans.

Combine remaining eggs, ¼ cup sugar, vanilla and syrup. Pour over pecans. Bake at 375° for 35-40 minutes or until center is firm. Pie will be golden brown. Layers will change in baking, with pecans floating to top, cream cheese layer next, and egg-syrup mixture sinking to bottom. May serve with vanilla ice cream or whipped topping. Serves 6 - 8.

Loaves and Fishes (Alabama)

Peanut Butter Pie

This is delicious and similar to a peanut butter cheesecake.

CHOCOLATE CRUNCH CRUST:

⅓ cup butter
1 (6-ounce) package chocolate chips
2½ cups Rice Krispies

In heavy saucepan, over low heat, melt ⅓ cup butter and 1 small package chocolate chips. Remove from heat and gently stir in cereal until completely coated. Press into bottom and side of greased 9-inch pie plate. Chill 30 minutes.

PIE:

1 (8-ounce) package cream cheese, softened
1 (14-ounce) can sweetened condensed milk (not evaporated)
1 cup peanut butter
1 teaspoon vanilla
1 (8-ounce) carton Cool Whip, thawed
1 (6-ounce) jar Smuckers Chocolate Fudge Sauce

In large bowl, beat cream cheese until fluffy; beat in condensed milk, peanut butter, and vanilla until smooth. Fold in Cool Whip. Turn into Chocolate Crunch Crust. Top with fudge sauce (it helps to place pie in freezer for a time to make spreading easier). Chill in freezer for about 2 hours. Serves 8.

Ship to Shore I (North Carolina)

Peanut Butter Pie

1 (8-ounce) package cream cheese
½ cup sugar
½ cup creamy peanut butter
1 teaspoon vanilla
1 (8-ounce) carton whipping cream
1 (9-inch) graham cracker crust
1 - 2 tablespoons chopped salted peanuts (optional)

Combine cream cheese and sugar until smooth. Add peanut butter and vanilla. Beat well. Beat whipping cream to peaks. Fold into first mixture. Pour into crust. Sprinkle on peanuts. Chill 3 hours.

Generations of Good Cooking (Iowa)

Angel Pie

Gorgeous looking and a heavenly taste.

MERINGUE:
4 egg whites
¼ teaspoon cream of tartar
1 cup sugar
Pinch of salt
1 teaspoon vanilla extract

Preheat oven to 275°. Beat egg whites until frothy. Add cream of tartar and beat until stiff, gradually adding sugar and salt. Fold in vanilla. Spread in a 9-inch buttered pie pan covering bottom and sides; shape with the back of a spoon, making the bottom ¼ inch thick and the sides 1 inch thick. Bake for 1 hour; leave in the oven to cool for 1 hour.

FILLING:
4 egg yolks
½ cup sugar
¼ cup lemon juice
2 tablespoons grated lemon peel
2 cups whipping cream, whipped, divided
Toasted almonds, for garnish

Beat egg yolks until lemon-colored, gradually adding sugar, lemon juice and peel. Cook in the top of a double boiler over hot water (not touching pan) until thick, stirring constantly. (This will take between 5 and 8 minutes.) Cool. Fold in half of whipped cream. Spread over meringue and cover with remaining whipped cream. Sprinkle toasted almonds over the top. Refrigerate a minimum of 12 hours. May be made the day before serving. Serves 8.

Cook and Deal (Florida)

German Chocolate Angel Pie

SHELL:

2 egg whites
1/8 teaspoon salt
1/8 teaspoon cream of tartar
1/2 cup sugar
1/8 teaspoon vanilla
1/2 cup finely chopped nuts

Beat egg whites with salt and cream of tartar until foamy. Add sugar, 2 tablespoons at a time, beating well after each addition; continue beating until stiff peaks form. Fold in vanilla and nuts. Spoon into lightly greased 8-inch pie pan to form nest-like shell, building sides up to 1/2 inch above the edge of pan. Bake at 300° 50-55 minutes. Cool.

CHOCOLATE CREAM FILLING:

1 (4-ounce) bar Baker's German Sweet Chocolate (or 5 ounces milk chocolate)
3 tablespoons water
1 teaspoon vanilla
1 cup heavy cream, whipped

Stir chocolate in water over low heat until melted; cool until thick. Add vanilla. Fold whipped cream into chocolate mixture. Pile into cooled shell. Chill 2 hours. Serves 6 - 8.

Variation: Double amounts of egg whites, sugar, cream of tartar, and vanilla for deeper meringue crust; use larger pie pan.

Out of Our League (North Carolina)

Strawberry Angel Pie

3/4 cup sugar
4 tablespoons cornstarch
1 1/2 cups boiling water
3 egg whites
3 tablespoons sugar
1 teaspoon vanilla flavoring
1 package frozen strawberries
10 individual baked tart shells or meringue shells
1 cup whipping cream

Combine sugar and cornstarch. Stir sugar mixture into boiling water and cook, stirring constantly, until clear. Pour slowly into well-beaten egg whites beaten with 3 tablespoons sugar. Add vanilla. Fold in 2 tablespoons strawberries; pour mixture into baked tart shells or meringue shells. Cool. Serve with whipped cream and remaining strawberries. If fresh strawberries are in season, garnish each serving with one or two.

I Promised A Cookbook (Mississippi)

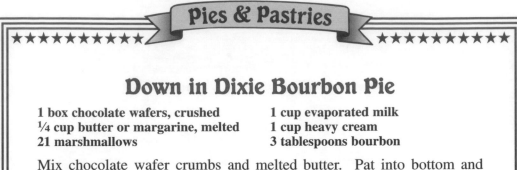

Down in Dixie Bourbon Pie

1 box chocolate wafers, crushed
¼ cup butter or margarine, melted
21 marshmallows
1 cup evaporated milk
1 cup heavy cream
3 tablespoons bourbon

Mix chocolate wafer crumbs and melted butter. Pat into bottom and sides of a 9-inch pie pan. Bake at 350° until set, about 15 minutes.

In saucepan, heat marshmallows and milk until marshmallows melt and mixture is smooth. Do not boil. Remove from heat. Whip cream until stiff. Fold into marshmallow mixture. Add bourbon and pour into cooled chocolate crumb crust. Refrigerate 4 hours or until set. Additional whipped cream and chocolate crumbs make an attractive garnish. Yields 6 - 8 servings.

Vintage Vicksburg (Mississippi)

★ **Editor's Extra:** If you can't find chocolate wafers, scrape the cream off Oreo halves. Works great!

In the 1830s a ten-dollar note was issued by a New Orleans bank which read "Dix" (which is French for ten). Riverboat workers returning to the north boasted that they had "a pocketful of Dixies" or ten-dollar notes. With the help of a minstrel tune, the Deep South soon became known as "Dixie."

Pawleys Island Cobbler

¼ cup butter, softened
½ cup sugar
½ cup milk
1 cup sifted flour
2 teaspoons baking powder
¼ teaspoon salt
Fruit and juice*
Sugar

Cream butter and sugar; add milk and dry ingredients. Pour batter into a 2-quart greased casserole. Place fruit, sugar, and juice over batter in that order. Bake at 375° for 45 minutes or until batter rises to top, browns, and cobbler is bubbly.

*For filling, use enough fresh fruit of any kind, sugared, to cover bottom of 2-quart casserole, or use canned cherries, blackberries, etc. If using canned fruit, use ¼ cup sugar and 1 cup of juice.

Feeding the Faithful (South Carolina)

Ricotta Raspberry Tart

An excellent brunch dessert.

2 cups ricotta cheese
Zest of 1 orange
3 eggs
½ cup granulated sugar
4 cups raspberries

Preheat oven to 350°. Grease well a 12-inch springform pan. In a large bowl, mix together ricotta and orange zest. Lightly beat eggs and add them and granulated sugar to ricotta; mix well. Pour mixture into prepared pan and top with raspberries; set aside.

TOPPING:
¾ cup unsalted butter
½ cup confectioners' sugar
1 egg
1½ cups all-purpose flour
½ cup toasted almonds
½ teaspoon almond extract
½ teaspoon salt

In a medium bowl, mix well butter and confectioners' sugar. Add egg and mix again. Add flour, almonds, almond extract, and salt; mix well. Crumble this topping over raspberries and bake for 35-40 minutes or until a tester inserted in center of cheese custard comes out clean. Allow to cool completely before chilling for an hour before serving. Serve chilled.

Home Cookin': Almont Elementary PTA (Michigan)

Pear-Raspberry Cobbler

2½ pounds firm pears, sliced (5 or 6)
½ cup sugar or Sugar Twin
2½ tablespoons flour
⅛ teaspoon cinnamon
⅛ teaspoon nutmeg
1 tablespoon lemon juice
1 cup raspberries, fresh or frozen

Preheat oven to 350°. Peel, halve, core, and slice pears. Combine sugar, flour, spices, and sliced pears. Add lemon juice and raspberries. Mix and spoon into 2-quart dish.

TOPPING:
¾ cup flour
1 tablespoon plus 1 teaspoon sugar or Sugar Twin
¾ teaspoon baking powder
¼ teaspoon soda
¼ teaspoon salt
3 tablespoons cold butter
¼ cup nonfat buttermilk

Combine flour, 1 tablespoon sugar, baking powder, soda, and salt. Cut butter into small pieces and blend with pastry cutter into flour mixture until coarse meal texture; then add buttermilk. Stir, roll between 2 pieces waxed paper sprayed with Pam. Peel off waxed paper and place over fruit and sprinkle with remaining teaspoon sugar. Bake for 35-45 minutes, till lightly browned. Serves 8.

Beyond Loaves and Fishes (New Mexico)

Kolachy

A rich, fancy, finger pastry.

1 (3-ounce) package cream cheese, softened
½ cup butter, softened
1 cup sifted flour
4 ounces apricot or raspberry jam, approximately

Combine the cream cheese, butter, and flour. Divide the dough in half. Chill. Roll out half at a time, approximately ¼ inch thick. Cut with a small square-shaped, circular-shaped, or diamond-shaped cookie cutter. Place ½ teaspoon of jam on each cookie. Bring 2 sides of the cookies up to meet in the middle and crimp. Bake on ungreased cookie sheets at 350° for 20 minutes or until lightly browned. Cool on racks. Sprinkle with powdered sugar. Yields 2 dozen.

Variation: Recipe may be doubled using 8 ounces of cream cheese. Add 3 tablespoons sugar and ¼ teaspoon salt.

A Pinch of Sunshine (Florida)

Peach Cobbler

¾ cup flour
⅛ teaspoon salt
2 teaspoons baking powder
2 cups sugar, divided
¾ cup milk
½ cup margarine
2 cups freshly sliced peaches

Sift flour, salt, and baking powder. Mix with 1 cup sugar; slowly stir in milk to make batter. Melt butter in 8x8x2-inch pan. Pour batter over melted butter. Do not stir. Mix peaches with remaining 1 cup sugar and carefully spoon over batter. Bake 1 hour at 350°. Serve hot or cold, with cream if desired.

Southwest Cookin' (Arkansas)

Peach Crisp with Maple Sauce

Wonderful taste.

PEACH CRISP:
1 cup flour
½ cup packed brown sugar
½ cup granulated sugar
½ teaspoon cinnamon
¼ teaspoon nutmeg
¼ teaspoon salt
½ cup butter
8 medium, fresh peaches, peeled, sliced (5 - 6 cups)
2 tablespoons maple syrup
Juice and rind of ½ lemon

Combine flour, sugars, cinnamon, nutmeg, and salt. Cut into butter with pastry blender or fork until crumbly. Combine peaches with maple syrup, lemon juice, and rind. Place in 9-inch square baking pan. Sprinkle with crumb mixture. Cover with foil. Bake at 375° for 30 minutes. Remove foil. Bake 15 minutes more, or until crisp on top. Serve warm or cold with Creamy Maple Sauce. Makes 6 - 8 servings.

CREAMY MAPLE SAUCE:
1½ cups whipping cream
⅓ cup maple syrup
3 tablespoons light corn syrup

Combine ingredients and simmer about 30 minutes or until thickened and reduced. Chill.

Soupçon II (Illinois)

Apple Turnovers

2½ cups flour
1 cup margarine
¾ teaspoon salt
1 egg, separated
⅔ cup milk
8 -12 baking apples
¾ cup sugar
½ teaspoon cinnamon
1 tablespoon flour
2 tablespoons tapioca

Mix flour, margarine, and salt like you would a pie crust. Combine egg yolk and milk. Stir into flour mix. Take half of this dough and press into 10x15-inch baking sheet. Slice apples onto pastry. Combine sugar, cinnamon, flour, and tapioca. Sprinkle on the apples. Roll out remaining dough and lay on top, sealing edge as best you can. Beat egg white and brush on top of dough. Bake for 10 minutes at 425°. Then bake 20 minutes at 350°. Cool. Swirl a powdered sugar glaze over the top (1 cup powdered sugar and hot water, enough to make a glaze).

Saint Mary Catholic Church Cookbook (Iowa)

Apple Dumplings

2 cups all-purpose flour
2 teaspoons baking powder
1 teaspoon salt
1 tablespoon butter or margarine, softened
1 tablespoon shortening
1 cup milk
½ cup butter or margarine, melted
1 teaspoon ground cinnamon
4 tablespoons brown sugar
6 tart apples, peeled, cored and chopped
Apple Dumpling Sauce

Combine flour, baking powder and salt in a large mixing bowl. Cut in butter and shortening until mixture resembles coarse meal. Gradually add milk to make a soft dough. Roll dough into a ¼-inch-thick rectangle on a lightly floured surface. Brush with melted butter; sprinkle with cinnamon and brown sugar. Spread apples over pastry. Roll up jellyroll fashion; cut into 10 slices. Place flat in a greased 9x13x2-inch baking pan; bake at 350° for 20 minutes. Pour Apple Dumpling Sauce over top, and continue baking 20 minutes. Yields 10 servings.

APPLE DUMPLING SAUCE:

1 cup sugar
1 tablespoon all-purpose flour
Dash of salt
1 tablespoon butter or margarine
½ teaspoon lemon juice
1 cup hot water

Combine all ingredients in a saucepan over medium heat. Bring to a boil; cook 2 minutes, stirring constantly. Yields 1½ cups.

The Apple Barn Cookbook (Tennessee)

Apple Spoon-Ups

2 cans apple pie filling
1 teaspoon cinnamon
1 can crescent-shaped dinner rolls
1½ cups sour cream
1 cup brown sugar

Preheat oven to 375°. Spread apple pie filling in greased 9x13-inch pan. Sprinkle with cinnamon. Unroll crescent rolls and place over apples. Combine sour cream and brown sugar. Spread over roll dough. Bake for 40-45 minutes. Serve warm.

The Pick of the Crop (Mississippi)

Apple Crisp

This is by far the best apple crisp you have ever tasted! The sugar and water combine to make a wonderful "caramelly" thick sauce on the bottom with the apples.

½ cup water
½ cup sugar
1 teaspoon cinnamon
4 cups diced apples
1 cup brown sugar
1 cup flour
7 tablespoons butter

Stir water, sugar, and cinnamon together in bottom of 7x11-inch baking dish; stir in apples. Mix brown sugar, flour, and butter with fingers until crumbly, and sprinkle on top. Bake in 350° oven for 35 minutes and serve warm. Yields 8 servings.

Variations: English Apple Pie. Slice 8 medium tart apples into buttered 9-inch pie pan and sprinkle with ½ cup sugar. Mix 1 cup flour, ½ cup brown sugar, ½ cup chopped pecans (optional) and ½ cup butter together; pat on top and bake at 350° for 30 minutes.

The Guild Cookbook IV (Indiana)

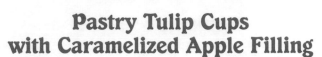

Pastry Tulip Cups with Caramelized Apple Filling

Mastering the art of working with frozen phyllo pastry is a fun activity. (No need to tell your awed guests how easy it was!) Easily made hours ahead, this apple filling can be reheated in the microwave or in a heavy pan over gentle heat. If you don't have the apple brandy, Calvados, substitute some good cognac.

6 large tart cooking apples, peeled, cored, and diced
6 tablespoons unsalted butter
6 tablespoons sugar
½ vanilla bean, split lengthwise
¼ cup Calvados
1 tablespoon fresh lemon juice
1 cup whipping cream
2 tablespoons confectioners' sugar

In a large skillet, stir apples with butter and sugar over medium heat until butter melts. Add vanilla bean to mixture. Increase heat to medium-high and cook, stirring frequently, until apples are brown and caramelized—about 30 minutes. Remove vanilla bean. Pour off any excess butter and add the Calvados. Cook for 1 minute more over high heat, scraping up any caramel from bottom of the pan. Stir in lemon juice.

Whip cream until thickened; add confectioners' sugar gradually and continue to whip until very stiff. While still warm, spoon apple mixture into Pastry Tulip Cups and top each with a large dollop of the freshly whipped cream. Makes 6 servings.

PASTRY TULIP CUPS:
4 sheets phyllo
Melted unsalted butter

Stack phyllo with butter brushed between the sheets. Cut into 4-inch squares. Press each square into a buttered muffin tin, pressing the bottom flat and folding excess dough to create a petal effect on the sides. Bake in the bottom third of a 375° oven for 10-12 minutes or until golden. Remove from muffin tins and cool on a rack.

Cooking with Marilyn (Ohio)

★ **Editor's Extra:** Filling is good in pastry cups, too. Yum!

Amaretto Cream Puffs

CREAM PUFFS:

½ cup butter
1 cup water
1 cup flour
4 eggs
¼ teaspoon salt

Preheat oven to 450°. Grease a large cookie sheet. Bring butter and water to boil and add flour. Stir until it forms a ball. Remove from heat and cool slightly. Beat eggs in 1 at a time. Beat well and add salt. Drop by teaspoonfuls onto cookie sheet, 2 inches apart. Bake at 450° for 15 minutes; lower heat to 350° for 10-25 minutes. Remove immediately and cool on rack.

FILLING:

1 cup heavy cream
4 teaspoons sugar
¼ cup amaretto

Whip cream until stiff then add sugar and amaretto.

SAUCE:

20 ounces frozen red raspberries in syrup, thawed
2 teaspoons cornstarch
1 tablespoon water

Place raspberries and syrup in blender. Purée for 10 seconds. Press through sieve (discard seeds). In a small saucepan, mix cornstarch with 1 tablespoon water. Add purée. Heat, stirring until mixture thickens and starts to boil. Cool.

Assembly: Slit cream puffs, fill with cream filling, and pour sauce over each one before serving. Serves 8.

Just Desserts (Pennsylvania)

Sopapillas

1 package active dry yeast
½ cup warm water (110°)
1 teaspoon sugar
3 cups flour
1 tablespoon melted butter, cooled
1 teaspoon salt
1 egg
Oil for frying

Dissolve yeast in warm water with sugar.

Mix flour, butter, salt, and egg. Pour into yeast mixture. Add enough water to make firm, springy bread-like dough.

Knead 15 minutes. Cover with towel or plastic wrap. Place in warm, draft-free area; let rise 30 minutes or longer until doubled in bulk.

Punch down dough. Roll half of dough to ¼-inch thickness on lightly floured board. Cut into 2-inch squares.

Heat oil to 375°. Stretch squares gently and drop into hot oil. Hold down in oil until dough begins to puff, then turn squares over. Fry only three or four at a time and turn often until golden. Drain on absorbent paper. Repeat with remaining dough. Serve hot with butter and lots of honey. Yields 3 dozen.

Houston Fine Arts Cookbook (Texas)

Frozen Desserts

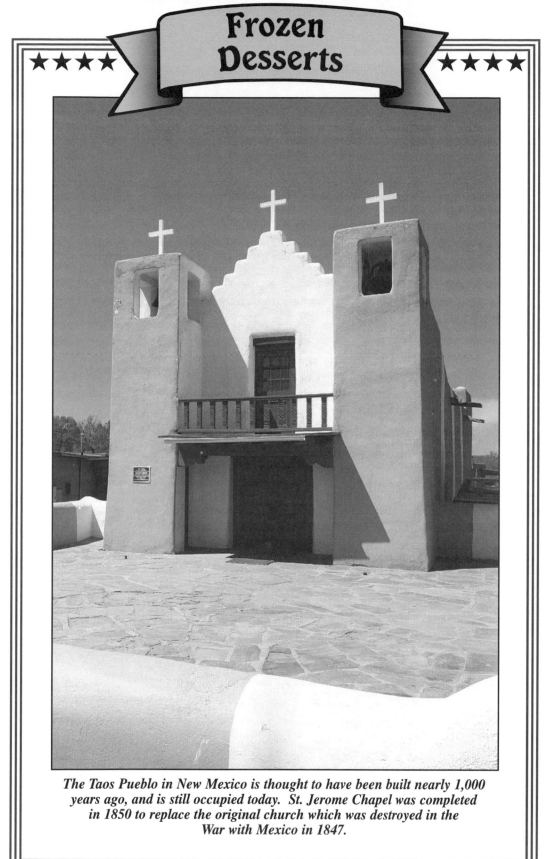

The Taos Pueblo in New Mexico is thought to have been built nearly 1,000 years ago, and is still occupied today. St. Jerome Chapel was completed in 1850 to replace the original church which was destroyed in the War with Mexico in 1847.

Ice Cream

4 eggs, beaten until light
2 heaping cups sugar
1 teaspoon salt
2 cups cream
2½ tablespoons vanilla
1 package instant vanilla pudding
Milk to fill can (1 quart)

Mix together first 6 ingredients well and put into ice cream freezer. Fill can with whole milk, allowing 2 inches from top of can. Churn freezer according to directions.

The Berns Family Cookbook (Iowa)

★ **Editor's Extra:** For those concerned about raw eggs, pasteurized liquid eggs or pasteurized liquid egg whites can usually be successfully substituted.

Aunt Clara's Peach Ice Cream

2 cups fresh peeled, sliced peaches
1½ - 3 cups sugar to taste, divided
3 whole eggs
2 teaspoons vanilla
1 quart milk (including 1 large can evaporated milk)
2 cups whipping cream, whipped

Purée the peaches or mash well with a fork. Let stand an hour or two with sugar to sweeten. Mix eggs, some sugar, vanilla, and milk. Fold in whipped cream and peaches and freeze in ice cream freezer.

When freezing, remember to fill the barrel about ⅓ full of ice, and then pour in a layer of ice cream salt. Pour more ice, then more salt. Keep the freezer full of ice, but be careful that no salty water gets into the freezing container. When you have turned until hard, remove dasher and pack tightly with ice and salt to ripen and harden. Or you can remove container to your own freezer. Serve when hard.

Chattanooga Cook Book (Tennessee)

French Chocolate Ice Cream

¼ cup sugar
½ cup water
6-9 ounces semisweet chocolate pieces
4 egg yolks
3 cups heavy cream, whipped

In a small saucepan combine sugar and water. Bring to boil and boil rapidly for 3 minutes. Into a blender container put semisweet chocolate pieces (more for real chocolate lovers!). Add the hot syrup; cover and blend on high speed until chocolate sauce is smooth. Add egg yolks. Stir to combine; cover and blend for 10 seconds. Fold chocolate mixture into whipped cream. Spoon into plastic container; cover with waxed paper, and freeze 2 - 3 hours. This needs no stirring and will not form ice crystals no matter how long you store it in your freezer. Makes 1½ quarts.

VARIATIONS:

1. Add mini-chips for chocolate chip ice cream.
2. Add almonds for chocolate almond.
3. Add instant coffee to sugar-water for mocha ice cream.

The Philadelphia Orchestra Cookbook (Pennsylvania)

The Attic's Almond Amaretto Ice Cream

½ gallon vanilla ice cream
8 tablespoons amaretto liqueur
Almond Crunch Topping

Freeze parfait or wine glasses. Just before serving, spoon in ice cream, splash with amaretto and sprinkle with Almond Crunch Topping. Serves 8.

ALMOND CRUNCH TOPPING:

2 ounces sliced almonds
2 tablespoons butter
1 cup sugar
1 tablespoon water

Spread sliced almonds in a buttered pan. In a small, heavy saucepan, stir together the sugar with a tablespoon of water over low heat until the sugar has melted. Then pour it over the almonds and let harden. When the topping is completely cold, break it up with your fingers or a kitchen hammer and grind it in a blender into smaller bits. Store the topping in a covered jar in the refrigerator.

Georgia's Historic Restaurants (Georgia)

Tin Can Ice Cream

1 (1-pound) can with lid
1 (3-pound) can with lid
¾ cup ice cream salt
1 egg
¾ cup milk
½ teaspoon vanilla
1 cup cream
⅓ cup sugar
Pinch salt

Fill large can half-full of crushed ice and ice cream salt. Mix egg, milk, vanilla, cream, sugar and salt in smaller can and put lid on. Place in larger can with lid and roll around about 10 minutes or until frozen. Serves 4.

Sisters Two II (Great Plains)

★ **Editor's Extra:** Nifty if you don't have an ice cream freezer. Be sure to fill large can with ice after small can is inserted, and be sure all lids are on tight—I rolled mine upright back and forth with a pair of oven mitts.

Gold Brick

1 stick margarine
1 (12-ounce) package chocolate chips
⅓ cup evaporated milk
1 cup chopped walnuts, pecans, or peanuts (optional)

Melt margarine, chocolate and milk in double boiler. Stir until chocolate is melted. Remove from heat and add nuts, if desired. Serve over ice cream (it will harden). Store in glass jar in refrigerator. Reheat in pan of warm water.

Lost Tree Cook Book (Florida)

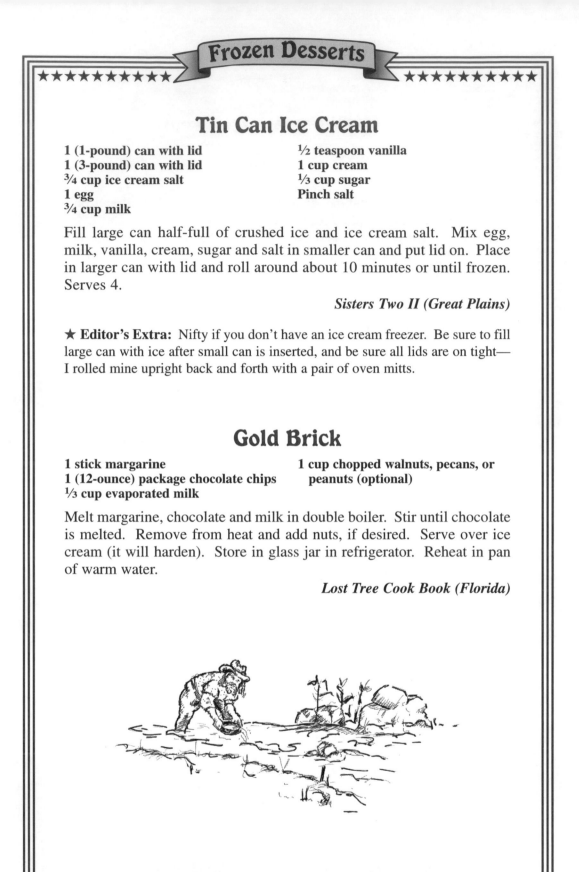

Apple Ice Cream Sauce

½ cup firmly packed brown sugar
1 tablespoon cornstarch
½ teaspoon cinnamon
¼ teaspoon nutmeg
1 teaspoon lemon juice
½ teaspoon grated lemon rind (optional)
1 (20-ounce) can pie-sliced apples, undrained

Combine the first 6 ingredients in a saucepan; blend well. Stir in apples; cook, stirring constantly, until thickened. Serve hot over vanilla ice cream. Yields about 6 servings.

Flavor Favorites (Texas)

Sherwood Forest Orange Cream Sauce

Serve on angel food cake or ice cream. This always gets rave notices.

2 egg yolks
½ cup sugar
½ cup orange juice
1 cup cream, whipped

Put egg yolks, sugar and juice on stove. Cook until thick. When cooled, add 1 cup cream that has been whipped until stiff. Serve immediately on angel cake slices or vanilla ice cream.

The Virginia Presidential Homes Cookbook (Virginia)

Here's the scoop: Charles Menches sold ice cream at the 1904 World's Fair in St. Louis, Missouri. On one particularly hot day he sold so much ice cream that he ran out of cups. Nearby, a Syrian friend of his named Ernest Hamwi was selling a wafflelike Middle Eastern pastry known as *zalabia*. In desperation, Menches bought some of Hamwi's pastries, rolled them into cones, and plopped a scoop of ice cream on top. Ingenious!

Chambord Melba Sauce

Place fresh, poached or frozen peaches in tall stemmed glasses, add vanilla ice cream and top with sauce.

1 (10-ounce) package frozen raspberries
½ cup currant jelly
¼ cup sugar
1 teaspoon cornstarch
⅓ cup Chambord liqueur
½ teaspoon fresh lemon juice

Combine the raspberries, currant jelly, sugar, and cornstarch in a saucepan. Stir over moderate heat until boiling. Then simmer gently for 10 minutes. Remove from heat and add the Chambord and lemon juice. Strain and chill before serving.

Raleigh House Cookbook II (Texas II)

Old-Fashioned Lemon Sauce

1 cup sugar
½ cup butter or margarine
¼ cup water
1 egg, well beaten
¾ teaspoon grated lemon peel
3 tablespoons lemon juice

In medium saucepan, combine all ingredients. Heat to boiling over medium heat, stirring constantly. Makes about 1 cup. Delicious over gingerbread.

Campbellsville College Women's Club Cookbook (Kentucky)

Fruited Ice

Many people have requested this fruit recipe.

1 cup sugar
1 cup water
1 (20-ounce) can crushed pineapple
1 (16-ounce) can apricot halves, drained and chopped
1 (16-ounce) package frozen strawberries
2 bananas

Boil sugar and water and add to mixture of pineapple, apricots, and strawberries. Slice in bananas; fill foil muffin cups and freeze. Makes about 30 foil cups.

Thank Heaven for Home Made Cooks (Wisconsin)

Watermelon Sorbet

2 cups watermelon, puréed
Juice of 2 lemons
2 cups simple syrup (2 cups water, 1 cup sugar, boiled 5 minutes)

Mix all together. Freeze overnight. Whip in food processor. Form into balls with ice cream server. Garnish with mint. Serves 12.

Twickenham Tables (Alabama)

Chunky Watermelon Sherbet

1 cup sugar
3 tablespoons lemon juice
4 cups diced, seeded watermelon
1/8 teaspoon salt
1 envelope unflavored gelatin
1/4 cup cold water
1 cup whipping cream

Combine sugar, lemon juice, watermelon, and salt; refrigerate 30 minutes. Spoon mixture into container of electric blender; process until smooth.

Soften gelatin in cold water; place over low heat, and stir until gelatin is dissolved. Add to watermelon mixture, stirring well. Add whipping cream, and beat until fluffy.

Pour into freezer can of a 1-gallon ice cream freezer. Freeze according to manufacturer's instructions. Yields 1 quart.

Cooking with Ms. Watermelon (Arkansas)

Caramel Delight

This is a very rich dessert, but it is worth every calorie.

1 large package (50) caramels
⅔ cup water
1 cup (8 ounces) sour cream
1 large container (1 pound) Cool Whip, slightly thawed

Melt caramels with water. (I use the microwave and it takes about 7 minutes.) You have to stir them until all the caramel is melted. You can also use a double boiler to melt the caramels. Allow the mixture to cool slightly (won't burn your finger when touched). After mixture has cooled, add the sour cream and Cool Whip. Stir until blended; do not beat.

Pour mixture into the Graham Cracker Crust. Sprinkle reserved mixture on top, cover with Saran Wrap and freeze.

Allow to stand at room temperature about 10-15 minutes before cutting into squares. Refreeze if all is not eaten at once. (I don't usually have any left.)

This is a great dessert for any occasion, and every time I take it to a social function, I am always asked for the recipe. This will feed about 15, depending on how large you cut your squares.

GRAHAM CRACKER CRUST:
1 package graham crackers, crushed
1 stick margarine, melted
1 tablespoon sugar

Pour melted butter over crackers and sugar; mix well and press into a 7x11-inch glass dish. Reserve about 2 tablespoons to sprinkle on top. (I spray my dish with Pam, or you could grease it with butter.)

The Junior Welfare League 50th Anniversary Cookbook (Kentucky)

Will's Ice Cream Cake

1 package Oreo cookies
1/3 cup butter, melted
1/3 cup slivered toasted almonds
2 pints softened coffee ice cream
1 pint softened vanilla ice cream
2 cups semisweet chocolate chips
1/4 cup milk or cream
1/4 cup Grand Marnier

Crush cookies and mix 4 cups crumbs with melted butter and toasted almonds. Reserve a few almonds and a small amount of cookie crumbs for topping. Place crumb mixture in a 10-inch springform pan and pat. Bake at 375° for about 15 minutes or until mixture forms a crust. Cool.

Fill crust with ice cream, layering flavors. Sprinkle top with reserved crumbs and almonds and freeze solid. Make a chocolate sauce by melting the chocolate chips over low heat. Add cream to thin, then stir in liqueur. Serve cake with drizzled chocolate sauce over each slice. Serves 12.

Kitchen Keepsakes by Request (Colorado)

Coffee Toffee Ice Cream Pie

1 (9-inch) graham cracker crust, baked
1 jumbo-size chocolate almond bar (1/2 pound)
1/4 cup coffee
1 quart coffee ice cream, slightly softened
3 Heath candy bars

Melt chocolate almond bar with coffee in double boiler. Spread over crust and cool. Fill chocolate-lined pie crust with coffee ice cream. Top with crushed Heath bars (crush better when frozen). Freeze. Remove 10-15 minutes before serving. Serves 6 - 8.

Note: The size of Heath candy bars makes no difference. The more the better!

The Cook Book (Missouri)

★ **Editor's Extra:** A heatproof bowl can become a double boiler by setting it over a right-sized pot—be sure the bottom of the bowl doesn't touch the boiling water in the pot.

Butter Brickle Ice Cream Pie

The caramel sauce can be made up to three days in advance and refrigerated . . . if you trust yourself to have this sweet treat in your house that long!

1½ cups pecans, coarsely chopped (save 8 whole pecans for garnish)
2 egg whites
¼ cup sugar
¼ teaspoon salt
1 quart butter brickle ice cream (or butter pecan or butter crunch), softened

Lightly toast all the pecans in a 350° oven for 5 - 8 minutes. Cool on a paper towel before using. Beat egg whites until frothy. Gradually add sugar and salt and beat until stiff. Fold in cooled chopped nuts and spread meringue in bottom and up side of well-buttered 9-inch pie pan. Prick bottom and sides with fork to eliminate bubbles. Bake at 350° for 15-20 minutes. Watch closely. Cool completely. Spread ice cream over crust. Cover with foil and freeze. To serve, cut into wedges, top with sauce and 1 whole pecan. Serves 8.

CARAMEL SAUCE:
1 cup firmly packed brown sugar
½ cup half-and-half or evaporated milk
¼ cup light corn syrup
2 tablespoons butter or margarine
1 tablespoon vanilla

Combine all ingredients except vanilla. Bring to a boil over medium heat, stirring occasionally. Boil about 4 minutes, stirring occasionally. Remove from heat, stir in vanilla, and let cool 30 minutes. Store in refrigerator.

Presentations (Great Plains)

Frozen Crème de Menthe Pie

2 cups crushed chocolate wafers
5½ tablespoons butter, softened
½ gallon vanilla ice cream
7 tablespoons green crème de menthe
2 (1-ounce) squares unsweetened chocolate
6 tablespoons light cream
½ cup sugar
Dash of salt
3 tablespoons butter
1 teaspoon vanilla

Combine wafer crumbs with softened butter. Press into a 9-inch springform pan. Refrigerate at least 1 hour.

Turn ice cream into large bowl to soften. Stir crème de menthe into ice cream. Fill wafer shell with ice cream mixture and freeze.

Melt chocolate squares in cream over low heat. Add sugar and salt. Remove from heat and add butter and vanilla. Stir until cooled. Let stand until cooled thoroughly.

When pie is frozen, spread chocolate sauce over top. Return to freezer until firm. Serves 10.

Well Seasoned (Tennessee)

Peanut Pie

From the heart of the peanut country.

1 (3-ounce) package soft cream cheese
½ cup creamy peanut butter
1 cup confectioners' sugar
½ cup milk
1 (8-ounce) carton whipped topping
1 (1-inch deep) graham cracker crust
Crushed peanuts, garnish, optional

Beat cream cheese, peanut butter, sugar and milk. Add whipped topping and pour mixture into pie shell and place in freezer until ready to serve. Crushed peanuts may be sprinkled on top. Serves 6 - 8.

The VIP Cookbook: A Potpourri of Virginia Cooking (Virginia)

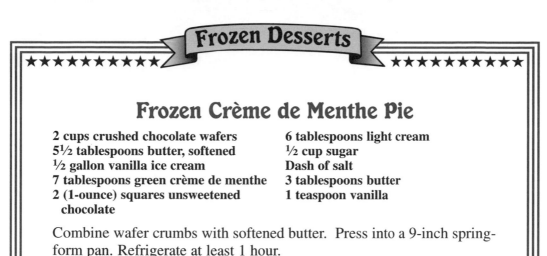

The Natural Bridge in Virginia is 215 feet high (17 stories) and 90 feet long. Thomas Jefferson bought the bridge and 157 surrounding acres from King George of England in 1774. The price of the purchase was 20 schillings. George Washington's initials are carved in it. It is one of the Seven Natural Wonders of the World.

Frozen Key Lime Pie

This pie was chosen as the Best Key Lime Pie in Florida by Burton Wolf (James Beard's associate) in a 1977 cooking competition. It still is!

CRUST:

1¼ cups graham cracker crumbs
¼ cup softened butter or margarine
¼ cup firmly packed dark brown sugar
1 teaspoon cinnamon
¼ teaspoon fresh ground nutmeg

Combine ingredients for crust. Spray pie plate with Pam Spray and "tamp" crumbs into pan, gently (do not pack firmly). Reserve 2 tablespoons crumbs for topping. Bake at 350° for 10 minutes.

FILLING:

2 eggs, separated
1 can sweetened condensed milk
½ cup (generous) Key lime juice
Grated peel of 2 lemons (coarse grated)

Beat yolks until thick and lemon-colored. Add milk and blend. Add juice, 2 tablespoons at a time. Blend well after each addition. Add one-half of grated lemon peel and blend again.

Beat whites stiff. Fold one-half of whites into milk-juice mixture. (Discard remaining whites or use to make meringue cookies). Pour into prepared crust.

Sprinkle reserved crumbs and remaining half of lemon peel over top. Freeze until firm. Then cover with aluminum foil and keep frozen until ready to use.

Remove from freezer about 5 minutes before serving. After 10 minutes, pie will no longer seem "frozen." Serves 6 - 8.

Seasons in the Sun (Florida)

Margarita Pie

1 (8-ounce) package cream cheese, softened
2 packages dry margarita mix
½ - ¾ cup sugar
1 (8-ounce) carton Cool Whip
1 graham cracker crust

Cream the cream cheese until fluffy. Add margarita mix and sugar and beat until smooth. Add Cool Whip. Freeze in graham cracker crust until ready to serve.

More of the Four Ingredient Cookbook (Texas II)

★ **Editor's Extra:** Add a drop or 2 of green food coloring and put in margarita glasses with 2 pretzel sticks. Fun and delicious—and E-Z!

Amaretto Dessert

Five-star recipe.

2 cups heavy cream
1 cup sugar
½ cup finely crushed Amaretto di Saronno cookies
3 ounces semisweet chocolate, grated
6 egg whites
½ cup Amaretto di Saronno cookies, whole
Chocolate Whipped Cream for garnish

Beat heavy cream until thick. Gradually add sugar and cookie crumbs. Beat until stiff peaks form. Fold in chocolate. In separate bowl, beat egg whites until stiff. Gently fold in cream mixture.

Line 9x5-inch loaf pan with wax paper. Arrange whole cookies in bottom of pan. Spoon cream mixture into pan. Cover with plastic wrap. Freeze overnight until firm. Garnish with Chocolate Whipped Cream.

CHOCOLATE WHIPPED CREAM:
1 cup whipping cream
2 tablespoons powdered sugar
1 teaspoon vanilla extract
½ cup chocolate syrup

In a small mixing bowl, combine all ingredients. Beat until soft peaks form.

Great Beginnings, Grand Finales (Indiana)

Bailey's Irish Cream Turtle Torte

A wonderful frozen ice cream pie.

1½ cups shortbread cookie crumbs (like Keebler's Pecan Sandies)
¼ cup light brown sugar, packed
¼ teaspoon ground nutmeg
¼ cup butter, melted
1 quart butter pecan ice cream
¾ cup Bailey's Irish Cream liqueur, divided
1 (12-ounce) jar caramel ice cream topping
1 cup coarsely chopped pecans, toasted, divided
1 quart chocolate ice cream
1 (12-ounce) jar fudge ice cream topping

Lightly butter sides of a 10-inch springform pan. Line the sides with strips of waxed paper, then butter the bottom and paper-lined sides. In a bowl, combine the cookie crumbs, sugar, and nutmeg. Stir in melted butter. Pat evenly on bottom of pan and refrigerate.

Spoon slightly softened butter pecan ice cream into a bowl and swirl in ½ cup of the Irish Cream. (Do not overmix.) Pack this into the chilled crust. Pour caramel topping into a small bowl and stir in 2 tablespoons of the Irish Cream. Drizzle over the butter pecan layer, then sprinkle with ¾ cup of pecans. Freeze 1 hour.

Spread slightly softened chocolate ice cream on top of frozen first layer. Pour fudge topping into another small bowl and stir in the remaining 2 tablespoons of Irish Cream. Spoon this over chocolate ice cream. Cover with foil and freeze until firm, 6 hours or overnight.

To serve, remove sides of pan. Carefully peel off waxed paper. Place bottom of springform pan on serving plate. Garnish top with remaining ¼ cup pecans. Let torte stand for 10 minutes before slicing. If desired, serve with a dollop of whipped cream atop each serving. Serves 14-16.

It's About Thyme (Indiana)

Pistachio Dessert

45 Ritz crackers, crushed
1 stick margarine, softened
2 boxes instant pistachio pudding
1½ cups milk
1 quart vanilla ice cream, softened
1 (8-ounce) carton Cool Whip
Milk chocolate for garnish

Mix cracker crumbs and softened margarine. Press into greased 9x13-inch pan. Bake 12-15 minutes at 325°. Cool. In bowl, mix pudding and milk; stir until blended, then add ice cream and stir until smooth. Spread on crust; freeze. Spread layer of Cool Whip over pudding mixture. Sprinkle grated chocolate on top.

Wyndmere Community Alumni Cookbook (Great Plains)

Buster Bar Dessert

½ cup melted butter
1 pound Hydrox or Oreo cookies, crushed
2 cups powdered sugar
⅔ cup chocolate chips
1½ cups evaporated milk
½ cup butter
1 teaspoon vanilla
½ gallon vanilla ice cream
2 cups Spanish peanuts (or more to taste)

Mix together melted butter and Hydrox (or Oreo) cookies. Put into a 9x13-inch pan; refrigerate until firm.

Mix together in saucepan powdered sugar, chocolate chips, evaporated milk, and butter. Boil this mixture for 8 minutes, then stir and add vanilla. Cool. Place ice cream (softened) on top of crust, then peanuts. Pour cooled chocolate mixture on top layer; freeze.

Salem Cook Book II (Minnesota)

International Falls was the inspiration for Frostbite Falls, the hometown of cartoon characters Bullwinkle Moose and Rocket J. Squirrel, "the sleepy little town where nothing ever happens." International Falls is also the home of the Smokey the Bear statue, which is 26 feet high and weighs 82 tons, and a 22-foot tall thermometer that stands in Smokey Bear Park in Minnesota.

Ice Cream Sugar Cookie Sandwiches

1 cup powdered sugar
1 cup white sugar
1 cup butter
1 cup vegetable oil
2 eggs
1 teaspoon vanilla flavoring
4 cups flour
1 teaspoon baking soda
1 teaspoon salt
1 teaspoon cream of tartar
Ice cream

Cream powdered sugar, white sugar, butter, and vegetable oil; beat well. Add eggs and vanilla; beat until fluffy. Sift flour, baking soda, salt, and cream of tartar; add to creamed mixture. Roll into balls the size of walnuts and roll in granulated sugar. Place on ungreased cookie sheet and bake at 350° for 10 minutes.

Once cooled, place 1 dip of softened ice cream between cookies and slightly press together. Wrap in clear plastic and store in freezer. When serving, top with fudge sauce, whipped cream and a cherry.

Blue Willow's "Sweet Treasures" (Iowa)

Polar Creams

16 ounces semisweet chocolate
2 tablespoons butter
2 eggs
1 cup brown sugar
⅔ cup butter, melted
½ cup crushed Heath bars
½ cup blanched, slivered almonds, toasted
1 teaspoon vanilla
1 cup whipped cream

Melt chocolate with butter and pour in paper-lined muffin cups (any size). Paint chocolate up sides of cups. Chill thoroughly. Beat eggs until thick and light. Add sugar, blending until dissolved. Add butter, candy, almonds, and vanilla. Fold in whipped cream. Spoon into chocolate shells and freeze. Peel off muffin cups and let set for 10 minutes.

Tasting Tea Treasures (Mississippi)

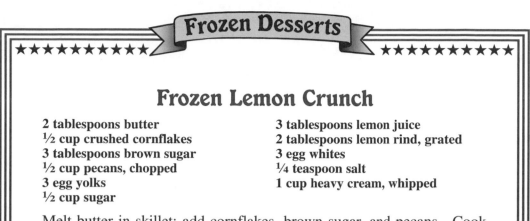

Frozen Lemon Crunch

2 tablespoons butter
½ cup crushed cornflakes
3 tablespoons brown sugar
½ cup pecans, chopped
3 egg yolks
½ cup sugar
3 tablespoons lemon juice
2 tablespoons lemon rind, grated
3 egg whites
¼ teaspoon salt
1 cup heavy cream, whipped

Melt butter in skillet; add cornflakes, brown sugar, and pecans. Cook and stir until sugar melts and caramelizes slightly. Set aside.

In small saucepan, beat egg yolks and sugar until light and foamy. Cook over low heat until thick. Add lemon juice and rind. Cool.

In large bowl, beat egg whites with salt until stiff. Fold in cooled egg yolk mixture and whipped cream. Place half of cornflakes mixture on bottom of springform pan. Pour in lemon mixture and top with remaining cornflakes mixture. Freeze a minimum of 4 hours. Serves 10.

Company's Coming (Missouri)

Chocolate Coronet

Lovely at Christmas.

18 ladyfingers (split)
½ cup orange juice
1 pound cream cheese, softened
¾ cup granulated sugar
½ teaspoon salt
2 teaspoons vanilla
3 eggs, separated
3 (4-ounce) packages chocolate pieces, melted and cooled
2 cups heavy cream, whipped
½ cup chopped nuts (optional)

Stand ladyfingers in a 9-inch springform pan. Arrange remaining ladyfingers on bottom of the pan. Combine orange juice, cream cheese, sugar, salt and vanilla. Beat until well blended and smooth. Add egg yolks and beat until smooth. Blend in melted chocolate. Beat egg whites until stiff and fold them in along with whipped cream. Pour mixture into pan over ladyfingers. Put in freezer. Prior to serving, set out a few minutes until soft enough to cut.

Canopy Roads (Florida)

Frangelico White and Dark Chocolate Mousse

A chocolate lover's dream.

CRUST:

⅔ cup crushed chocolate wafer cookies
⅓ cup crushed graham crackers
¼ cup butter, melted

Preheat oven to 350°. Combine cookies, graham crackers, and butter. Press into a springform pan. Bake for 8 minutes. Cool crust on rack.

BOTTOM LAYER:

1½ cups heavy whipping cream, chilled
4 ounces semisweet chocolate
2 ounces unsweetened chocolate
6 egg yolks
¾ cup sugar
½ cup hazelnut liqueur (Frangelico)

Whip cream until soft peaks form and set aside. Melt chocolates over double boiler. Beat egg yolks and gradually add sugar until mixture is pale yellow and batter falls in ribbons. Beat in liqueur, then add melted chocolates. Gradually fold in whipped cream, ⅓ at a time. Pour chocolate mousse onto crust and freeze 30 minutes or until set.

TOP LAYER:

1⅓ cups heavy whipping cream, chilled
10 ounces good quality white chocolate
¾ cup heavy whipping cream, chilled
3 tablespoons hazelnut liqueur (Frangelico)

Whip 1⅓ cups cream until soft peaks form and set aside. Chop white chocolate into tiny pieces. In a large saucepan, bring ¾ cup cream to a boil; simmer for 2 minutes. Add white chocolate to cream, blend until smooth. Add liqueur. Gradually fold in whipped cream, ⅓ at a time. Pour white chocolate mousse on top of chocolate mousse layer. Freeze for at least 8 hours. Remove from freezer 10-15 minutes before serving. Separate from edges with a warm knife.

CHOCOLATE TOPPING:

2 ounces semisweet chocolate
1 tablespoon butter

After mousse is set, melt chocolate with butter. Drizzle on top for decoration. Serve immediately. Serves 10-12.

The Bountiful Arbor (Michigan)

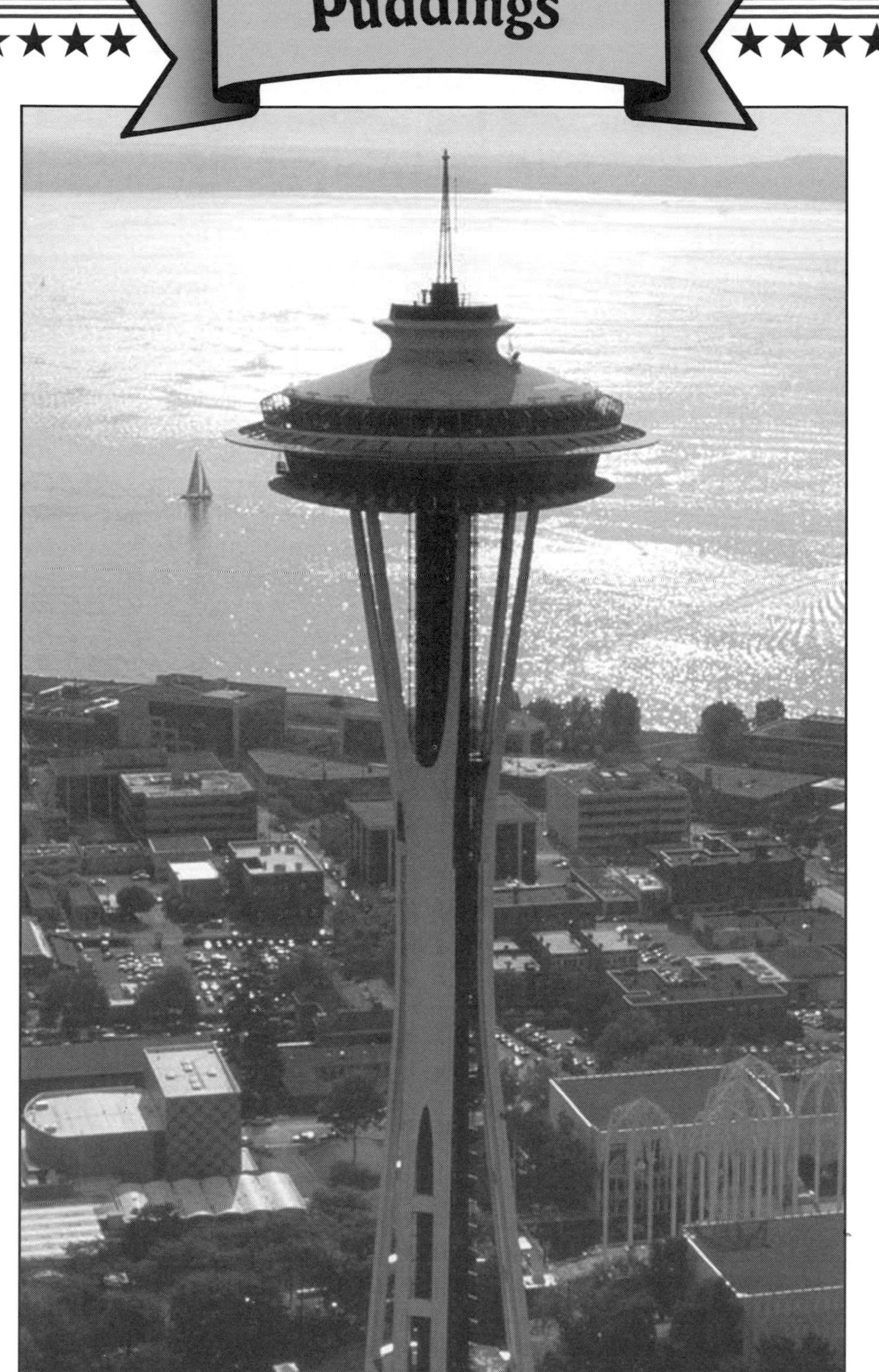

The futuristic Space Needle in Seattle was designed and built for the 1962 World's Fair, whose theme was "Century 21." During the fair, nearly 20,000 people per day went up its elevators.

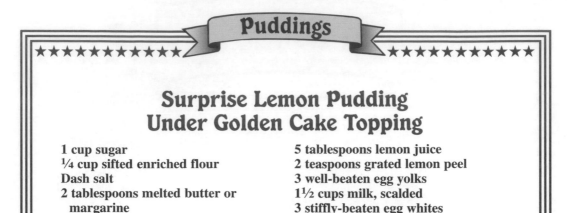

Surprise Lemon Pudding Under Golden Cake Topping

1 cup sugar
¼ cup sifted enriched flour
Dash salt
2 tablespoons melted butter or margarine
5 tablespoons lemon juice
2 teaspoons grated lemon peel
3 well-beaten egg yolks
1½ cups milk, scalded
3 stiffly-beaten egg whites

Preheat oven to 325°. Combine sugar, flour, salt, and butter; add lemon juice and peel. Combine the beaten egg yolks and milk; add to first mixture. Fold in beaten egg whites and pour into 8 greased 5-ounce custard cups (Pyrex).

Bake in pan of hot water in slow oven (325°) 45 minutes. When baked, each dessert will have custard on the bottom and sponge cake on top. Makes 8 servings.

Covered Bridge Neighbors Cookbook (Missouri)

Bride's Bread Pudding

Your next family favorite!

1 (10-ounce) loaf stale French bread
2 tablespoons water
2¼ cups evaporated milk
7 eggs, beaten
1 can Eagle Brand Milk
½ cup sugar
½ cup raisins
1 (8-ounce) can pineapple, crushed
2 tablespoons vanilla extract
¼ cup butter, melted

Preheat oven to 350°. Lightly coat 9x12-inch baking dish with cooking spray. Tear bread into pieces and sprinkle lightly with water. Blend in all other ingredients. Prepare a large pan of water and place on middle rack in oven. Fill baking dish with pudding and place in water pan. Bake for 1 hour or until set. Serve warm with Bourbon Sauce.

BOURBON SAUCE:
1 cup butter, softened
2 cups super-fine granulated sugar
Nutmeg to taste
½ cup bourbon

Using an electric mixer, combine butter and sugar until light and fluffy. Add nutmeg and bourbon, beating until smooth. Sugar should be completely dissolved. Place a small scoop of sauce on top of warm pudding and serve immediately. Makes 8 servings.

Applause! (Oklahoma)

Gran Sally's Bread Pudding

Ruthmary refers to this old-time dessert as "a rich version of a Depression Era staple from my childhood."

1 dozen brown-and-serve rolls, cooked and dried
Approximately 1 cup whole milk
½ cup sugar
1 teaspoon vanilla
½ teaspoon nutmeg
½ teaspoon cinnamon
4 eggs, beaten

Crumble rolls in small pieces. Cover with milk. Add remaining ingredients and mix well. Grease baking dish with generous amount of butter or margarine and heat in oven until very hot. Then pour bread mixture into hot dish immediately and return to 350° oven to bake until a knife comes out clean, approximately 25 minutes. Pride House uses individual gelatin molds for baking dishes.

To serve: Spoon Praline Sauce in bottom of individual dishes. Place serving of pudding over the Praline Sauce and top with rich cream.

PRALINE SAUCE:
1 (16-ounce) box dark brown sugar
¾ cup cream
¼ cup Karo syrup, light or dark
2 tablespoons butter
¼ teaspoon vanilla

Mix sugar, cream, and syrup and boil 5 minutes. Add butter and vanilla. Cool and refrigerate. Serves 6.

Texas Historic Inns Cookbook (Texas)

Amaretto Bread Pudding

Better than the average bread pudding—don't pass this one by!

12 pieces sliced bread
4 cups milk
¼ cup butter
3 eggs
1½ cups sugar
1 teaspoon almond extract
½ cup sliced almonds

Preheat oven to 350°. Tear up bread into medium-size pieces and place in a large greased baking dish. Heat milk and butter in a large saucepan over low heat until butter melts. Pour over bread. Beat eggs; add sugar and almond extract. Pour over bread and gently stir. Sprinkle with almonds. Bake about 40 minutes until set.

SAUCE:
½ cup butter
1 cup powdered sugar
1 egg
¼ cup amaretto

Melt butter and powdered sugar in a small saucepan over low heat. Remove from heat and quickly whisk in 1 egg. Stir in amaretto and beat until smooth.

To serve, cut bread pudding into squares and top with sauce. Serve warm, even if made ahead. Can be reheated in microwave. Serves 12.

Kay Ewing's Cooking School Cookbook (Louisiana II)

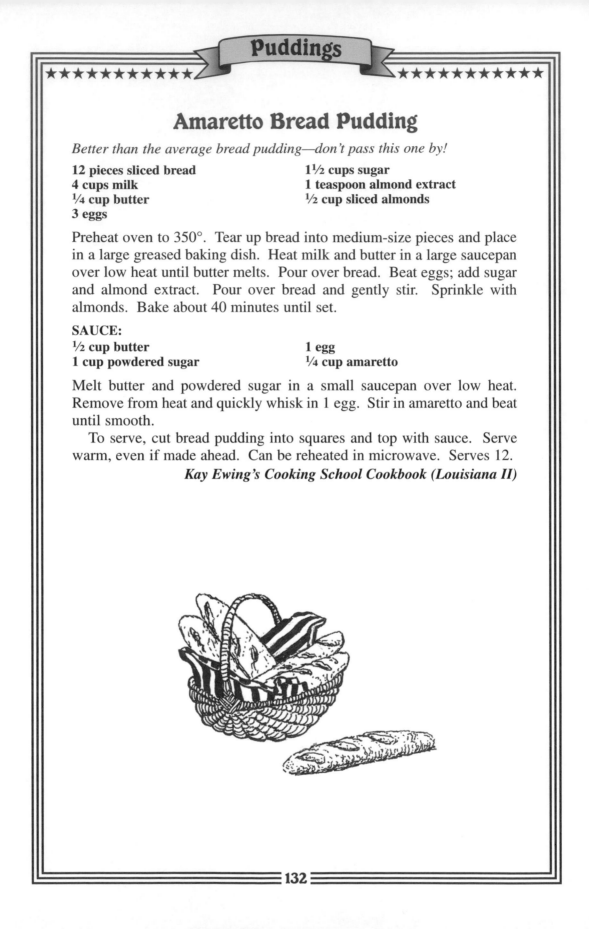

Grandma's Bread Pudding

At long last, our Bread Pudding & Brandy Sauce recipe! For all of you who call in on Sunday mornings to see if we have it, here you go—now you can treat yourself every day!

BREAD PUDDING:

6 cups sourdough bread (ends are okay), cut in ½-inch cubes
1 Granny Smith apple, peeled, cored, and diced
¼ cup raisins
4 large eggs
1 cup granulated sugar
¼ cup brown sugar
½ teaspoon nutmeg
1½ teaspoons ground cinnamon
1 teaspoon vanilla extract
2 cups whole or 2% milk
Whipped cream and cinnamon for garnish

Preheat oven to 400°. Prepare 9x13-inch pan by spraying with Pam or buttering. Place bread cubes in large bowl and add diced apples and raisins. Beat eggs in medium-sized bowl until frothy. Add sugars, spices, and vanilla. Mix well. Blend in milk. Pour mixture over bread and toss to coat. Pile into prepared pan, and press down lightly, spreading evenly in pan. Cover tightly with foil. Place pan in slightly larger pan. Place in oven. Pour boiling water into larger pan (be careful not to pour too much water into pan). Bake for 1 hour. Take foil off last 10 minutes until lightly brown. Serve with Gram's Brandy Sauce and top with whipped cream and a touch of cinnamon. Serves 10-12.

GRAM'S BRANDY SAUCE:

½ cup butter or margarine
1 cup sugar
1 large egg
¼ cup brandy

Melt butter or margarine in small heavy saucepan, being careful not to burn. In a medium bowl, mix sugar and egg with wire whisk, until well blended. Gradually pour in melted butter and blend well. Return mixture to saucepan. Stir with whisk over low heat for 60 seconds or until sugar is dissolved (do not boil). Add brandy and blend. Remove from heat immediately after blending or egg will set and turn brown. Serve over Bread Pudding or your favorite crisp.

Incredible Edibles (California)

Sourdough bread has long been a symbol of San Francisco since Isadore Boudin opened his North Beach bakery in 1849. The bread's tangy taste comes from a special yeast starter, though some claim that San Francisco's air gives the yeast a characteristic flavor that cannot be exported. The Acme Bread Company in Berkeley produces 30,000 sourdough baguettes a week.

Homestead Inn Banana Pudding with Walnut Crust

CRUST:

½ cup margarine
1 cup flour
1 cup finely chopped walnuts

Blend margarine, flour, and walnuts. Press in bottom of 9x13-inch pan and bake at 350° until light brown. Cool.

FIRST LAYER:

1 (8-ounce) package cream cheese
1 cup powdered sugar
10 ounces whipped topping
Sliced bananas (4 - 6)

Beat first 3 ingredients together and spread on prepared crust. Top with sliced bananas, then pudding layer.

PUDDING LAYER:

3 egg yolks
1 cup sugar
3 tablespoons cornstarch
2 cups milk
Banana flavoring

In saucepan, blend ingredients and cook over medium heat until thick. Cool before spreading over cream cheese and banana layer, then top with whipped topping or sweetened whipped cream. Refrigerate, and cut into 12 squares and serve.

Dining in Historic Ohio (Ohio)

Layered Banana Pudding

⅔ cup sugar
¼ cup cornstarch
¼ teaspoon salt
2 cups milk, scalded
3 egg yolks, slightly beaten
2 tablespoons butter
½ teaspoon vanilla
2 - 3 ripe bananas, sliced
1 (11-ounce) box vanilla wafers
½ cup heavy cream, whipped
Vanilla wafer crumbs

Mix sugar, cornstarch, and salt together in top of double boiler. Gradually add milk to sugar mixture. Stir constantly over boiling water for 10 minutes, or until mixture thickens and forms a pudding. Remove from heat. Stir small amount of pudding into egg yolks. Stir egg yolk mixture into remaining pudding. Cook, stirring constantly, for an additional 5 minutes. Remove from heat. Stir in butter and vanilla. Cool. Fold in bananas.

Line bottom and sides of serving dish with vanilla wafers. Pour in pudding. Chill. Garnish with whipped cream and a sprinkle of crumbs. Makes 6 servings.

The Elsah Landing Restaurant Cookbook (Illinois)

Effie Romberger's Old-Fashioned Rice Pudding

I still hunger for mother's rice pudding!

1 cup uncooked rice
6 eggs
1 cup sugar
1 teaspoon nutmeg
1 teaspoon salt
½ cup milk
1 stick butter, no substitute

Cook rice. Beat eggs; add sugar, nutmeg, salt, milk, and cooked rice. Pour into 2-quart baking dish in which 1 stick butter has been melted. Bake at 400° about 30 minutes. Do not overcook. Center should be a little shaky.

GRANDMOTHER ROMBERGER'S LEMON SAUCE:

3 tablespoons cornstarch
½ cup water
¾ cup sugar
⅛ teaspoon salt
⅓ cup lemon juice
1 tablespoon butter
1 egg, beaten
Yellow food coloring, optional

Mix cornstarch with water. In saucepan, mix sugar, salt, lemon juice, butter, and egg. Add cornstarch mixture. Stir and cook slowly until thick. Add coloring if desired. Makes 1 cup. Pour over pudding.

Four Generations of Johnson Family Favorites (Oklahoma)

Dirt

1 (8-ounce) package cream cheese, softened
½ stick margarine, softened
1 cup confectioners' sugar
2 small packages instant chocolate pudding
3½ cups milk
1 (12-ounce) container Cool Whip
1 bag Oreos, crushed

Cream together cream cheese, margarine and sugar. Mix together pudding, milk and Cool Whip. Combine chocolate mixture with creamed mixture. Stir well.

In clean flowerpot, layer mixture with crushed Oreo cookies, ending with cookies on top. Add silk flowers and plastic shovel for serving.

The PTA Pantry (Ohio)

Date Pudding II

SYRUP:
1 cup brown sugar
1 cup water
1 tablespoon butter

BATTER:
½ cup brown sugar
1 cup flour
2 teaspoons baking powder
¼ teaspoon salt
½ cup milk
1 cup dates, chopped
½ cup chopped nuts

Combine 1 cup brown sugar and water; cook together 3 minutes to make syrup. Remove from heat and add butter.

To make batter; sift sugar, flour, baking powder, and salt together. Add milk and stir until smooth. Fold in chopped dates and nuts, blending well into mixture. Pour syrup in a greased baking dish. Pour batter on top of hot syrup and bake at 350° for 35-40 minutes. Serve plain or with whipped cream. Makes 6 servings.

Mennonite Community Cookbook (Virginia)

The Medjool Date, the largest, juiciest, and most flavorful variety available, is grown near the banks of the Colorado River near Yuma, Arizona.

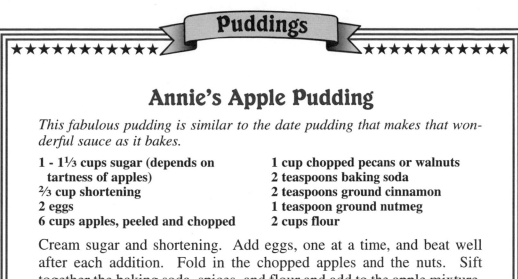

Annie's Apple Pudding

This fabulous pudding is similar to the date pudding that makes that wonderful sauce as it bakes.

1 - 1⅓ cups sugar (depends on tartness of apples)
⅔ cup shortening
2 eggs
6 cups apples, peeled and chopped
1 cup chopped pecans or walnuts
2 teaspoons baking soda
2 teaspoons ground cinnamon
1 teaspoon ground nutmeg
2 cups flour

Cream sugar and shortening. Add eggs, one at a time, and beat well after each addition. Fold in the chopped apples and the nuts. Sift together the baking soda, spices, and flour and add to the apple mixture. Spread the apple mixture into a greased 9x13-inch pan and pour the following sauce over the top.

SAUCE:
1½ cups brown sugar, packed
2 tablespoons flour
1 cup water
¼ cup butter
1 teaspoon vanilla

Stir together the sugar and the flour, then add remainder of ingredients in a heavy saucepan. Bring to a boil and boil gently for 3 minutes, stirring often. Pour this hot sauce over the batter. Do not stir. Bake at 325° for 1 hour. Serves 10-12.

Christmas Thyme at Oak Hill Farm (Indiana)

White Chocolate Mousse with Strawberry Sauce

MOUSSE:

1 cup heavy cream
¼ cup water
½ cup sugar
¼ cup egg whites
½ pound white chocolate, cut into small cubes

Whip cream until stiff and refrigerate. Heat water and sugar to 250°. Meanwhile, when sugar reaches about 240°, beat egg whites until they form soft peaks. When sugar reaches 250° add to whites in a slow, steady stream and blend for 3 minutes. Add chocolate cubes and beat for 1 minute more. Fold in whipped cream and chill several hours. When chilled, put a little strawberry sauce onto each dessert plate and then spoon mousse onto sauce.

Suggested garnishes: candied violets, chocolate leaves, grated dark chocolate, amaretti or amarettini cookies.

STRAWBERRY SAUCE:

2 (10-ounce) packages frozen strawberries and/or raspberries
¼ cup sugar
2 tablespoons cornstarch
¼ teaspoon almond extract (I use 3 tablespoons Grand Marnier at restaurant)

Thaw berries, drain and reserve syrup, add water to make 1½ cups of liquid. Mix sugar and cornstarch in saucepan and gradually add syrup/water mixture. Cook and stir until simmers, 2 minutes, remove from heat and add berries and flavoring. Chill well. Berries may be puréed before adding to sauce.

Recipe from Jamie's French Restaurant
Fiesta (Florida)

Trifles & Tortes

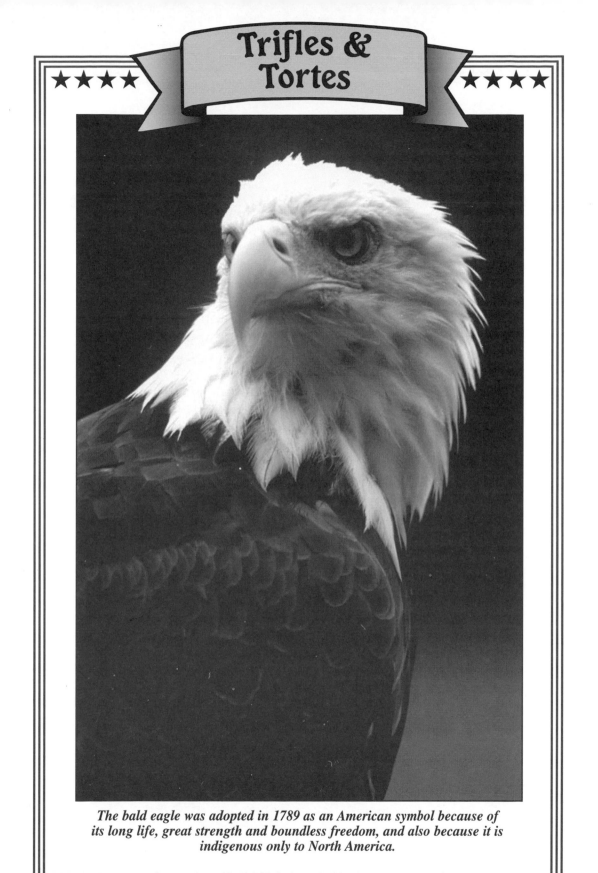

The bald eagle was adopted in 1789 as an American symbol because of its long life, great strength and boundless freedom, and also because it is indigenous only to North America.

Raspberry Sherry Trifle

A winner at family get-togethers, Thanksgiving, and Christmas. A traditional English dessert.

Angel food or yellow cake
Raspberry jam
1 (8-ounce) package frozen raspberries (defrosted)
3 - 4 ounces pecans
1 (3-ounce) package raspberry Jell-O
2 ounces sherry
½ pint (1 cup) half-and-half or milk
3 egg yolks
1 teaspoon cornstarch
1 ounce (⅛ cup) sugar
½ pint heavy whipping cream

Slice cake and spread raspberry jam on each piece. Then line a glass trifle bowl with them about ⅓ of the way, with jam face up. Drain raspberries; reserve juice. Spread raspberries and half of the pecans over cake. Make Jell-O (per box instructions) substituting juice of raspberries for part of water. Pour over cake when lukewarm, just enough to soak. Sprinkle sherry on top (optional). Refrigerate.

To make custard, heat half-and-half (or whole milk) in pan. Blend egg yolks, cornstarch, and sugar together. When milk is hot, slowly pour over egg mixture, while constantly stirring. Return mixture to pan and stir until thick, over low heat. Pour over cake and refrigerate until cool. When ready to serve, whip cream and pipe or spread over top. Decorate with remaining pecans, chocolate shavings, or some extra raspberries. Serves 6 - 8.

Dining Door to Door in Naglee Park (California)

Trifle

Tipsy cake or English Trifle has been popular with Virginians for 200 years. It is served today most often during the Christmas season. The ingredients have been traditionally ladyfingers, fruit, custard, and sherry.

4 eggs
½ cup sugar
2 cups milk
⅛ teaspoon salt
24 ladyfingers
1 cup apricot jam
½ cup muscatel
½ pint heavy cream, whipped and sweetened
½ cup sliced almonds, toasted

Beat eggs slightly; combine with sugar, milk, and salt in double boiler. Cook over hot, not boiling, water, stirring constantly until mixture thickens slightly and coats spoon. Cool. Split ladyfingers and sandwich together with apricot jam. Place in serving dish, making 2 layers; sprinkle each layer with muscatel. Pour custard over and chill several hours or overnight. Before serving, top with cream; sprinkle with almonds. Serves 8 -10.

Virginia Hospitality (Virginia)

The Grand Finale Grand Trifle

4 cups pound or yellow cake chunks
1 cup fresh or frozen, thawed strawberries in syrup
4 ounces port wine
4 ounces cream sherry
8 large scoops rich vanilla ice cream or custard
1 cup fresh or frozen, thawed raspberries in syrup
1½ - 2 cups heavy cream, whipped
¼ cup toasted slivered almonds
8 maraschino or chocolate-covered cherries for garnish

In 8 large brandy snifters or a 2-quart clear bowl, layer ingredients in order given and garnish with cherries. Chill about an hour to blend flavors. Serves 8.

Dining in Historic Ohio (Ohio)

Built in just over four years, the Golden Gate Bridge was completed in 1937 at a cost of $35 million. An all-time record of 162,414 vehicles crossed the bridge on October 27, 1989, due to an earthquake which closed other nearby routes.

Strawberry Tiramisu

Guaranteed rave reviews from guests.

¾ pound mascarpone cheese (1½ cups) room temperature
3 tablespoons confectioners' sugar
3 tablespoons orange-flavored liqueur
1½ cups heavy cream
1 pint strawberries, rinsed and hulled
¼ cup granulated sugar
¼ cup orange juice
24 ladyfingers

In medium bowl, whisk mascarpone cheese, confectioners' sugar, and 1 tablespoon of the orange liqueur until well blended. In large chilled bowl with electric mixer at medium speed, beat heavy cream until soft peaks form; gently fold whipped cream into mascarpone mixture until blended. In blender or food processor, blend together remaining liqueur, the strawberries, granulated sugar, and orange juice to a smooth purée. Pour strawberry mixture into shallow bowl.

Dip 12 ladyfingers in strawberry mixture to coat; arrange in a 9-inch square glass dish, side-by-side, in 2 rows touching. Spread ½ cup of the strawberry mixture evenly over rows. Spread ½ of the cream mixture on top. Arrange remaining ladyfingers over cream layer. Spread with remaining strawberry mixture. Spread with remaining cream, smoothing top with spatula. Cover and refrigerate at least 8 hours or overnight.

To serve, cut into 9 squares. Place on dessert plates and dust each with cocoa powder and top with a sliced fanned strawberry.

Note: If mascarpone cheese is unavailable, purée in blender or food processor 2 tablespoons of the heavy cream with 1¼ cups ricotta cheese, 3 tablespoons softened cream cheese, and 1 teaspoon fresh lemon juice until smooth.

Recipes from Our House (Colorado)

Lime Angel Dessert

1 small package lime gelatin
1 cup sugar
1¼ cups boiling water
⅓ cup lime juice
1 can (1 cup) flaked coconut
1 cup heavy cream, whipped
1 small angel food cake, torn into pieces

Dissolve gelatin and sugar in boiling water. Add juice and chill until thickened. Fold in coconut and whipped cream. Make layers of cake bits and gelatin mixture in 9x13-inch pan. Chill overnight and cut into squares. Serves 12.

Mushrooms, Turnip Greens and Pickled Eggs (North Carolina)

Charlotte Russe with Raspberry Sauce

Every year Marie takes this charlotte to the Willing Workers' Christmas party. The ladies love it!

1 tablespoon plain gelatin
⅓ cup cold water
1 cup heavy cream
3 large eggs, separated
Pinch of salt
5 tablespoons sugar, divided
3 tablespoons rum
1 (3-ounce) package ladyfingers, halved and split

Dissolve gelatin in cold water placed over boiling water; cool. Whip cream until nearly stiff; put in refrigerator. Beat egg whites with salt. Gradually add 3 tablespoons sugar; beat until very stiff and refrigerate. Beat egg yolks, add 2 tablespoons sugar and beat until light and fluffy. Add cooled gelatin to egg yolks, then add rum. Fold in egg whites, then fold in whipped cream. Put 3 ladyfinger pieces in each sherbet glass (work fast); fill each glass with charlotte. Refrigerate 3 - 4 hours or overnight. Top with Raspberry Sauce just before serving. Serves about 8.

RASPBERRY SAUCE:

1 (10-ounce) box frozen raspberries, thawed
½ cup sugar
1 heaping teaspoon cornstarch

Add a little water to berries and bring to a boil. Press through a strainer to remove seeds and return to stove. Mix sugar and cornstarch; add a little water to make a paste. Stir into boiling berries and cook a few minutes. Cool and refrigerate till serving time.

Cookbook (Alabama)

Peaches and Cream Soufflé

Butter and sugar for coating
1 cup water
1 cup sugar, divided
6 eggs, separated
2 envelopes unflavored gelatin
2 teaspoons grated lemon peel
½ teaspoon almond extract
½ teaspoon vanilla
¼ teaspoon ground ginger
4 cups sliced ripe peaches
3 tablespoons lemon juice
¾ teaspoon cream of tartar
1 cup whipping cream, whipped
Peach slices, optional
Mint leaves, optional

Make a 4-inch band of triple-thickness aluminum foil long enough to go around 1½-quart soufflé dish or casserole, and overlap 2 inches. Lightly butter 1 side of band and sprinkle with sugar. Wrap around outside of dish with sugared side in. Fasten with tape, paper clip or string. Collar should extend 2 inches above rim of dish. Set aside.

In medium saucepan, combine water, ¼ cup sugar and egg yolks. Sprinkle with gelatin and let stand 1 minute. Cook over medium heat, stirring until gelatin is dissolved, about 5 minutes. Stir in lemon peel, flavorings and ginger.

Combine peaches with lemon juice, and mash to form a pulp mixture. Stir into gelatin mixture. Chill, stirring occasionally, until mixture mounds slightly when dropped from spoon.

In large mixing bowl, beat egg whites with cream of tartar at high speed until foamy. Add remaining ¾ cup sugar, 1 tablespoon at a time, beating constantly until sugar is dissolved and whites are glossy and stand in soft peaks.

Gently but thoroughly, fold chilled gelatin mixture and whipped cream into whites. Carefully pour into prepared dish. Chill until firm, several hours or overnight. Just before serving, carefully remove foil band. Garnish with peach slices and mint leaves, if desired. Serves 6.

A Very Special Treat (Arkansas)

Three ships, named *Discovery, Godspeed,* and *Susan Constant,* brought the first colonists to Jamestown in 1607. "James Towne," the first permanent English settlement, was named in honor of King James I of England.

Heavenly Cherry Angel Food Trifle

5 cups angel food cake cubes
¼ cup cherry liqueur, optional
1 cup powdered sugar
1 (3-ounce) package cream cheese, softened
1 (8-ounce) package frozen non-dairy whipped topping, thawed and divided
½ cup toasted chopped pecans
1 (21-ounce) can cherry filling or topping

Place cake cubes in large bowl. Sprinkle with liqueur, if desired; let stand 30 minutes. In medium bowl, combine powdered sugar and cream cheese; beat until blended. Reserve 2 tablespoons whipped topping; fold remaining topping into cheese mixture. Stir topping mixture and pecans into cake cubes; mix well.

Spoon cake mixture into a pretty glass or crystal bowl. Spread cherry filling evenly on top. (Or if desired, layer ½ cake mixture and cherry filling. Repeat layers.) Cover and refrigerate at least 3 hours. Garnish servings with reserved whipped topping. Yields 8-10 servings.

Good Food from Michigan (Michigan)

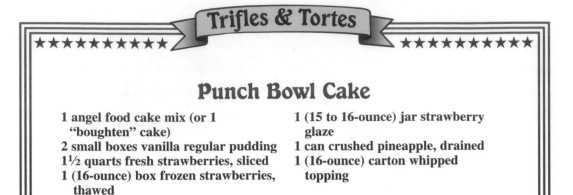

Punch Bowl Cake

1 angel food cake mix (or 1 "boughten" cake)
2 small boxes vanilla regular pudding
1½ quarts fresh strawberries, sliced
1 (16-ounce) box frozen strawberries, thawed
1 (15 to 16-ounce) jar strawberry glaze
1 can crushed pineapple, drained
1 (16-ounce) carton whipped topping

Make cake as directed and bake. While cake is baking, make pudding according to directions on box. Allow cake and pudding to cool. Crumble half of cake into the bottom of a punch bowl. Mix the berries and the glaze together. Top cake with ½ each of the pudding, pineapple, berries, and whipped topping. Repeat the layers, beginning with remaining cake. Cover and refrigerate at least overnight.

First Christian Church Centennial Cookbook (Iowa)

Death by Chocolate

1 chocolate cake, baked in 9x13-inch pan
1 cup Kahlua
3 boxes chocolate mousse
6 Skor or Heath bars, frozen
1 (16-ounce) carton Cool Whip

Bake cake and cool. Poke large holes with fork; pour Kahlua over cake, cover and refrigerate 4 - 5 hours or overnight. Mix mousse according to directions. Break and crunch candy bars in package. In punch bowl, layer ⅓ crumbed cake, ⅓ mousse, ⅓ Cool Whip, and 2 candy bars. Repeat for 2 more layers. Chill 3 hours or overnight. This is much better made the day before.

Gardener's Delight (Ohio)

No Cook Cake

2 small boxes (or 1 large) French vanilla pudding
1 angel food cake
1 (8-ounce) container sour cream
1 can pie filling (I like strawberry)

Mix pudding according to package directions. Break or cut cake in pieces in 9x13-inch pan. Pour sour cream and pudding mix over cake, then top with pie filling. Chill.

Southwest Cookin' (Arkansas)

Toffee Crunch Trifle

Dynamite dessert looks and tastes spectacular, but is easy to make.

1 (18-ounce) chocolate cake mix
Eggs, oil and water (as directed on cake mix)
½ cup Kahlua
1 (16-ounce) jar chocolate or fudge sauce
3 Skor or Heath candy bars, broken into bite-size pieces
1 (12-ounce) carton frozen whipped topping, thawed

Prepare cake according to package directions, baking in a 9x13-inch pan. Cool. Poke holes all over top of cake with a large fork. Pour Kahlua slowly over cake, allowing it to soak in. Cover tightly with plastic wrap; refrigerate at least 3 hours or overnight.

Assemble the day you want to serve (trifle gets watery assembled too far ahead) in a 3-quart trifle or straight-sided, see-through bowl. Layer ingredients beginning with about a 1-inch layer of cake, ¼ fudge sauce, 1 candy bar, and ¼ whipped topping. Repeat layers 2 more times, reserving the last candy bar and ¼ of fudge sauce to decorate top of trifle. Drizzle fudge sauce over top layer of whipped topping and sprinkle with candy pieces. Refrigerate until ready to serve. Yields 10-12 servings.

Note: A 3-quart trifle dish (about 7 inches in diameter and 5 inches deep) will only use about half of cake. Freeze remaining cake in a plastic bag for later use. If you have a larger container or make 2 trifles at the same time, double the fudge sauce, candy, and whipped topping.

Palates (Colorado)

Twinkie Treat

This is an easy, but delicious, dessert. Your friends will think you have spent hours on this luscious treat.

2 boxes or 24 Twinkie snack cakes
1 large box strawberry Jell-O
1 large package instant vanilla pudding
1 can strawberry pie filling
1 medium-sized container whipped topping
½ cup chopped pecans

Place all the Twinkies in a 9x13-inch pan (may have to squeeze them to fit). Mix Jell-O according to directions on package. Pour over Twinkies. Prepare pudding mix as directed on package. Pour over Jell-O. Spread pie filling over pudding. Top with whipped topping and sprinkle nuts over all. Chill at least 2 hours before serving. Even better to refrigerate overnight.

Centennial Cookbook (Oklahoma)

★ **Editor's Extra:** Pudding comes in two sizes, small and large. Though ounces vary among brands, the small size is around 3 ounces, and the large around 6.

Angel Food Orange Delight

1 (6-ounce) package orange Jell-O
2 cups boiling water
1 pint orange sherbet
1 small container Cool Whip
1 (11-ounce) can mandarin oranges, drained
1 small can crushed pineapple, drained
1 angel food cake, baked

Mix Jell-O with boiling water; cool. Add orange sherbet and then add Cool Whip. Cut oranges into small pieces. Add drained oranges and drained pineapple. Trim brown off the cake and cut into cubes.

Line 9x13-inch dish with cake cubes, and pour ½ of mixture over cake. Add another layer of cake and add rest of Jell-O mix. Refrigerate overnight before serving.

Cook Book: Favorite Recipes from Our Best Cooks (Illinois)

★ **Editor's Extra:** Cool Whip sizes have changed a little over the years, but currently they come in 8-ounce (small), 12-ounce (medium), and 16-ounce (large).

Black Forest Trifle

This is one of my favorite "party" recipes because it looks so festive and elegant.

1 (19.8-ounce) package fudge brownie mix
1 (3.5-ounce) package instant chocolate pudding mix
¼ cup coffee or chocolate-flavored liqueur (optional)
1 can cherry pie filling (you will use only about ⅔ of can)
1 (12-ounce) carton frozen whipped topping, thawed
Garnish: Chocolate curls, mini-chocolate morsels, or maraschino cherries

Prepare brownie mix according to package directions for cake-like brownies in a 9x13x2-inch pan. Cool and crumble.

Prepare chocolate pudding according to package directions. Chill and divide in half. Place ½ crumbled brownies in bottom of a 3-quart trifle bowl; drizzle ½ of liqueur over brownies in the bowl. Dot with ⅓ of the cherry pie filling (make sure some of them show through sides of bowl), layer with ½ pudding, then ½ whipped topping. Repeat layers: brownies, liqueur, cherries, pudding, and whipped topping. Garnish with 1 - 2 of the items listed for garnishing. Chill 8 hours. Yields 16-18 servings.

Recipes from the Cotton Patch (New Mexico)

Cherry-Berries on a Cloud

6 egg whites
½ teaspoon cream of tartar
¼ teaspoon salt
1¾ cups sugar

Heat oven to 275°. Grease a 9x13x2-inch pan. Beat egg whites, cream of tartar and salt until frothy. Gradually beat in sugar. Beat until stiff and glossy, about 15 minutes. Spread in pan. Bake 60 minutes. Turn oven off and leave meringue in oven until cool, about 12 hours or overnight.

FILLING:
2 (3-ounce) packages cream cheese, softened
1 cup sugar
1 teaspoon vanilla
2 cups whipped cream (½ pint)
2 cups miniature marshmallows

Mix cream cheese with sugar (add gradually) and vanilla. Gently fold in whipped cream and marshmallows. Spread over meringue and refrigerate 12 hours or overnight. Cut into serving pieces and top with Topping.

TOPPING:
1 can cherry pie filling
1 teaspoon lemon juice
2 cups sliced, fresh strawberries or 1 package frozen strawberries, thawed

Stir the can of cherry pie filling with juice into the sliced strawberries. Serves 12-16.

Cherry Berries on a Cloud and More (Wisconsin)

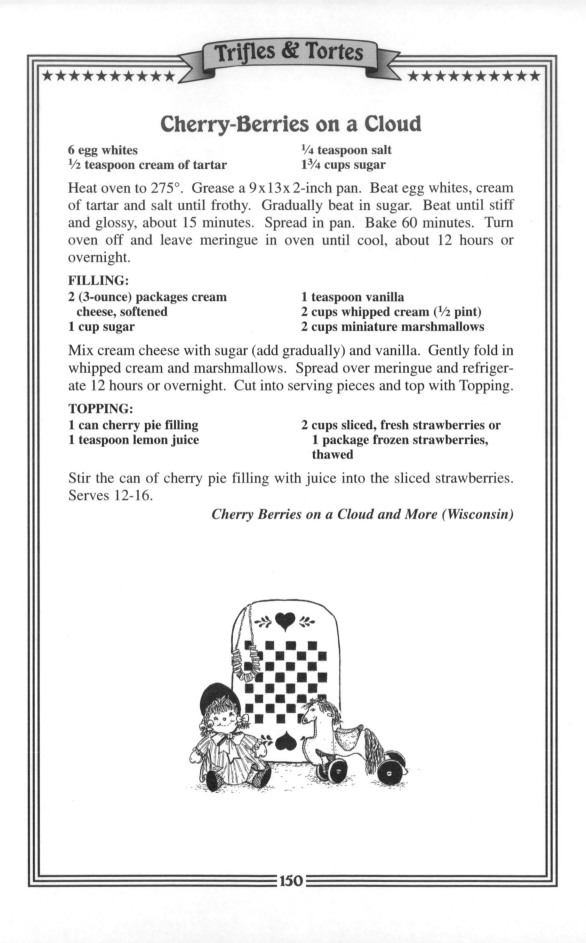

Mocha Polka Walnut Torte

1 package brownie mix (or your own recipe)
2 eggs
¼ cup water
¾ cup coarsely chopped nuts
2 cups whipping cream
½ cup brown sugar, firmly packed
2 tablespoons instant coffee
Walnut halves

Follow cake-like method for preparing brownie mix, adding eggs and water as directed; add nuts. Spoon into 2 greased 9-inch cake pans. Bake at 350° for 20 minutes. Turn onto racks to cool. Whip cream until it begins to thicken. Gradually add brown sugar and instant coffee. Continue beating until of spreading consistency. Spread between layers of torte and swirl over top and sides. Polka-dot with walnut halves. Chill overnight. This is very rich, so 1 torte serves 10-12.

Mammoth Really Cooks, Book II (California)

Chocolate Torte Royal

2 egg whites
¼ teaspoon salt
½ teaspoon vinegar
½ cup sugar
¼ teaspoon cinnamon
¼ teaspoon instant coffee
½ cup ground nuts

Beat egg whites with salt and vinegar to make soft peaks. Blend in sugar, cinnamon, coffee, and nuts, gradually. Beat until stiff peaks form. Put on brown paper on a cookie sheet. Shape like a pie shell with high sides. Bake in 275° oven for 1 hour. Turn off heat and dry shell in oven for 2 hours.

FILLING:
1 (6-ounce) package chocolate bits
2 egg yolks, beaten
¼ cup water
1 cup heavy cream
¼ teaspoon cinnamon
¼ cup sugar
¼ teaspoon instant coffee

Melt chocolate over hot water (or microwave 2 minutes), cool slightly, and spread 2 tablespoonfuls over bottom of cooled shell. Add egg yolks and water to rest of chocolate, blend well. Chill until thick. Whip cream with cinnamon, sugar, and coffee. Beat until stiff. Spread half over chocolate in shell. Fold remaining whipped cream mixture into remaining chocolate mixture. Spread over top of torte. Decorate with pecan halves or cut-up pecans. Chill several hours or overnight.

Recipe Jubilee! (Alabama)

Black Forest Cake

1 cup egg whites
1 small pinch cream of tartar
2 cups plus 2 tablespoons sugar
1 teaspoon vanilla
4½ ounces slivered almonds, finely chopped

Cut 4 (9-inch) parchment paper discs. Place on cookie sheets and grease discs. (The same paper discs may be used many times; just be sure to grease them each time.) Whip egg whites until foamy and add cream of tartar. Continue whipping egg whites until stiff enough to follow the beater around. With mixer on low speed, blend sugar (⅓ cup at a time) and vanilla into whites. If you stir it too much, the sugar will melt the whites. Fold in almonds with a wooden spoon. Use rubber spatula and gently spread meringue on discs. Be sure the meringue is not higher in the center. Cook for 2½ hours at 225°; then turn off the oven and leave inside at least 6 hours with the doors closed so that the discs can dry thoroughly.

CHOCOLATE FILLING:

3 egg whites
¾ cup sugar
3 tablespoons cocoa
3 ounces German sweet chocolate, melted
3 sticks butter, very soft

Whip egg whites over hot, but not boiling water. Add sugar and whip until stiff. Add cocoa. Take off fire. Add German chocolate; then fold in butter. Let chocolate mixture get cold enough to spread. Then use a rubber spatula and smooth it right on top of each disc and set in the refrigerator to chill. (Do not stack.)

WHIPPED CREAM ICING:

3 cups whipping cream
⅓ cup sugar
2 tablespoons vanilla
3 ounces German sweet chocolate, grated

Whip cream very stiff. Add sugar and vanilla. Remove meringue and chocolate discs from refrigerator. To build the cake, simply ice the first disc with whipped cream, place the second on top of this and ice it, and so on until all 4 layers are arranged. Then ice the sides and top with remainder of whipped cream, and sprinkle grated German chocolate on top. Store in refrigerator or freezer.

Suggestions: Start the cake in the early evening. First, break off six one-inch squares from a 4-ounce package of the chocolate to grate later for top of cake. Rewrap the rest and save to melt in top of double boiler when making chocolate filling later. Remove butter from refrigerator so it will soften. Preheat ovens. Make meringue; put each one on a cookie sheet and bake one above the other in double ovens. If you have

(continued)

(continued)

only 1 oven, it might be necessary to mix and bake just 2 at a time. (There must be room for the heat to circulate, or the meringues will melt.) After they are baked, turn off the ovens and leave them in there overnight. After putting the meringues in the ovens, mix the chocolate filling and leave it at room temperature. It will be the right consistency to spread the next morning.

Confectioners' sugar blends with whipping cream better than granulated sugar.

When you run out of confectioners' sugar, blend 1 cup granulated sugar and 1 tablespoon cornstarch in blender on medium-high or in food processor for 2 minutes.

Recipe from Chef "Shorty" Lenard
Revel (Louisiana)

Bavarian Apple Torte

CRUST:

½ cup butter, softened
⅓ cup sugar
¼ teaspoon vanilla
1 cup flour

Cream butter, sugar, and vanilla; blend in flour. Spread dough onto bottom and 2 inches high around sides of 9-inch springform pan.

FILLING:

1 (8-ounce) package cream cheese
¼ cup sugar
1 egg
½ teaspoon vanilla
⅓ cup sugar
½ teaspoon cinnamon
4 cups apple slices
¼ cup sliced almonds

Combine cream cheese and sugar, mixing well until blended. Add egg and vanilla; mix well. Pour into pastry-lined pan.

Combine sugar and cinnamon; toss with apples. Spoon apple mixture over cream cheese layer; sprinkle with nuts. Bake at 450° for 10 minutes. Reduce oven temperature to 400°; continue baking 25 minutes. Serves 8 - 10.

What's Cooking at Trinity (Pennsylvania)

Mocha Nut Torte

Make this topping first and let it cool while making the cake.

MOCHA TOPPING:
½ cup sugar
2 tablespoons cornstarch
1 cup strong cold coffee
1 ounce unsweetened chocolate
1 tablespoon butter
2 teaspoons vanilla
1 cup whipping cream, whipped

In saucepan, mix sugar and cornstarch and gradually stir in coffee and chocolate. Cook, stirring constantly, until mixture thickens and boils. Boil 1 minute. Blend in butter and vanilla. When thoroughly cool, fold in whipped cream.

TORTE:
6 egg yolks
1 cup sugar, divided
½ cup flour
1 teaspoon baking powder
6 egg whites
1 cup finely ground walnuts
½ cup fine dry bread crumbs

Grease 2 (9-inch) pans. Line with wax paper, then grease paper.

Beat egg yolks with ¾ cup sugar until thick and pale. Add flour and baking powder and beat again until smooth.

In separate bowl, beat egg whites until foamy; add remaining ¼ cup sugar and beat to soft peaks. Mix together the walnuts and crumbs. Add to yolk mixture. Stir to mix well. Fold egg whites into yolks and nut mixture. Spoon into prepared pans. Bake 30 minutes at 350° until slight imprint remains. Cool in pans 10 minutes. Invert onto rack, loosen, and peel off paper. Fill and frost when cool. Refrigerate. Serves 10.

The Steinbeck House Cookbook (California)

Pineapple Cheese Torte

PAT-IN-THE-PAN-CRUST:

1/3 cup butter or margarine, softened
1 cup flour
1 1/4 cups powdered sugar
1/4 cup finely chopped almonds

Combine crust ingredients; pat into bottom of an 8 x 12-inch baking dish. Bake at 350° for 20 minutes.

FILLING:

2 (8-ounce) packages cream cheese
1/2 cup sugar
2 eggs
2/3 cup unsweetened pineapple juice

Beat cream cheese in bowl until fluffy. Beat in sugar and eggs. Stir in juice. Pour filling over crust. Bake at 350° for 20 minutes or until center is set. Cool.

PINEAPPLE TOPPING:

1/4 cup flour
1/4 cup sugar
1 (20-ounce) can crushed pineapple, drained, save juice
1/2 cup whipping cream

Combine flour and sugar in a saucepan. Stir in 1 cup of reserved pineapple juice. Bring to boil, stirring constantly. Boil and stir 1 minute. Remove from heat; fold in pineapple. Cool. Whip cream until stiff peaks form; fold into topping. Spread carefully over dessert. Refrigerate 6 hours or overnight. Garnish with strawberries, if desired. Yields 12-16 servings.

Favorite Recipes (Ohio)

Edelweiss Torte

Simple, but delicious . . . make two, freeze one.

1/2 bar German sweet chocolate
1/2 cup butter
3 eggs, beaten
1 cup sugar
1/2 cup flour
1 1/2 teaspoons vanilla

Melt chocolate and butter in a small pan over low heat. Beat eggs with a whisk until light and foamy. Gradually beat in sugar, flour, and vanilla to eggs. Add butter/chocolate mixture. Pour into a well buttered 9-inch pie pan. Bake at 325-350° for 25-30 minutes. (Do not overbake...will sink slightly in middle.) Serve warm or cold. Top with whipped cream and chocolate slivers. Freezes beautifully! Makes 6 - 8 servings.

A Thyme For All Seasons (Minnesota)

Rhubarb Torte

We've lost count of how many times this has been requested and printed in The Daily Globe.

FIRST LAYER:

1 cup flour
2 tablespoons sugar
Pinch of salt
½ cup butter

Combine ingredients and press in an 8x10-inch pan. Bake at 325° for 20 minutes.

SECOND LAYER:

1¼ cups sugar
2 tablespoons flour
⅓ cup milk
2¼ cups cut rhubarb
3 egg yolks (save whites)

Cook until thick; pour over baked crust.

THIRD LAYER:

3 egg whites
6 tablespoons sugar
¼ teaspoon cream of tartar

Beat egg whites, sugar and cream of tartar. Spread atop cooked rhubarb mixture. Brown in 325° oven for 10-15 minutes.

Dorthy Rickers Cookbook: Mixing & Musing (Minnesota)

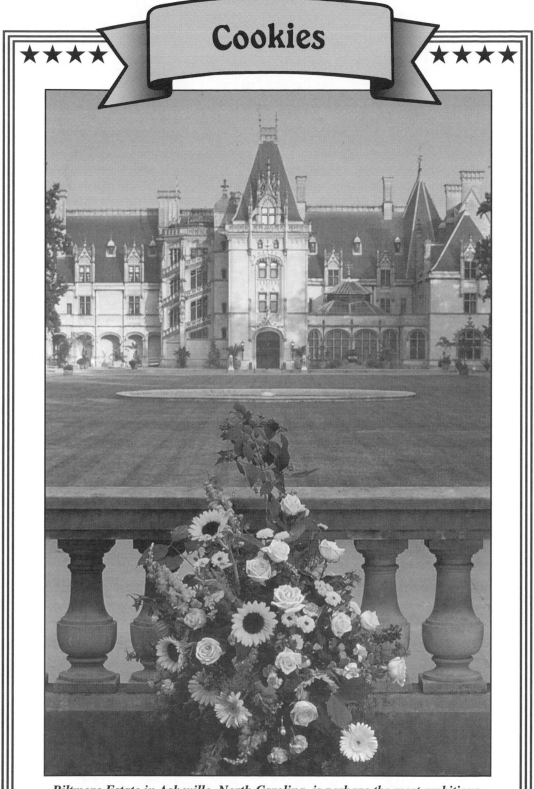

Biltmore Estate in Asheville, North Carolina, is perhaps the most ambitious home ever conceived in America. Boasting four acres of floor space, the 250-room mansion features 34 bedrooms, 43 bathrooms and three kitchens.

PHOTO COURTESY OF THE BILTMORE COMPANY

Old-Fashioned Sugar Cookies

As tender as love, and that's what they are made of, along with the essentials that make a rich cookie. Eight dozen? You'll make a double batch of these the next time.

1 cup butter, softened
1 cup vegetable oil
1 cup granulated sugar
1 cup powdered sugar
1 teaspoon vanilla
2 eggs
4 cups flour
1 teaspoon baking soda
1 teaspoon cream of tartar
1 teaspoon salt

Thoroughly cream butter, vegetable oil, and both sugars. Add vanilla and eggs; beat well. Sift dry ingredients; stir in and blend.

Roll a teaspoon of dough into a small ball. Place on a lightly greased cookie sheet and press down with the bottom of a glass tumbler which has been dipped in sugar. Repeat with remaining dough. Bake 12 minutes in 375° oven.

Aren't You Going to Taste It, Honey? (Ohio)

Golden Sugar Cookies

Of all the cookies we made, this sugar cookie was the most popular. It is a handsome cookie and stays soft.

2½ cups flour
1 teaspoon baking soda
1 teaspoon cream of tartar
¼ teaspoon salt
1 cup butter, softened
½ teaspoon vanilla
½ teaspoon lemon flavoring
2 cups sugar
3 egg yolks

Sift first 4 ingredients together and set aside. Cream butter and extracts; gradually add sugar, creaming until fluffy after each addition. Add egg yolks, one at a time. Add dry ingredients in fourths to creamed mixture; beat just until blended after each addition. Form dough into 1-inch balls and place 2 inches apart on cookie sheet. Bake at 350° for 10 minutes.

Heirloom Recipes and By Gone Days (Ohio)

Molasses Cookies

¾ cup Crisco
1 cup sugar
1 egg
¼ cup molasses
2 cups flour, sifted
3 teaspoons baking soda
1 teaspoon cinnamon
1 teaspoon ground ginger
1 teaspoon ground cloves
1 teaspoon salt
Natural sugar

Cream Crisco and sugar. Add egg and molasses. Stir in flour, 1 cup at a time, along with other dry ingredients. Chill ½ hour. Shape dough into marble-sized balls, roll in natural sugar, and place 1 inch apart on baking sheet. Bake at 350° for 8 -10 minutes. Yields 3 - 4 dozen. May be halved or doubled.

Flavors (Texas)

★ **Editor's Extra:** Put a cinnamon candy on top while hot for an extra bit of color and spice.

Country Raisin Gingersnaps

1½ cups seedless raisins
¾ cup shortening
1 cup sugar
1 egg
¼ cup molasses
2¼ cups sifted flour
2 teaspoons soda
½ teaspoon salt
1 teaspoon ginger
½ teaspoon cinnamon
½ teaspoon cloves

Chop raisins, as this makes the cookie chewy as well as crunchy. Beat together shortening, sugar, and egg. Blend in molasses. Blend in flour sifted with soda, salt, and spices. Mix in raisins. Chill dough. Shape dough into small balls and roll in additional sugar, if desired. Place on lightly greased baking sheet. Bake in moderately hot oven 375°, 8 -10 minutes. Remove to cooling rack. Makes about 3 dozen cookies.

Maine's Jubilee Cookbook (New England)

Old recipes called for many eggs because the hens were not as richly fed and the eggs were smaller.

Oatmeal Pecan Dreams

With a recipe this simple, anyone can have home-baked cookies anytime!

1 cup (2 sticks) margarine, softened
½ cup sugar
1 cup flour
½ cup oatmeal
1¼ teaspoons vanilla
12 pecan halves cut in half lengthwise

Put all ingredients except pecans into food processor or blender. Blend until completely mixed. Drop by teaspoonful (or make into small balls) onto an ungreased cookie sheet. Press 1 pecan piece into each cookie. Bake at 350° for 10-15 minutes. Yields 2 dozen cookies.

Just Inn Time for Breakfast (Michigan)

Extra Special Chocolate Chip Cookies

⅔ cup butter, softened
⅔ cup shortening
1 cup brown sugar
1 cup white sugar
2 teaspoons vanilla
2 eggs, slightly beaten
3 - 4 cups flour
1 teaspoon salt
2 teaspoons baking soda
1 teaspoon baking powder
1 (12-ounce) bag chocolate chips
1 (12-ounce) bag Reese's peanut butter chips
½ cup chopped pecans

Cream butter and shortening. Add sugars; cream until sugar begins to dissolve. Add vanilla and eggs. Stir together 1 cup flour, salt, baking soda, and baking powder. Add to butter mixture. Keep adding flour until dough looks dry (approximately 3½ cups). Stir in chips and nuts. Bake 10 minutes at 350° on ungreased cookie sheets. Makes 6 - 8 dozen (depending on how much dough you eat).

Decades of Mason County Cooking (Texas II)

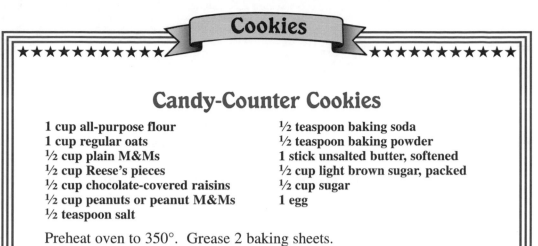

Candy-Counter Cookies

1 cup all-purpose flour
1 cup regular oats
½ cup plain M&Ms
½ cup Reese's pieces
½ cup chocolate-covered raisins
½ cup peanuts or peanut M&Ms
½ teaspoon salt
½ teaspoon baking soda
½ teaspoon baking powder
1 stick unsalted butter, softened
½ cup light brown sugar, packed
½ cup sugar
1 egg

Preheat oven to 350°. Grease 2 baking sheets.

In a medium bowl, stir together the flour, oats, M&Ms, Reese's pieces, chocolate-covered raisins, peanuts or peanut M&Ms, salt, baking soda, and baking powder.

In a large bowl, cream the butter and sugars. Beat in the egg. Stir in the dry ingredients until just combined. By ¼ cupfuls, drop the batter onto the prepared sheets, spacing 2 inches apart. Flatten slightly. Bake, reversing the position of the sheets in the oven once, until the cookies are crisp and golden brown, about 11 minutes. Cool the cookies 5 minutes on the sheets, then transfer them to racks to cool completely. Makes about 16 cookies.

Symphony of Flavors (California)

Dynamite Chocolate Chip Cookies

1 cup butter, softened
1 cup granulated sugar
½ cup brown sugar
2 eggs
2 teaspoons vanilla
2 cups flour
1½ teaspoons salt
1 teaspoon soda
1 (12-ounce) package semisweet chocolate bits
1 cup raisins
½ cup coconut

Cream together butter, sugars, eggs, and vanilla until light and fluffy. Stir in dry ingredients. Blend well.

Add chocolate chips, raisins, and coconut. Grease cookie sheet, drop by teaspoon and bake at 375° for 8 minutes. Yields 3 dozen medium cookies.

The Kettle Cookbook (Ohio)

Pecan Cocoons

1 cup butter
2¾ cups flour
4 tablespoons powdered sugar
4 teaspoons vanilla
1 cup finely chopped pecans
1 tablespoon ice water

Mix all ingredeints together. Work dough well with hands until it can be handled like pie pastry. Break into small pieces and roll between hands into cocoons. Place on ungreased cookie sheet 1 inch apart. Bake at 350° until very delicate brown. Remove from oven and roll in additional powdered sugar while still hot. When cool, roll in powdered sugar again. Yields approximately 3 dozen.

Recipes and Reminiscences of New Orleans I (Louisiana)

Butterfinger Cookies

⅓ cup shortening
¾ cup sugar
1 egg
1⅓ cups sifted flour
½ teaspoon soda
¼ teaspoon salt
2 Butterfinger candy bars, cut in small pieces

Cream shortening and sugar together. Beat in egg. Sift together dry ingredients. Sprinkle over candy bar pieces and combine with creamed mixture. Chill. Drop by spoonfuls on greased cookie sheet. Bake at 350° for about 12 minutes.

Recipes from Jan's Cake & Candy Crafts (Indiana)

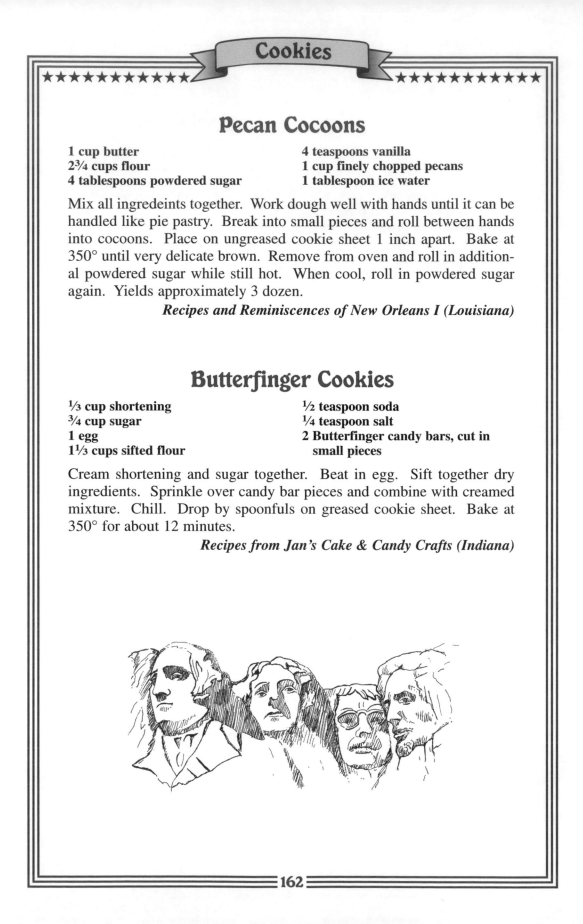

Guess-Again Cookies

The crisp bits in these are potato chips!

1 cup butter, softened (no substitutes)
½ cup sugar
1½ cups flour
1 teaspoon vanilla extract
¾ cup finely crushed fresh potato chips

Preheat oven to 325°. Mix butter and sugar in electric mixer until fluffy. Add flour and mix until smooth. By hand, add vanilla and potato chips; mix well. Drop on ungreased cookie sheet by small teaspoonfuls. Bake 15-20 minutes, until light brown. Cool and sprinkle with sifted confectioners' sugar. These freeze exceptionally well. Makes 5 dozen.

Cook and Deal (Florida)

Judy's Chocolate Crinkle Cookies

They look so pretty and taste like brownies.

½ cup vegetable oil
4 ounces unsweetened chocolate, melted
2 cups granulated sugar
4 eggs
2 teaspoons vanilla
2 cups unsifted flour
2 teaspoons baking powder
½ teaspoon salt
1 cup confectioners' sugar

Mix oil, chocolate and granulated sugar. Blend in 1 egg at a time till well mixed. Add vanilla; stir in flour, baking powder and salt; chill overnight.

Preheat oven to 350°. Drop dough by teaspoon into confectioners' sugar—don't attempt to shape yet. Coat lightly with confectioners' sugar—this makes it crinkle. Pick up, roll into a ball, and roll again in confectioners' sugar. Place 2 inches apart on greased baking sheets. Bake 10-12 minutes. Do not overcook. They will be a little soft to the touch. Makes about 4 dozen small cookies.

Hors D'Oeuvres Everybody Loves (Mississippi)

South Dakota's Black Hills provide the backdrop for Mt. Rushmore. Washington, Jefferson, Teddy Roosevelt, and Lincoln are the most famous men in rock.

Devil's Food Drop Cookies

This is a wonderful, old-fashioned cookie. Delicious, especially at holiday time. Great for chocolate freaks!

½ cup margarine, softened
1 cup brown sugar
1 egg
1 teaspoon vanilla
2 (1-ounce) squares unsweetened chocolate, melted and cooled
2 cups all-purpose flour
½ teaspoon baking soda
¼ teaspoon salt
¾ cup sour cream
½ cup finely chopped walnuts

Cream margarine and sugar till fluffy. Beat in egg and vanilla. Stir in chocolate. Sift together all dry ingredients, adding to chocolate mixture alternately with the sour cream. Mix well and stir in walnuts. Drop from teaspoon, 2 inches apart, on foil-covered cookie sheet (dull-side-up). Bake at 350° for 10 minutes or just until done. Remove and cool. Frost with Mocha Frosting.

MOCHA FROSTING:
¼ cup softened margarine
2 teaspoons instant coffee
2 tablespoons cocoa
Dash of salt
3 cups confectioners' sugar
3 tablespoons milk
1 teaspoon vanilla

Cream margarine, coffee, cocoa, and salt; slowly cream in 1 cup of the sugar, then add remaining 2 cups sugar, milk, and vanilla. Beat until smooth. Makes about 4½ dozen cookies.

Recipes and Memories (Michigan)

Lace Cookies

1 cup sifted flour
1 cup chopped flaked coconut (or chopped nuts)
½ cup light syrup
½ cup firmly packed brown sugar
½ cup margarine
1 teaspoon vanilla

Mix flour and coconut. Combine syrup, sugar, and margarine in heavy saucepan. Bring to a boil over medium heat, stirring constantly. Remove from heat; gradually blend in flour mixture, then vanilla. Drop onto foil-covered cookie sheets by scant teaspoonfuls, 3 inches apart. Bake at 350° for 8 -10 minutes. Cool on wire racks until foil peels off easily. Place cookies on absorbent paper (brown).

The Prima Diner (Florida)

★ **Editor's Extra:** Can also substitute quick-cooking oatmeal for coconut.

Whoopie Pies

COOKIE:

½ cup salad oil
1 cup sugar
½ cup cocoa
1 cup milk
1 egg
2 cups flour
1½ teaspoons baking soda
½ teaspoon salt
1 teaspoon vanilla

Mix ingredients in order and beat until well mixed. Drop on ungreased cookie sheet from a tablespoon. Bake for 7 -10 minutes in a 375° oven or until done. Yields 40 cookies. Spread Filling between 2 cookies.

FILLING:

1 cup milk
4 tablespoons cornstarch
½ cup margarine, softened
1 cup Crisco
1 cup sugar
1 teaspoon vanilla
¼ teaspoon salt

Cook milk and cornstarch together. This will be very thick. Cool completely. Cream together the margarine, Crisco, and sugar. Add vanilla and salt. Add cooled, cooked mixture and beat with electric mixer on high speed for at least 5 minutes. Will be very creamy.

By Our Cookstove (Ohio)

Cream Cheese Cookies

½ cup butter or margarine, softened
1 (3-ounce) package cream cheese, softened
1 cup sugar
1 cup flour
½ cup chopped pecans
1 teaspoon vanilla

Blend butter with cream cheese. Mix in sugar and flour. Add nuts and vanilla. Drop from teaspoon onto ungreased cookie sheets. Bake in 350° oven for 10-12 minutes or until edges of cookies are brown. Makes about 5 dozen chewy cookies.

Hullabaloo in the Kitchen (Texas)

Mexican Wedding Cakes

This traditional holiday cookie is rich and delicious. "Nothing makes the inn smell as warm and wonderful as a batch of Mexican Wedding Cakes baking in the oven," comments innkeeper Julie Cahalane. "My guests can't wait to enjoy them."

2 cups butter, softened
1 cup powdered sugar
2 teaspoons vanilla extract
4½ cups flour
½ teaspoon salt
2 cups chopped pecans
Additional powdered sugar

Preheat oven to 325°. Grease cookie sheets.

With an electric mixer, cream the butter, powdered sugar, and vanilla. Beat in the flour, salt and pecans. Roll stiff dough into bite-sized balls. Place 8 across and 9 down on a cookie sheet. Bake for 20 minutes. After cooling for 5 minutes, roll still-warm cookies in a bowl of powdered sugar. Allow to cool. Roll again to cover completely. Makes 6 dozen cookies.

Inn on the Rio's Favorite Recipes (New Mexico)

Best-Ever Thumb Print Cookies

1 cup butter, softened
½ cup brown sugar
2 egg yolks (save whites)
1 teaspoon vanilla
2 cups flour
½ teaspoon salt
2 egg whites, slightly beaten
Finely chopped nuts (½ cup)
Butter Cream Frosting
Crabapple jelly or maraschino cherries

Cream butter and brown sugar. Add yolks and vanilla; mix well. Stir in flour and salt. Roll into 1-inch balls. Dip each ball into egg whites then roll in chopped nuts. Place on ungreased cookie sheet. Bake 5 minutes at 375°. Make thumb print in center of each cookie. Bake 8 minutes longer. At Christmas, these are pretty filled with green Butter Cream Frosting and topped with a spoonful of crabapple jelly or a maraschino cherry.

BUTTER CREAM FROSTING:
⅓ cup butter
3 cups powdered sugar
1½ teaspoons vanilla
2 - 3 tablespoons milk

Cream butter and sugar, stir in vanilla and add enough milk to make frosting smooth and of spreading consistency. Makes 30-36 cookies.

Kitchen Keepsakes (Colorado)

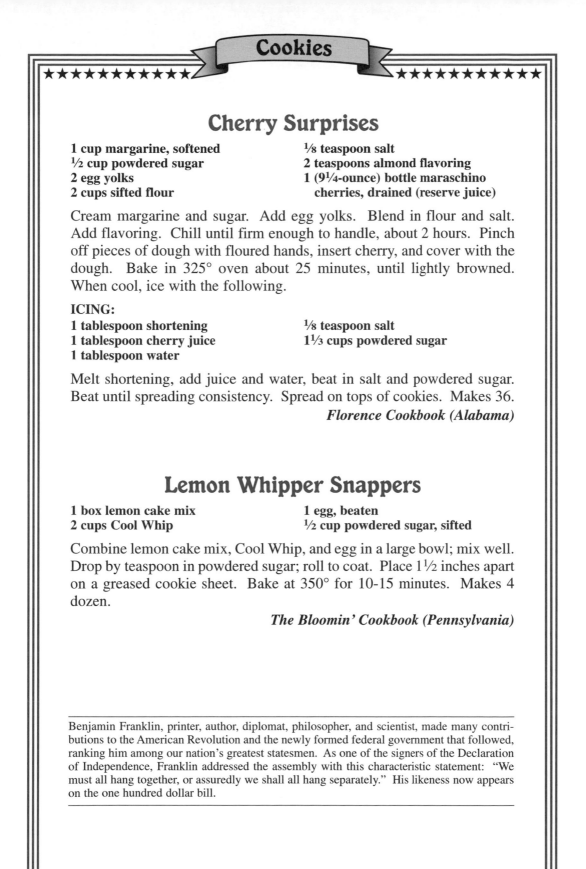

Cherry Surprises

1 cup margarine, softened
½ cup powdered sugar
2 egg yolks
2 cups sifted flour
⅛ teaspoon salt
2 teaspoons almond flavoring
1 (9¼-ounce) bottle maraschino cherries, drained (reserve juice)

Cream margarine and sugar. Add egg yolks. Blend in flour and salt. Add flavoring. Chill until firm enough to handle, about 2 hours. Pinch off pieces of dough with floured hands, insert cherry, and cover with the dough. Bake in 325° oven about 25 minutes, until lightly browned. When cool, ice with the following.

ICING:
1 tablespoon shortening
1 tablespoon cherry juice
1 tablespoon water
⅛ teaspoon salt
1⅓ cups powdered sugar

Melt shortening, add juice and water, beat in salt and powdered sugar. Beat until spreading consistency. Spread on tops of cookies. Makes 36.

Florence Cookbook (Alabama)

Lemon Whipper Snappers

1 box lemon cake mix
2 cups Cool Whip
1 egg, beaten
½ cup powdered sugar, sifted

Combine lemon cake mix, Cool Whip, and egg in a large bowl; mix well. Drop by teaspoon in powdered sugar; roll to coat. Place 1½ inches apart on a greased cookie sheet. Bake at 350° for 10-15 minutes. Makes 4 dozen.

The Bloomin' Cookbook (Pennsylvania)

Benjamin Franklin, printer, author, diplomat, philosopher, and scientist, made many contributions to the American Revolution and the newly formed federal government that followed, ranking him among our nation's greatest statesmen. As one of the signers of the Declaration of Independence, Franklin addressed the assembly with this characteristic statement: "We must all hang together, or assuredly we shall all hang separately." His likeness now appears on the one hundred dollar bill.

Chocolate-Glazed Shortbread Cookies

1 cup (2 sticks) butter, softened
1 cup confectioners' sugar
2 cups flour
2 cups almonds or pecans, finely chopped, divided
6 ounces semisweet chocolate

Cream butter and sugar; gradually add flour; stir in half the nuts. Chill dough 1 hour. Preheat oven to 325°.

Form 1 tablespoon dough into a 2-inch-long finger. Cut in half lengthwise and place cut-side-down on ungreased cookie sheet. Bake 15 minutes or until pale golden brown. Cool. Melt chocolate. Dip 1 end of cookie into chocolate then into chopped nuts. Cool on waxed paper until set. Yields about 5 - 6 dozen.

Christmas Memories Cookbook (New England)

Linzer Tarts

Great at Christmastime!

¾ pound butter, softened
6 tablespoons sugar
4 egg yolks (save whites)
4 cups all-purpose flour
1 teaspoon baking powder
1 teaspoon vanilla extract
2 egg whites
½ cup walnuts, finely chopped
1 (12-ounce) jar seedless raspberry preserves

In a large bowl, cream butter, sugar and egg yolks. Sift flour and baking powder together; blend into butter mixture along with vanilla. Divide dough into 4 pieces. Roll ¼ of dough at a time into ¼-inch thickness on a floured board. Cut into rounds using a 2-inch biscuit cutter. Use a thimble to cut holes in center of ½ of the cookies. Combine holes into remaining dough; roll and cut as before. Bake on an ungreased cookie sheet at 350° for 8 - 9 minutes or until lightly brown. Brush top half of cookies (ones with holes) with egg white; then dip into nuts. Spread raspberry preserves on bottom half of cookies. Put top in place, making a sandwich. Makes 2 - 3 dozen.

Note: The same dough makes wonderful cut-out cookies for children. Decorate as desired.

Suncoast Seasons (Florida)

The Girl Scout Cookie Sale began in Philadelphia, Pennsylvania, in 1933.

Forgotten Kisses

2 egg whites
Pinch of salt
Pinch of cream of tartar
⅔ cup sugar
Green food coloring (or red)
1 package chocolate chips
¼ teaspoon mint extract

Heat oven to 350°. Beat whites until frothy. Add salt and cream of tartar. Keep beating, gradually adding sugar. Fold in food coloring and chips. Drop onto ungreased baking sheets. Turn oven off and leave cookies in oven several hours or overnight. Makes about 24 cookies.

Variations:

SANTA'S KISSES:

2 egg whites
¼ teaspoon cream of tartar
½ cup sugar
⅓ teaspoon salt
½ teaspoon vanilla
1 (3¼-ounce) can flaked coconut

Preheat oven to 350°. Beat egg whites; while beating, gradually add cream of tartar and sugar. When stiff, add salt and vanilla. Fold in coconut. Drop onto brown paper on a cookie sheet. Bake 20 minutes at 325°. Peel off paper when cool.

WITCHES' KISSES:

Fold in 1 (6-ounce) package chocolate chips, melted with coconut. Can be decorated with candy corn or other Halloween candy.

Colorado Cookie Collection (Colorado)

Brownie Meringues

1 (6-ounce) package semisweet chocolate pieces, melted and slightly cooled
2 egg whites
Dash of salt
½ teaspoon vinegar
½ teaspoon vanilla
½ cup sugar
¾ cup broken walnuts

Preheat oven to 350°. Beat egg whites with salt, vinegar, and vanilla until soft peaks form. Gradually add sugar, beating to stiff peaks. Fold in chocolate and nuts. Drop from teaspoon onto greased cookie sheet. Bake for 8 -10 minutes. Makes 3 dozen.

Connecticut Cooks (New England)

Coconut Cookies

2 cups sifted flour
½ teaspoon salt
2 teaspoons baking powder
½ cup shortening
1 cup sugar
2 eggs
½ teaspoon vanilla
1½ cups coconut

Sift together flour, salt, and baking powder. Mix until creamy the shortening, sugar, eggs, and vanilla. Mix in flour mixture, then add coconut. Mix well. Refrigerate for 1 hour or more.

Form dough into 1-inch balls. Place on cookie sheet; flatten with bottom of a glass covered with cheesecloth or dipped in sugar. Bake in a 350° oven, about 12 minutes or until done.

Recipes Old and New (Missouri)

Cornflake Macaroons

2 eggs, well beaten
½ cup sugar
¼ cup brown sugar
1 teaspoon vanilla
2 cups cornflakes
1 cup angel flake coconut
½ cup nuts, chopped

Beat eggs; add sugars and vanilla and beat until light lemon in color. Add remaining ingredients, drop onto parchment-lined cookie sheet and bake at 350° for 10-12 minutes. It's important to line your cookie sheet with parchment paper, as these macaroons will stick. Don't remove cookies until cool. Makes approximately 2 dozen medium-size cookies.

Cooking Pure and Simple (California)

Coconut Macaroons

2 ounces chocolate
2 (3½-ounce) cans coconut
1 can Eagle Brand Milk
1 cup chopped nuts
½ cup flour

Melt chocolate in double boiler. Remove from heat and add remaining ingredients. Drop from teaspoon on greased cookie sheet. Bake 20 minutes in 275° oven.

Company Fare II (Oklahoma)

Goof Balls

1 bag large marshmallows
2 (8-ounce) packages caramel candy
1 (14-ounce) can sweetened condensed milk
1 cup butter or margarine
1 (10-ounce) box Rice Krispies cereal

Cut marshmallows in half and freeze. Melt caramels, butter, and milk in double boiler. Dip marshmallows in caramel mixture and roll in Rice Krispies cereal. Refrigerate to set. Yields 4 - 5 dozen.

Potluck on the Pedernales (Texas II)

Peanut Butter Blossoms

1⅓ cups flour
1 teaspoon baking soda
1 teaspoon salt
½ cup shortening
½ cup creamy peanut butter
1 cup white sugar, divided
½ cup brown sugar
1 egg, unbeaten
2 tablespoons milk
1 teaspoon vanilla
1 package chocolate candy kisses

Sift together flour, baking soda, and salt. Cream together shortening, peanut butter, ½ cup white sugar, and brown sugar. Add egg, milk, and vanilla, and mix well. Add dry ingredients. Using teaspoon, shape into walnut-sized balls. Roll balls in ½ cup white sugar and place on ungreased baking sheet. Bake at 375° for 8 minutes. Remove from oven and press 1 chocolate candy kiss on each cookie, pressing down until the cookie cracks around the edges. Bake another 3 - 5 minutes.

Favorite Recipes from Quilters (Pennsylvania)

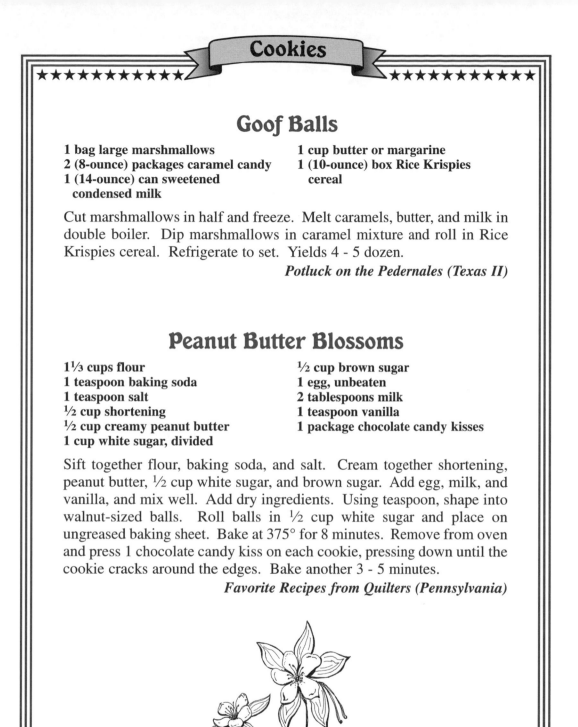

Kahlua-Filled Cookie Cups

1/3 cup sugar
1/2 cup butter, softened
1/2 teaspoon vanilla extract
1/8 teaspoon almond extract
1 egg yolk
1 cup flour
Dash of salt

Heat oven to 350°. Grease 24 miniature muffin cups. Beat sugar and butter until fluffy. Add vanilla, almond, and egg yolk. Blend well. Stir in flour and salt. Mix well. Chill 1 hour. Place 2 teaspoons dough into muffin cups and press up sides to form shell. Bake 10-15 minutes.

FILLING:
2 tablespoons unsweetened cocoa
1/2 cup butter, softened
1 cup powdered sugar
2 tablespoons coffee liqueur (Kahlua)
Grated chocolate

Carefully remove from cups. Cool. In small bowl, beat cocoa and butter until fluffy. Add powdered sugar and liqueur. Blend well. Spoon filling into pastry bag and pipe into cookies. Sprinkle with grated chocolate.

A Sprinkling of Favorite Recipes (Ohio)

★ **Editor's Extra:** A Ziploc bag can substitute for a pastry bag—just snip off a corner and pipe away!

The Indianapolis Motor Speedway is a National Historic Landmark. The Speedway was built as a combination racetrack and testing facility in 1909. The 500-Mile Race was first held in 1911. The Brickyard 400, a NASCAR event, was first held in 1994.

Brownies & Bars

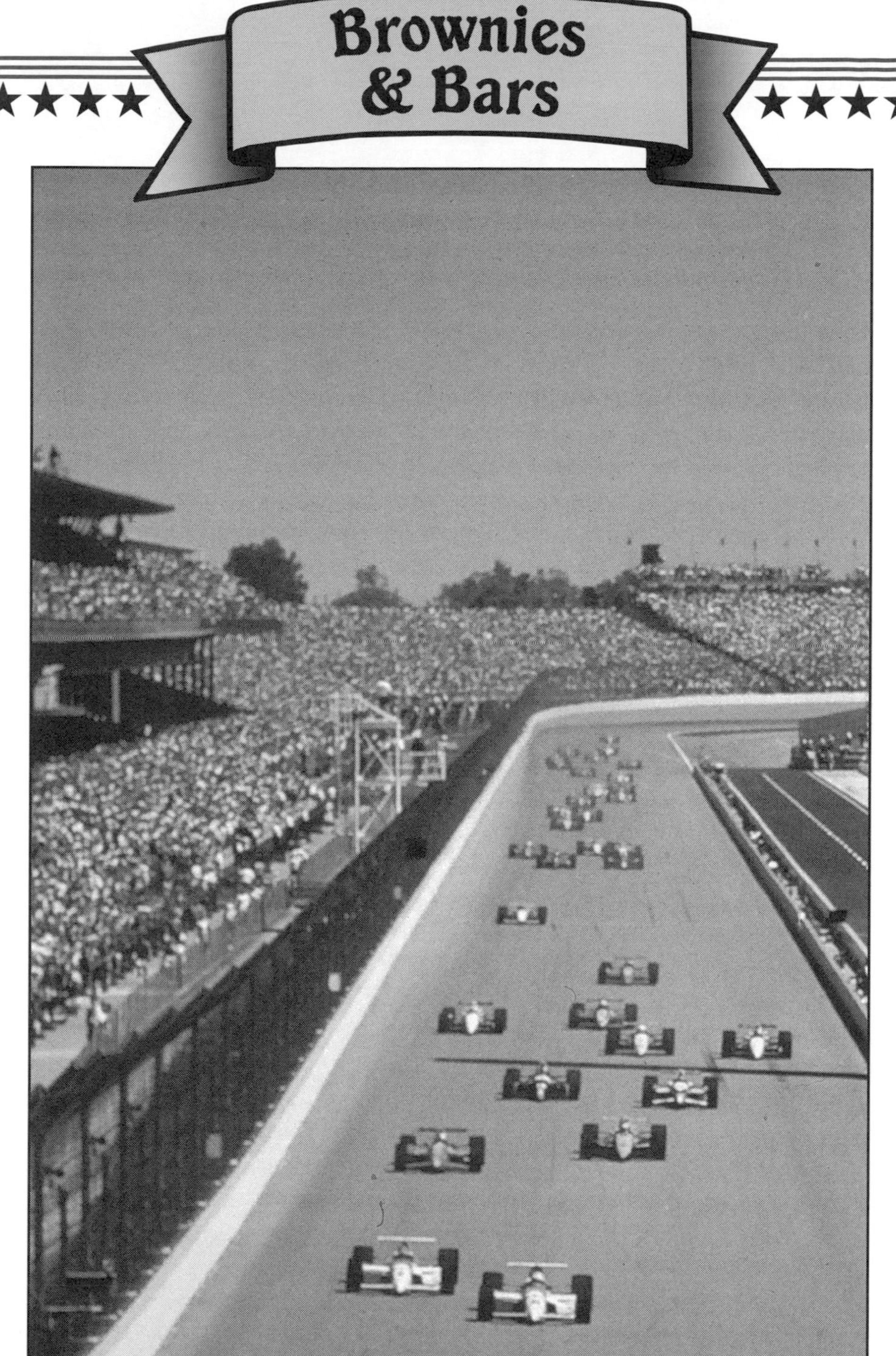

Each year more than 400,000 spectators fill the infield and the stands that circle the famed 2.5 mile track of the Indianapolis Motor Speedway to witness the world's largest single-day sporting event, the Indianapolis 500-Mile Race.

PHOTO COURTESY OF INDIANAPOLIS MOTOR SPEEDWAY

Fudgy Iced Brownies

1 stick margarine, softened
1 cup sugar
4 eggs
1 cup flour
1 (16-ounce) can chocolate syrup
1 cup pecans, chopped

Cream margarine until fluffy. Gradually add sugar and beat. Add eggs, one at a time, beating after each addition. Stir in flour and beat until smooth. Add syrup and nuts and mix. Pour into greased 9x13x2-inch pan and bake at 350° for 25 minutes. Do not overbake.

ICING:
1 stick margarine
1½ cups sugar
⅓ cup evaporated milk
½ cup chocolate morsels
1 cup pecans, chopped

In saucepan, combine margarine, sugar, and milk and cook over low heat to boiling, stirring constantly. Let boil for 1 minute without stirring. Remove from heat and add morsels. Stir until melted. Add nuts and mix. Pour icing over brownies while both are hot. Cool. Cut into squares.

When Dinnerbells Ring (Alabama)

Chocolate Delicious

24 chocolate sandwich cookies
¼ cup butter or margarine, melted
1 (14-ounce) can sweetened condensed milk
12 ounces chocolate chips, divided
4 ounces chopped nuts

Crush cookies and combine with butter. Press into 9x13-inch greased Pyrex pan. In a saucepan, combine milk and ½ of chips. Heat until melted. Spread evenly over cookie crust. Sprinkle with remaining chips and chopped nuts. Bake at 350° for 20 minutes. Do not overbake. Makes 1 dozen.

Tradition in the Kitchen 2 (Illinois)

★ **Editor's Extra:** "A spoonful of sugar helps the medicine go down." Nothing soothes as much as a piece of chocolate or your favorite sweet. When things go wrong, a little sugar treat makes everything seem rosy again.

Hawaiian Caramac Brownie Wedges

CRUST:

2 cups ground Oreo cookies
2 tablespoons melted butter
½ cup semisweet chocolate chips
½ cup chopped macadamia nuts
20 caramels
2 tablespoons heavy cream

Preheat oven to 350°. Spray a 9-inch springform pan with nonstick spray. Combine cookie crumbs and butter. Press into bottom of pan. Bake for 15 minutes. Remove from oven and sprinkle with chocolate chips and nuts. Combine caramels with cream in a microwave-safe bowl. Microwave on high 1 minute. (Stir to melt.) Drizzle over nuts and refrigerate while preparing Brownie.

BROWNIE:

¾ cup unsalted butter
4 ounces unsweetened chocolate, chopped
3 large eggs
2 cups sugar
3 tablespoons macadamia nut liqueur or 2 tablespoons crème de cacoa
1 cup flour
¼ teaspoon salt
¾ cup chopped semisweet chocolate

Melt butter and unsweetened chocolate in large saucepan, stirring until smooth. Remove from heat. Whisk eggs, sugar, and liqueur. Stir in flour, salt, and semisweet chocolate. Pour over crust. Bake until wooden pick inserted in center comes out with moist crumbs, 60-65 minutes. Cool on rack. Refrigerate until firm. Remove from pan; cut into wedges. Brownies will be thick and fudgy, not like cake.

GANACHE:

½ pint heavy whipping cream
10 ounces high quality semisweet chocolate, chopped

For ganache, heat whipping cream in medium saucepan until hot. Add chocolate and stir until completely blended. Pour ganache over top and sides of each wedge, covering completely. Refrigerate until set. Decorate with chocolate hibiscus leaves, macadamia nuts, and caramel drizzle, if desired.

Del Mar Fair's Fare (California)

★ **Editor's Extra:** This is so rich and luscious. Serve small wedges with a scoop of vanilla ice cream. Incredible!

Peanut Butter Brownies

1 cup butter
⅓ cup cocoa
2 cups sugar
4 eggs
1½ cups flour
½ teaspoon salt
1 teaspoon vanilla
1 cup crunchy peanut butter

Preheat oven to 350°. Melt 1 cup butter and cocoa in double boiler or microwave. Cool. Blend in sugar and eggs. Combine flour, salt and vanilla; to this add first mixture. Bake in greased 9x13x2-inch pan for 20-30 minutes. Spoon peanut butter over hot cake and spread while melting.

FROSTING:
½ cup butter
¼ cup cocoa
⅓ cup milk
8 large marshmallows
¼ teaspoon salt
1 teaspoon vanilla
1 box confectioners' sugar, sifted

Melt together butter, cocoa, milk, marshmallows, salt and vanilla. Beat in confectioners' sugar. Spread over cooled peanut butter. Yields 4 dozen 1½-inch squares.

Some Like It South! (Florida)

Chocolate Cream Cheese Brownies

1 (4-ounce) package German sweet chocolate
2 tablespoons butter or margarine
2 eggs
1 teaspoon vanilla
¾ cup sugar
½ cup flour
½ teaspoon baking powder
¼ teaspoon salt

Melt chocolate and butter together and cool. Beat eggs, vanilla, and sugar together in small bowl until thick. Sift together flour, baking powder, and salt; then add to the egg mixture and beat well. Blend in cooled chocolate mixture. Set aside. Spread half of chocolate mixture into greased and floured 8x8-inch pan. Pour Cheese Mixture over. Top with rest of chocolate mixture and swirl to marble. Bake at 350° for 40-45 minutes. Cut in squares when cool.

CHEESE MIXTURE:
1 (3-ounce) package cream cheese
¼ cup sugar
1 egg
½ teaspoon vanilla

Cream cheese and sugar until fluffy. Blend in egg and vanilla.

Centennial Cookbook (Minnesota)

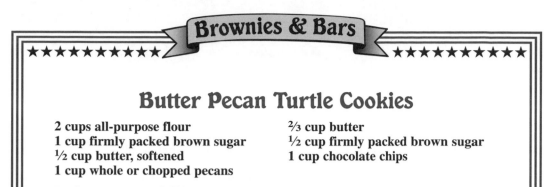

Butter Pecan Turtle Cookies

2 cups all-purpose flour
1 cup firmly packed brown sugar
½ cup butter, softened
1 cup whole or chopped pecans
⅔ cup butter
½ cup firmly packed brown sugar
1 cup chocolate chips

Preheat oven to 350°. In a 3-quart bowl, combine flour, 1 cup brown sugar, and ½ cup softened butter. Mix at medium speed, scraping sides of bowl often for 2 - 3 minutes or until well-mixed and particles are fine. Pat firmly into an ungreased 9x13x2-inch pan. Sprinkle pecans evenly over unbaked crust and press in lightly.

In a heavy 1-quart saucepan combine ⅔ cup butter and ½ cup brown sugar. Cook over medium heat, stirring constantly, until entire surface of mixture begins to boil. Boil 1 minute, stirring constantly.

Pour caramel mixture over pecans and crust. Bake near the center of the oven for 18-22 minutes, or until entire caramel layer is bubbly and crust is light golden brown. Remove from oven, and immediately sprinkle with chocolate chips. Allow chips to melt slightly (1 - 2 minutes), then swirl chips as they melt. Leave some whole for a marbled effect, and do not spread. Cool completely, and cut into desired size. Makes about 75 bite-size squares.

Le Bon Temps (Louisiana)

Chocolate Squares

A chocolate lover's cookie. This is great to pass around at a cookout.

2 cups graham cracker crumbs
12 ounces chocolate chips
1 can sweetened condensed milk

Mix all ingredients together. Place in a greased oblong pan. Bake at 350° for 20 minutes. Cool before cutting into squares.

The What In The World Are We Going To Have For Dinner? Cookbook (Virginia)

Deluxe Chocolate Marshmallow Bars

A family favorite.

¾ cup margarine, softened
1½ cups sugar
3 eggs
1 teaspoon vanilla
1⅓ cups flour
½ teaspoon baking powder
½ teaspoon salt
3 tablespoons cocoa powder
½ cup chopped nuts (optional)
4 cups miniature marshmallows

Cream margarine and sugar together thoroughly. Add eggs and vanilla, beating until fluffy. Sift dry ingredients together and add. Fold in nuts. Spread in greased 11x15-inch pan. Bake at 350° for 15-18 minutes. Sprinkle marshmallows evenly over chocolate layer as soon as you remove it from oven. Return to oven for 2 minutes to slightly melt. Use knife to spread evenly. Cool.

DELUXE TOPPING:
1⅓ cups chocolate chips
3 tablespoons butter or margarine
1 cup peanut butter
2 cups Rice Krispies cereal

Combine chocolate chips, butter and peanut butter in saucepan. Stir constantly over low heat until melted. Remove from heat. Stir in Rice Krispies. Spread over top of bars.

OPTIONAL CHOCOLATE TOPPING:
3 tablespoons cocoa powder
3 tablespoons soft margarine
3 or 4 tablespoons hot coffee to mix
¼ teaspoon vanilla

Beat together until smooth. Spread over bars. Dip knife in water occasionally to aid in spreading, if necessary.

Mennonite Country-Style Recipes (Virginia)

Gillie Whoopers

¾ cup sifted flour
¼ teaspoon baking powder
¼ teaspoon salt
2 tablespoons cocoa
¾ cup sugar
½ cup shortening
2 eggs
1 teaspoon vanilla
½ cup walnuts
1 package miniature marshmallows

Combine flour, baking powder, salt, cocoa, and sugar. Blend in shortening, eggs, and vanilla. Add walnuts. Spread in greased baking pan and bake at 350° for 20 minutes. Take from oven; sprinkle miniature marshmallows over the top, keeping away from sides. Put back into oven for 3 minutes.

FROSTING:

½ cup brown sugar
¼ cup water
2 squares baking chocolate
3 tablespoons butter
2 tablespoons vanilla
1½ cups powdered sugar

Combine brown sugar, water, chocolate. Boil for 3 minutes; take from burner and add butter, vanilla, and powdered sugar (enough to make smooth icing). Spread over marshmallows and let cool. Cut in squares.

All-Maine Cooking (New England)

Choco-Chewies

FILLING:

1 (12-ounce) package semisweet chocolate bits
1 (15-ounce) can sweetened condensed milk
2 tablespoons butter

DOUGH:

1 cup butter, melted
1 pound brown sugar
½ cup chopped nuts
2 eggs
2 cups flour
1 teaspoon salt
1 teaspoon vanilla

Melt filling ingredients in top of double boiler. In a large bowl, mix dough ingredients. Spread half the dough on a greased cookie sheet (10x15x1-inches); drizzle filling over it, and top with the remaining dough. Bake at 350° for 30-35 minutes. Cut squares before cooling. May be frozen. Do not double.

The Belle Grove Plantation Cookbook (Virginia)

Snicker Bars

2 cups chocolate chips, divided
½ cup butterscotch chips, divided
¾ cup creamy peanut butter, divided
1 cup sugar
¼ cup milk
¼ cup margarine
1 cup marshmallow creme
1 teaspoon vanilla
1½ cups dry-roasted peanuts
40 caramels
4 tablespoons water

Melt and spread 1 cup chocolate chips, ¼ cup butterscotch chips, and ¼ cup creamy peanut butter in buttered 9x13-inch pan. Cool. Boil sugar, milk, and margarine for 5 minutes to soft ball stage. Add marshmallow creme, ¼ cup peanut butter, and vanilla. Pour over first layer. Sprinkle peanuts over second layer. Melt together caramels and hot water, and pour over peanuts. Melt 1 cup chocolate chips, ¼ cup butterscotch chips, and ¼ cup creamy peanut butter and spread over caramel layer remaining. Cool and cut into squares.

Trinity Lutheran Church Centennial Cookbook (Iowa)

Raspberry-Filled White Chocolate Bars

1 cup butter
4 cups vanilla chips, divided
4 eggs
1 cup sugar
2 cups flour
1 teaspoon salt
2 teaspoons almond extract
1 cup seedless raspberry fruit spread or preserves
½ cup sliced almonds

Melt butter in a small saucepan over low heat. Remove from heat and add 2 cups of the vanilla chips. Let stand—do not stir.

In a large bowl, beat eggs until foamy. Gradually add sugar, beating at high speed, until lemon colored. Stir in vanilla chip mixture. Add flour, salt, and almond extract and mix on low speed until just combined. Spread ½ of the batter in a greased and floured 9x13-inch pan. Bake at 325° for 15-20 minutes, or until golden brown.

Stir remaining 2 cups of vanilla chips into remaining batter and set aside. Melt raspberry jam in a saucepan and spread evenly over cooked batter. Gently spoon remaining batter over fruit. (Some fruit may show through.) Sprinkle with almonds. Bake at 325° an additional 30-35 minutes. Test for doneness. Let cool completely and cut into 1x1-inch squares. Makes 9½ dozen.

Buffet on the Bayou (Texas II)

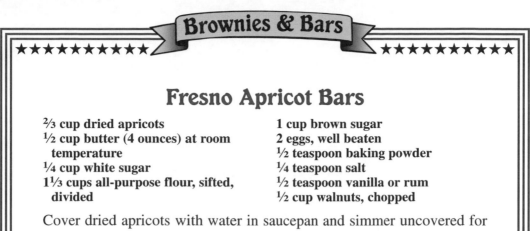

Fresno Apricot Bars

⅔ cup dried apricots
½ cup butter (4 ounces) at room temperature
¼ cup white sugar
1⅓ cups all-purpose flour, sifted, divided
1 cup brown sugar
2 eggs, well beaten
½ teaspoon baking powder
¼ teaspoon salt
½ teaspoon vanilla or rum
½ cup walnuts, chopped

Cover dried apricots with water in saucepan and simmer uncovered for 10 minutes. Drain and cool.

Mix butter with white sugar and 1 cup flour. Blend with your hands or a fork until mixture is crumbly. Lightly grease an 8-inch cake pan. Press crumbly mixture into bottom of pan. Bake at 350° for 25 minutes.

While this is baking, in a large mixing bowl, add brown sugar to beaten eggs and beat together until well blended. In a separate bowl, sift remaining ⅓ cup flour together with baking powder and salt. Chop apricots coarsely and add to egg mixture, along with flavoring, nuts, and flour mixture.

When bottom "crust" has baked, remove from oven and spread apricot mixture over it. Return pan to oven and bake at same temperature an additional 25 minutes. Cool pan on a rack. Cut into squares or bars. Makes 32 (2-inch) squares.

The California Cookbook (California)

Crème De Menthe Bars

BOTTOM LAYER:

3 squares unsweetened chocolate, melted
2 cups firmly packed brown sugar
3 eggs
1¼ cups flour
½ teaspoon salt
¼ teaspoon baking soda
1 teaspoon vanilla

Mix all ingredients together and spread on greased cookie sheet or 9x13-inch pan. Pop into 350° oven for 25-30 minutes. When toothpick comes out clean, cool.

MIDDLE LAYER:

4 cups powdered sugar
2 tablespoons coffee cream
2 sticks butter or oleo
3 shots of crème de menthe
½ teaspoon peppermint extract

Mix all ingredients together and spread over cooled bottom layer. Refrigerate until firm.

TOP LAYER:

12 ounces chocolate chips
3 tablespoons oil

Melt chocolate chips in oil. Spread over top of middle layer, refrigerate. Serves 24-36

From Our Kitchens With Love (Michigan)

Loch Ness Bars

½ cup margarine
1 (6-ounce) package chocolate chips
1 cup peanut butter
1 (10½-ounce) package miniature marshmallows
4¼ cups crisp rice cereal
1 cup peanuts, optional

Melt margarine, chocolate chips and peanut butter over low heat. Add marshmallows and stir until melted. Add cereal and nuts. Spread into 9x13-inch pan and refrigerate until set.

FROSTING:

1 (6-ounce) package chocolate chips
1 (6-ounce) package butterscotch chips

Melt chocolate chips and butterscotch chips together and spread on top. Makes 60 (2x1 inch) bars.

Children's Party Book (Virginia)

Chocolate Revel Bars

1 cup butter or margarine, softened
2 cups brown sugar
2 eggs
2 teaspoons vanilla
2½ cups sifted all-purpose flour
1 teaspoon baking soda
1 teaspoon salt
3 cups quick-cooking rolled oats

In large mixer bowl, cream together butter or margarine and brown sugar. Beat in eggs and vanilla. Sift together flour, soda, and salt. Stir in oats. Stir dry ingredients into cream mixture till blended; set aside.

FILLING:

1 (15-ounce) can sweetened condensed milk
1 (12-ounce) package (2 cups) semisweet chocolate pieces
2 tablespoons butter or margarine
½ teaspoon salt
2 teaspoons vanilla
1 cup chopped walnuts

In heavy saucepan over low heat, melt together sweetened condensed milk, chocolate pieces, butter or margarine, and salt, stirring till smooth. Stir in vanilla and nuts.

Pat ⅔ of oat mixture in bottom of a greased 10x15x1-inch pan. Spread chocolate mixture over dough. Dot with remaining oat mixture. Bake 25-30 minutes at 350°. Cool; cut into 2x1-inch bars. Yields about 75 bars.

Recipe from Bavarian Inn Restaurant
Cookies and Bars (Michigan)

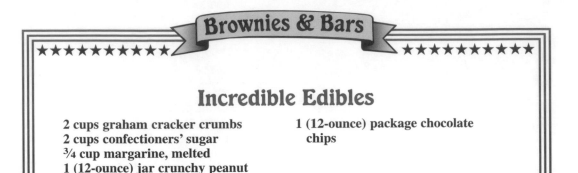

Incredible Edibles

2 cups graham cracker crumbs
2 cups confectioners' sugar
¾ cup margarine, melted
1 (12-ounce) jar crunchy peanut butter
1 (12-ounce) package chocolate chips

Mix cracker crumbs, sugar, margarine and peanut butter with hands. Pat in a greased 9x13-inch baking dish. Melt chocolate chips in the top of a double boiler or microwave. Spread over cookie mix. Let cool. Cut into squares. Store in refrigerator in an airtight container. Yields 24 cookies.

Jacksonville & Company (Florida)

Chocolate Sherry Cream Bars

I have copied this over so many times because they are absolutely out of this world. I am hoping this will be circulated enough so that I'll never have to copy it again. Amen!

4 ounces baking chocolate
1 cup butter or margarine
4 eggs
2 cups sugar
1 cup flour
½ teaspoon salt
1 teaspoon vanilla

Preheat oven to 350°. Melt chocolate and butter over hot water (in a double boiler); mix together and set aside to cool slightly. Beat eggs in mixing bowl until light. Gradually cream in sugar. Add remaining ingredients. Beat 1 minute. Stir in chocolate mixture and pour into greased and floured 10x14-inch pan. Bake 25 minutes. Cool!

FILLING:
½ cup butter or margarine
4 cups powdered sugar
¼ cup coffee cream
¼ cup sherry
1 cup chopped walnuts

Beat butter and sugar together while gradually adding cream and sherry; mixture should be light and fluffy. Mix in walnuts. Spread over base and chill.

TOPPING:
1 (6-ounce) package semisweet chocolate pieces
4 tablespoons butter or margarine
4 tablespoons water

Melt chocoalte pieces with butter and water over hot water. Mix well. Dribble over filling. Chill until firm. Cut into 1x2-inch bars.

Frederica Fare (Georgia)

Love Notes
(Lemon Bars)

CRUST:
2 cups sifted plain flour
½ cup powdered sugar
1 cup butter

Cut flour and powdered sugar into butter until mixture clings together. Press dough into 9x13-inch baking pan. Bake at 350° for 25 minutes. Cool to room temperature before putting on the topping. This is essential for a crisp crust.

TOPPING:
4 eggs, slightly beaten
2 cups granulated sugar
6 tablespoons lemon juice
1 teaspoon baking powder
¼ cup plain flour
Powdered sugar

Mix eggs, sugar, and lemon juice together. When well blended, add baking powder and flour. Mix well. Pour over baked crust. Bake at 350° for 25 minutes. Sprinkle with powdered sugar. Cool completely, then cut into bars. Yields 2½ dozen.

From Mrs. Tom Watson, wife of 1977 Masters' Champion
Tea-Time at the Masters® (Georgia)

Yummy Cherry Bars

2 cups flour
2 cups quick oatmeal
½ teaspoon soda
1¼ cups sugar
½ cup chopped pecans
1¾ cups melted butter
1 (21-ounce) can cherry pie filling
1 cup miniature marshmallows

In a large bowl, combine flour, oatmeal, soda, sugar, pecans, and butter. Mix at low speed, scraping sides of bowl often until crumbly (2 or 3 minutes). Reserve 1½ cups crumb mixture, and spread remaining mixture evenly in a buttered 9-inch pan. Bake at 350° for 12-15 minutes, until brown at edges. Gently spoon pie filling over crust and sprinkle with marshmallows, then remaining crumbs. Return to oven for 25 minutes or until lightly brown. Cool.

Iowa Granges Celebrating 125 Years of Cooking (Iowa)

Peach Meringue Bars

1 cup shortening
½ cup sugar
¼ teaspoon salt
4 eggs, separated
2½ cups flour
1 pint peach preserves
1 cup sugar
1 teaspoon vanilla
¾ cup chopped pecans or coconut

Cream together shortening, sugar, salt, egg yolks, and flour and spread on 9x13x2-inch pan. Cover with peach preserves. Beat egg whites until stiff. Add sugar and vanilla to whites. Spread on top of preserves. Sprinkle chopped pecans on top, or coconut, or both. Bake at 350° for 35-40 minutes.

Franklin County Homemakers Extension Cookbook (Illinois)

Butterscotch Cheesecake Bars

1 (6-ounce) package butterscotch chips
⅓ cup butter or margarine
2 cups graham cracker crumbs
1 cup chopped nuts
1 (8-ounce) package cream cheese
1 (14-ounce) can sweetened condensed milk
1 teaspoon vanilla
1 egg

Preheat oven to 350°. Melt butterscotch chips and butter. Stir in crumbs and nuts. Press half of mixture firmly into bottom of 9x13-inch pan.

In large mixing bowl, beat cheese until fluffy. Beat in condensed milk, vanilla, and egg. Mix well. Pour into prepared pan. Top with remaining crumb mixture. Bake 25-30 minutes, or until toothpick inserted in center comes out clean. Cool. Chill. Refrigerate leftovers.

Look What's Cookin' at Wal-Mart (Wisconsin)

Cinnamon Logs

Spicy and "short;" easy to make.

1 cup butter or margarine, softened
1 cup sugar
2 cups flour
2 teaspoons cinnamon
1 egg, separated
1 cup ground pecans

Cream butter and sugar. Sift flour and cinnamon together and add to butter-sugar mixture. Add egg yolk. Mix well and spread mixture on greased cookie sheet, 10x15 inches. Brush top with beaten egg white. Sprinkle nuts on top. Bake in 350° oven until slightly brown, about 15 minutes. Remove from oven and cut into bars. Makes 4 dozen 1 x 3-inch logs.

Cotton Country Cooking (Alabama)

The Georgia Peach Commission says when buying Georgia peaches, look for a creamy gold to yellow under-color. The red or "blush" is an indication of variety rather than ripeness. The crease should be well-defined and run from the stem end of the peach to the point. It should smell "peachy" and be soft to the touch. Refrigerate peaches and use within a week. To keep them from darkening after slicing, treat with lemon juice or ascorbic acid powder. To peel a peach, simply dip into boiling water for 30 seconds, then in cold water; the peeling should slide off easily.

Pecan Pie Squares

3 cups flour
¼ cup plus 2 tablespoons sugar
¾ cup margarine, softened
Dash of salt

Heat oven to 350°. Grease a jellyroll pan. Combine ingredients until crumbly. Press firmly in pan. Bake 20 minutes. Pour Filling over baked layer; spread evenly. Bake 25 minutes. Cool. Cut in 1½-inch squares. Makes 36.

FILLING:
4 eggs, slightly beaten
1½ cups sugar
1½ cups Karo syrup
3 tablespoons margarine, melted
1½ teaspoons vanilla
2½ cups chopped pecans

Mix first 5 ingredients until well blended. Stir in pecans.

Think Healthy (Virginia)

Lonesome Cowboy Bars

1 cup sugar
1 cup corn syrup
1½ cups crunchy peanut butter
6 cups cornflakes
12 ounces butterscotch chips

Over medium heat, bring sugar and syrup to a boil. Stir in peanut butter. Remove from heat and pour over cornflakes. Mix well, then pack into a 9x13-inch cake pan that has been greased with margarine. In a double boiler over a low heat, melt the butterscotch chips. Spread evenly on top of the cereal mixture. Cool completely and cut into bars. Makes 30 bars.

The Wild Wild West (Texas II)

Adobe Bars

Delicious warm or cold, these chewy bars have a rich brown topping that looks like New Mexico adobe.

¼ cup shortening
¼ cup butter
1 cup sugar
1 whole egg
2 eggs, separated
1½ cups flour
1 teaspoon baking powder
¼ teaspoon salt
1 cup nuts, chopped
½ cup semisweet chocolate pieces
1 cup miniature marshmallows
1 cup light brown sugar, packed

Preheat oven to 350°. Cream shortening, butter and sugar. Beat in the whole egg and 2 egg yolks. Sift flour, baking powder, and salt together; combine the 2 mixtures and blend thoroughly. Spread batter in a greased 9x13-inch pan. Sprinkle nuts, chocolate pieces and marshmallows over the batter. Beat 2 egg whites stiff; fold in brown sugar. Spread over top of cake. Bake 35 minutes. Cool and then cut into bars. Makes 32 bars.

Simply Simpatico (New Mexico)

Pecan Crunchies

The contributor of this recipe says she has never taken these cookies anywhere without people asking for the recipe. The happy surprise is that they are so easy to make.

½ (16-ounce) box graham crackers
½ pound butter
1 cup dark brown sugar
1 cup pecans, chopped

Lightly oil a jellyroll pan and line with graham crackers. Melt butter in a medium saucepan. Add brown sugar and stir until mixture bubbles vigorously. Add pecans and quickly spread over the graham crackers. Bake at 350° for 10 minutes. Cut along indentations of the crackers; leave in pan and freeze for 1 hour. Do not eliminate freezing, because this is what makes these so crunchy. Yields 5½ dozen.

Tastes & Tales From Texas . . . With Love (Texas)

Gail Borden, a Texas surveyor and patriot, discovered that milk could be condensed by evaporation, and patented condensed milk in 1856. He was the founder of the Borden Milk Company.

Heath Bars

Munchy, crunchy good!

2 cups flour
1 cup butter, divided
1½ cups brown sugar, divided
1 cup pecans, chopped
1 (6-ounce) package semisweet chocolate chips

Preheat oven to 350°. Mix flour, ⅓ cup butter and 1 cup brown sugar until fine. Spread mixture into 9x13-inch pan. Cover with pecans. In small saucepan, combine ⅔ cup butter and ½ cup brown sugar. Cook over medium heat, stirring constantly until entire surface boils ½ - 1 minute. Spread over nuts. Bake 18-22 minutes. Remove from oven. Immediately sprinkle chocolate chips over top; spread evenly. Cool. Cut into bars. Yields 32 cookies.

Fare by the Sea (Florida)

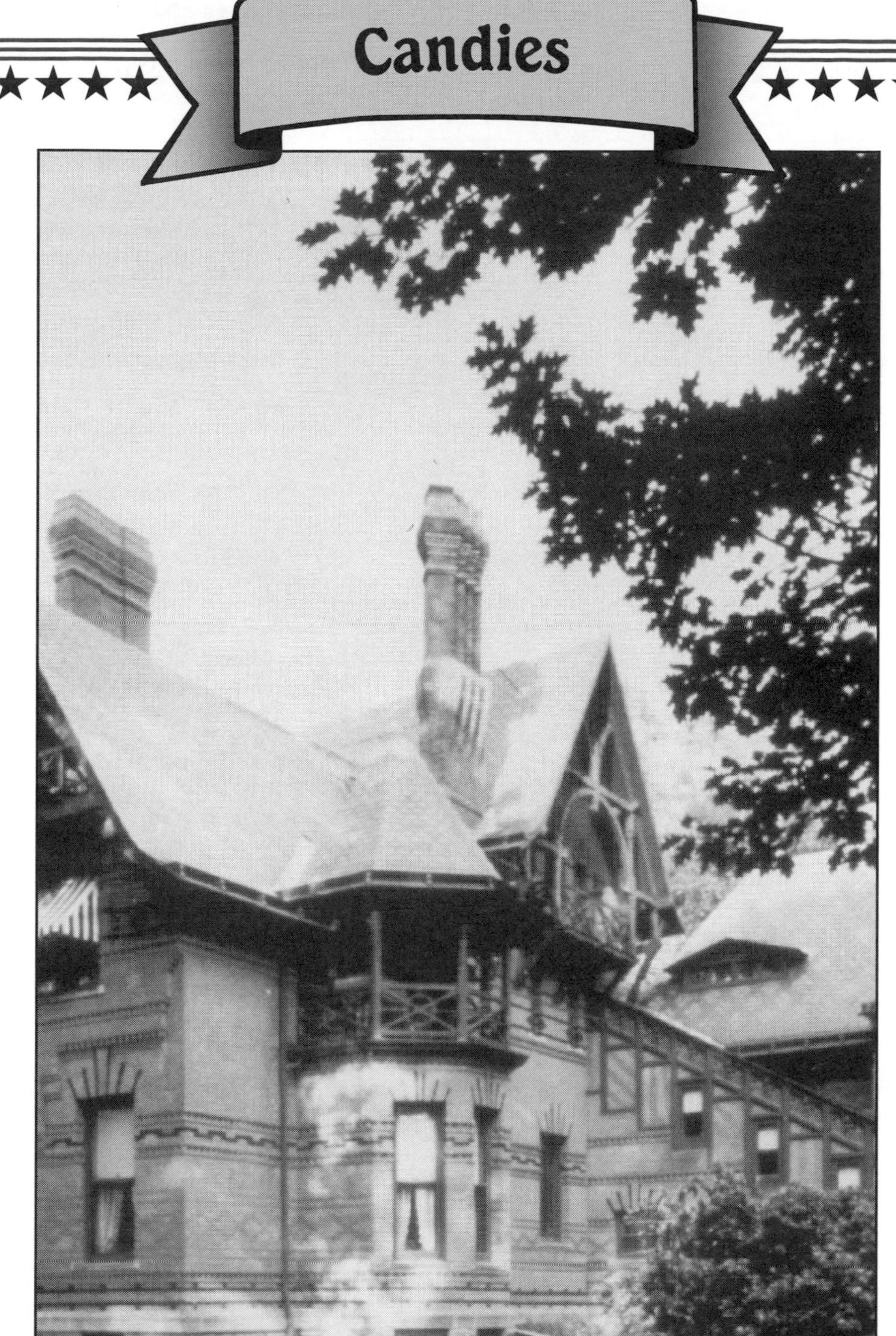

Mark Twain wrote several major works while living in this house in Hartford, Connecticut. During this incredibly creative period, Twain published **Tom Sawyer, Adventures of Huckleberry Finn, The Prince and The Pauper, Life on the Mississippi,** *and* **A Connecticut Yankee in King Arthur's Court.**

Peanut Butter Bon Bons

½ cup butter
½ cup peanut butter
2 cups powdered sugar
1 cup graham crackers
¾ cup chopped nuts
½ cup flaked coconut
1½ cups semisweet chocolate
3 tablespoons Crisco

Melt butter and peanut butter together. Add to dry (next 4) ingredients. Make 1-inch balls. Melt chocolate and shortening. Dip the balls into melted chocolate and put on waxed paper until hardened. Yields 3 - 4 dozen.

The Fine Art of Holiday Cooking (New England)

English Toffee

2 cups sugar
2 cups butter (this is a must)
6 tablespoons water
2 teaspoons vanilla
1 (4-ounce) bar chocolate, broken (or chocolate chips if you like dark chocolate)
1 cup chopped nuts

Combine sugar, butter, and water in heavy saucepan. Cook to 300° on candy thermometer, stirring constantly. Add vanilla and pour on buttered cookie sheet. Sprinkle chocolates on top and spread as they melt. Sprinkle nuts on top. Cool and break into pieces.

Seems Like I Done It This A-Way II (Oklahoma)

Coconut Bonbons

1 can sweetened condensed milk
½ stick margarine, melted
2 cups pecans, chopped
4 boxes powdered sugar
2 cans Angel Flake coconut
1 teaspoon vanilla
1 block paraffin
1 stick margarine
12 ounces chocolate chips

Mix milk, ½ stick margarine, pecans, powdered sugar, coconut and vanilla and form into walnut-sized balls. In double boiler, melt together paraffin, 1 stick margarine, and chocolate chips. Dip each ball until coated, using round toothpick. Put on dish to dry. Yields 10-12 dozen.

Joyce's Favorite Recipes (Tennessee)

★ **Editor's Extra:** Paraffin takes longer to melt, so get it started before you add the margarine and chips.

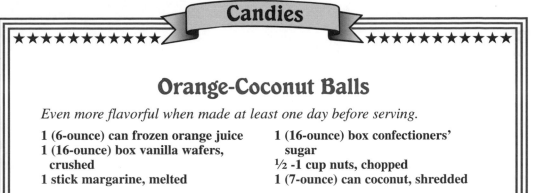

Orange-Coconut Balls

Even more flavorful when made at least one day before serving.

1 (6-ounce) can frozen orange juice
1 (16-ounce) box vanilla wafers, crushed
1 stick margarine, melted
1 (16-ounce) box confectioners' sugar
½ -1 cup nuts, chopped
1 (7-ounce) can coconut, shredded

Mix first 5 ingredients thoroughly. Form into small balls and roll in coconut. Makes 100.

When Dinnerbells Ring (Alabama)

Chocolate and Peanut Butter Truffles

1 cup peanut butter chips
¾ cup butter or margarine
½ cup cocoa powder
1 (14-ounce) can sweetened condensed milk
1 tablespoon vanilla extract

COATINGS:
Finely chopped nuts, or unsweetened cocoa, or graham cracker crumbs, or confectioners' sugar, or chocolate or candy sprinkles

In a heavy saucepan, over low heat, melt chips with butter. Stir in cocoa until smooth. Add milk and vanilla. Cook and stir until thickened and well blended, about 4 minutes. Remove from heat. Chill 2 hours or until firm enough to handle.

Shape into 1-inch balls and roll in any of the Coatings. Chill until firm, about 1 hour. Store covered in refrigerator.

The L.o.V.E. Chocolate Cookbook (Iowa)

Peanut Butter Cups

Candy freezes well—if it lasts that long.

1 pound butter, softened
2 cups peanut butter
3 teaspoons vanilla
2½ - 3 pounds powdered sugar
1 pound dipping chocolate*

Cream butter and peanut butter. Add vanilla. Add sugar; form into small balls. Pour little bit of chocolate in the bottom of paper candy cup. Drop ball in while chocolate is soft. Pour more chocolate on top to rim of cup. These balls can also be dipped in chocolate using a toothpick or dipping fork. Makes 125 pieces.

*Melt dark or milk chocolate pieces in a bouble boiler or microwave.

We're Cookin' in Cucamonga (California)

Fantasy Fudge

3 cups sugar
¾ cup margarine
1 (5⅓-ounce) can evaporated milk
1 (12-ounce) package semisweet chocolate pieces
1 (7-ounce) jar Kraft Marshmallow Creme
1 cup chopped nuts
1 teaspoon vanilla

Combine sugar, margarine, and milk in heavy 2½-quart saucepan; bring to a full rolling boil, stirring constantly. Continue boiling 5 minutes over medium heat, stirring constantly to prevent scorching. Remove from heat, stir in chocolate pieces until melted. Add marshmallow creme, nuts, and vanilla; beat until well blended. Pour into greased 9x13-inch pan. Cool at room temperature; cut into squares. Makes 3 pounds.

The Octagon House Cookbook (Wisconsin)

America's only national park located in a city, Hot Springs, Arkansas, has been famous for its healing waters from thermal springs for over a century. The "Valley of the Vapors" has long been a destination for tourists from around the world, beginning with the Spanish explorer, Hernando DeSoto, who discovered the famous hot springs.

Chocolate Marshmallow Slices

½ cup butter or margarine
1 (12-ounce) package Hershey's Semisweet Chocolate Chips (2 cups)
1 (10½-ounce) package miniature marshmallows (6 cups)
1 cup finely chopped nuts
Additional chopped nuts

In medium saucepan over low heat, melt butter and chocolate chips, stirring constantly until blended. Remove from heat; cool 5 minutes. Stir in marshmallows and 1 cup nuts; do not allow marshmallows to melt.

On wax paper, shape mixture into two 7-inch rolls. Wrap in foil; refrigerate about 20 minutes.

To coat rolls, roll in additional nuts. Wrap; refrigerate overnight. Cut rolls into ¼-inch slices. Store in airtight container in cool, dry place. Yields about 3 dozen slices.

Variation: Chocolate Rainbow Slices—Substitute colored and flavored miniature marshmallows for regular miniature marshmallows.

HERSHEY'S Fabulous Desserts (Pennsylvania)

Chocolate Fudge

Tools: large mixing bowl, stirring spoon.

3 cups powdered sugar
¼ cup cocoa powder
½ cup peanut butter
¼ cup skim milk

1) Put all ingredients in a large bowl and stir together until thoroughly mixed. 2) Shape into 1-inch squares. Yields 50 pieces.

Kids Cuisine (Arkansas)

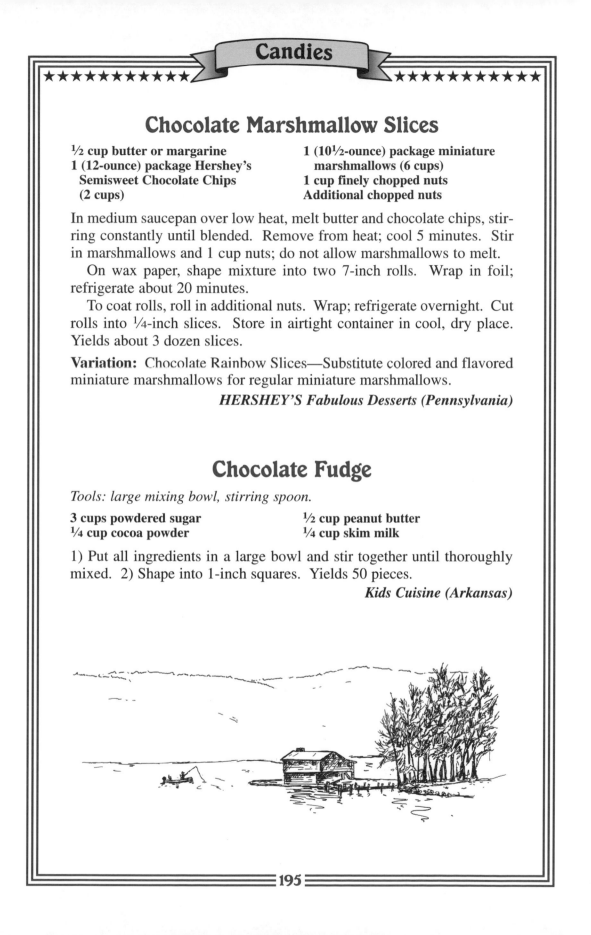

Cherry Divinity

3 cups granulated sugar
½ cup light corn syrup
Dash of salt
½ cup cold water
2 egg whites
1 teaspoon vanilla
½ cup candied red cherries
½ cup chopped nuts

Place sugar, syrup, salt and water in pan over low heat. Stir until sugar is dissolved. Cook until a small amount forms a soft ball in cold water (a candy thermometer takes the guesswork out of the job).

Beat egg whites until stiff and continue beating while pouring half of the syrup in gradually. Cook remaining syrup until it forms a hard ball in cold water. Beat egg whites slowly while remaining syrup cooks. Add remaining syrup gradually.

Continue beating until candy is thick enough to drop. Add vanilla, cherries and nuts. A few drops of red vegetable coloring gives a prettier pink color. Drop on waxed paper.

What Is It? What Do I Do With It? (North Carolina)

Salted Nut Rolls

1 (7-ounce) jar marshmallow cream
1 (12-ounce) package peanut butter chips
1 can Eagle Brand condensed milk
1 (24-ounce) jar dry roasted peanuts, divided
½ bag caramels
2 tablespoons milk

Melt marshmallow cream, chips, and condensed milk in microwave (2 - 3 minutes on HIGH). Chips may not be totally melted. Put half the peanuts on bottom of a greased 9x13-inch pan. Pour marshmallow mixture over peanuts. Microwave caramels and milk on HIGH until melted (about 2½ - 3 minutes). Pour melted caramels over marshmallow mixture. Top with remaining peanuts.

Regent Alumni Association Cookbook (Great Plains)

★ **Editor's Extra:** These are more squares than rolls, but whatever the shape, they are yummy!

Georgia Peanut Brittle

Use a candy thermometer and the brittle will be perfect!

3 cups sugar
1 cup white corn syrup (Karo)
½ cup water
3 cups raw Georgia peanuts
3 teaspoons margarine
1 teaspoon salt
2 tablespoons baking soda

Grease 2 long pieces of aluminum foil and have them ready on countertop. Combine sugar, syrup, and water in heavy 5- to 6-quart pan. On medium heat, stir until sugar melts, then add peanuts. Leave on medium to medium-high heat and stir occasionally. Cook until candy thermometer reaches 300°—hard crack stage. Syrup will be golden and peanuts will "pop" because they have roasted. Remove from heat and add margarine, salt, and soda, stirring well. Candy will "puff up." Pour candy on pieces of prepared, greased aluminum foil. Pour candy quickly and stretch, using a fork or hands, when cool enough. Cool and break into pieces. Yields 2½ - 3 pounds.

A Taste of Georgia (Georgia)

Almond Brittle

1 cup blanched whole almonds
2 tablespoons plus 1 teaspoon butter
½ cup sugar
1 teaspoon vanilla
Salt

In a heavy skillet combine almonds, butter, and sugar. Cook over medium heat, stirring constantly with a wooden spoon until mixture caramelizes (turns golden caramel brown). This process takes approximately 10 minutes. Immediately add vanilla and mix through quickly. Pour onto sheet of heavy duty aluminum foil and spread as thin as possible quickly. Sprinkle lightly with salt. Cool thoroughly. Break into clusters. Store in airtight containers up to 4 months.

If recipe is doubled, the caramelizing process will take approximately 10 minutes longer. Easy. Can do ahead.

Cooking in Clover (Missouri)

Plantation Pecan Crunch

2 cups butter (1 pound)
2 cups sugar
½ teaspoon salt
¼ cup water
2 tablespoons corn syrup
1 (6-ounce) package semisweet chocolate chips
2 cups finely chopped toasted pecans

Melt butter in heavy saucepan. Add sugar and cook, stirring constantly, until dissolved; do not burn. Add salt, water, and syrup. Cook to brittle stage or to register 290° on candy thermometer, stirring constantly. Remove from heat and pour into 2 shallow pans, spreading evenly to a thin layer. While candy cools, melt chocolate chips in top of double boiler over hot water, or microwave on HIGH for 2 minutes, then stir. Spread chocolate on candy layer and sprinkle with pecans. Let stand to cool, then break into pieces like peanut brittle. Makes 25-30 pieces.

Cane River's Louisiana Living (Louisiana II)

★ **Editor's Extra:** Easy to spread on greased foil. Breaks easy this way!

Easy Toffee

This is an amazing recipe.

1 stack of Saltine crackers
1 cup butter or margarine
1 packed cup light brown sugar
1 (12-ounce) package semisweet chocolate morsels

Line a large cookie sheet with foil. Lay crackers on foil in a solid cover, crackers touching. Boil butter and brown sugar for 3 minutes, stirring constantly. Pour over crackers, spreading to cover them all. Bake at 400° for 5 - 7 minutes; do not allow sugar mixture to burn. Remove from oven and allow to sit about 3 minutes. Sprinkle chocolate chips evenly over candy and spread with a spatula as chocolate begins to melt. Refrigerate. Chocolate will harden in about 30 minutes to an hour and candy can be broken into pieces.

Savannah Collection (Georgia)

Creamed Pecan Nuts

Most delicious!

½ cup brown sugar, packed
¼ cup white sugar
¼ cup sour cream
1½ teaspoons vanilla
1½ cups pecan halves

Combine sugars and sour cream in pan. Cook over low heat, stirring constantly, until sugars are dissolved. Cook until soft ball forms in cold water. Remove from heat. Add vanilla and pecans. Stir until light sugar coating begins to form on nuts. Turn out on wax paper. Separate nuts by hand; let cool.

Seasoned with Love (Illinois)

Pralines

2 cups sugar
1 teaspoon baking soda
1 cup buttermilk
¾ cup butter
1½ teaspoons vanilla
1½ cups chopped pecans

In heavy large saucepan, cook sugar, baking soda, buttermilk, and butter to soft ball stage (240° on candy thermometer). Stir frequently while cooking. When mixture reaches soft ball stage, remove from heat and beat until mixture lightens in color and thickens (about 5 minutes). Stir in vanilla and pecans. Drop by tablespoons on wax paper. Yields 3 dozen small pralines.

From A Louisiana Kitchen (Louisiana)

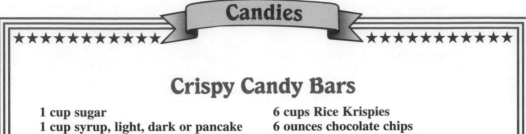

Crispy Candy Bars

1 cup sugar
1 cup syrup, light, dark or pancake syrup
1 cup peanut butter
6 cups Rice Krispies
6 ounces chocolate chips
6 ounces butterscotch chips

In a large saucepan, combine sugar and syrup. Bring to a boil over medium heat. Remove from heat; add peanut butter. Mix well. Add Rice Krispies; stir with a spoon until cereal is well coated. Press into a well-buttered 9x13-inch pan. In warm oven or microwave, melt together the chocolate and butterscotch chips. Stir until well blended. Spread over top of candy. Chill until topping is set. Cut in squares.

The candy does not require refrigeration after topping has hardened. You may want to cut just what will be eaten at that time. I usually serve these bars as cookies. I use about ⅔ cup each chocolate and butterscotch chips. This makes a thinner topping and requires more spreading.

Something Special Cookbook (Oklahoma)

Cinnamon Walnuts

1 cup sugar
¼ teaspoon salt
⅛ teaspoon cream of tartar
½ teaspoon cinnamon
¼ cup boiling water
½ teaspoon vanilla extract
1½ cups walnut halves

Combine sugar, salt, cream of tartar, and cinnamon in heavy saucepan. Add boiling water; mix well. Bring to a rolling boil, stirring constantly. Reduce heat. Cook to 240-248° on candy thermometer (236° at high altitude), firm ball stage. Remove from heat.

Add vanilla and walnuts, stirring until walnuts are coated and syrup begins to turn sugary. Spoon onto wax paper or greased baking sheet, separating walnuts. Cool. Store in airtight containers. Yields 24 servings.

Per serving: Cal 73; T Fat 4g; 46% Cal from Fat; Prot 1 g; Carbo 10g; Fiber <1g; Chol 0mg; Sod 23 mg.

The Flavor of Colorado (Colorado)

Baby Ruth Bars

Oh boy, are these good!

½ cup white sugar
½ cup brown sugar
1 cup corn syrup
1 cup peanut butter
6 cups cornflakes
1 cup salted peanuts
1 (8-ounce) Hershey chocolate bar, melted

Place sugars and syrup in saucepan and bring to a boil. Add the peanut butter, cornflakes, and nuts. Press firmly into greased 9-inch square or 9x13x2-inch pan. Melt chocolate and spread over top.

Recipe from Bavarian Inn Restaurant
Cookies and Bars (Michigan)

Easter Nests

¼ pound margarine
½ cup milk
2 cups sugar
6 tablespoons baking cocoa
1 teaspoon vanilla
½ cup peanut butter
2½ cups quick oatmeal
½ cup coconut
1 bag jelly beans

Combine oleo, milk, sugar, and cocoa; bring to a boil. Boil hard for 1 minute. Remove from stove. Add remaining ingredients, except jelly beans; mix well. On waxed paper, drop by heaping tablespoons. Make an indention in center and immediately lay 3 colored jelly beans in the center. Let set on waxed paper until dry on the outside. Wrap individually with plastic wrap and store in an airtight container, or freeze until the Easter Bunny needs them. These make nice favors at each plate on the table for Easter dinner.

Woodbine Public Library (Iowa)

Almond Apricot Delights

1½ cups dried apricots, coarsely chopped
2 tablespoons cognac
½ cup almond paste
½ cup powdered sugar
2 teaspoons instant coffee
2 teaspoons cocoa
¼ cup powdered sugar
1 teaspoon cocoa

Combine the first 6 ingredients in food processor or blender, and purée. Combine powdered sugar and 1 teaspoon cocoa. Roll apricot mixture into marble-size balls and shake in the powdered sugar mixture. Store in an airtight container with the leftover powdered sugar mixture to prevent them from sticking. Best kept in the freezer. Makes 50 balls.

Note: A quick way to roll out the balls is to do it assembly-line-fashion a dozen at a time. Scoop out about a dozen little spoonfuls on waxed paper, roll them one after the other, drop them into the bag and shake them all together.

Per serving (each): Cal 29; Prot 0g; Fat 0.7g; (trace saturated fat); Carb 5g; Dietary fiber 0g; Chol 0mg; Sod 3 mg; Cal 9mg; Iron 0.3mg. Exchanges: fruit ⅓; fat trace (not recommended for diabetics).

High Fit - Low Fat (Michigan)

Puppy Chow for People

½ pound margarine
12 ounces milk chocolate chips
¾ cup peanut butter
1 large box Crispix cereal
1 pound salted peanuts
1½ cups powdered sugar

Melt oleo, chocolate chips, and peanut butter. Place Crispix cereal and peanuts in a paper bag. Pour melted mixture over cereal and shake well. Pour powdered sugar in bag and shake well again.

Grade A Recipes (Colorado)

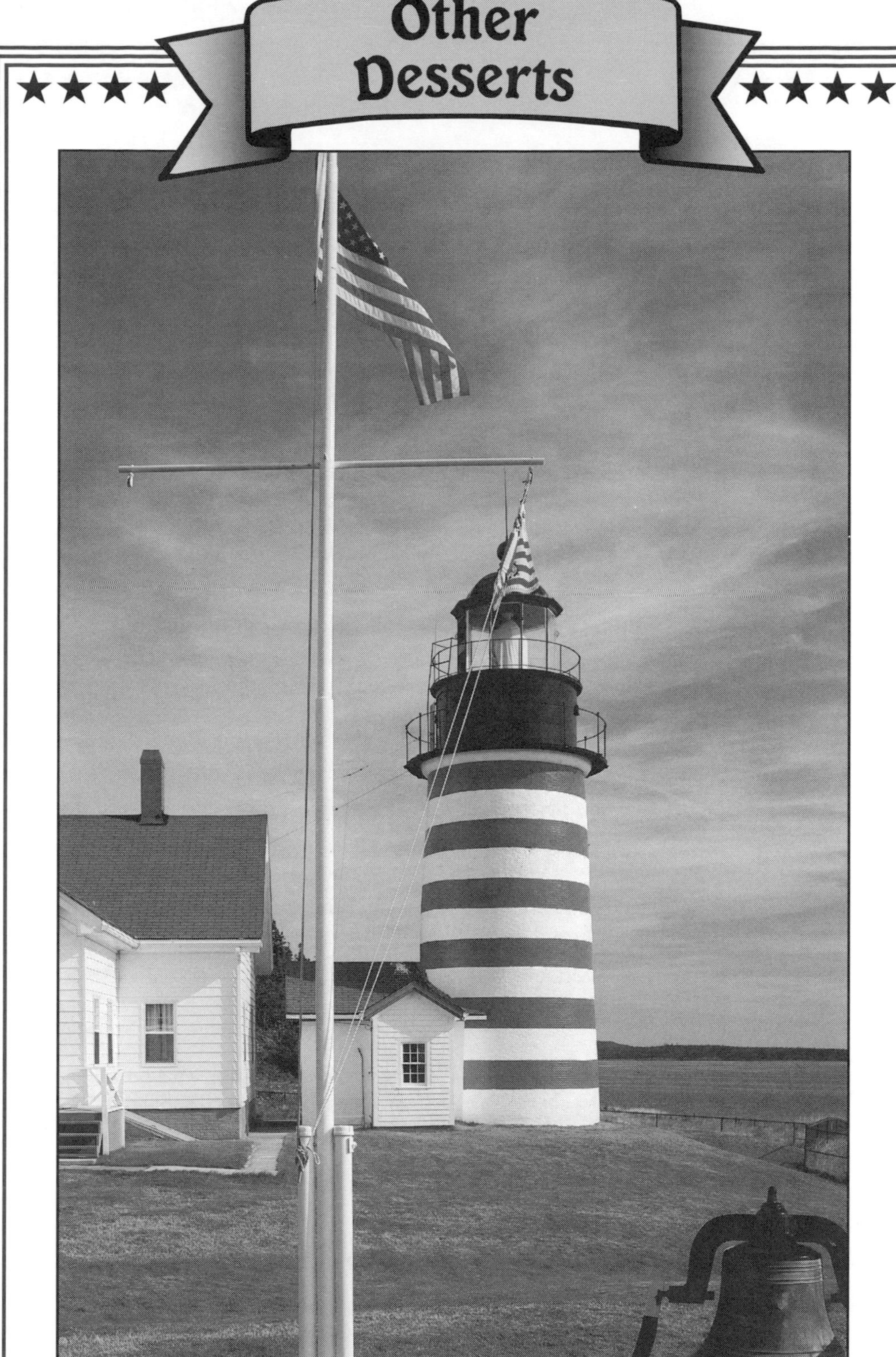

West Quoddy Head Light near Lubec, Maine, is one of the most frequently depicted American lighthouses, with its distinctive red and white bands. The lighthouse, built in 1858, stands on the easternmost point of the U.S. mainland.

Blueberry Dessert

BUTTER CRUNCH CRUST:

1 cup butter
½ cup brown sugar, packed
2 cups flour
1 cup pecans or walnuts, chopped (or coconut)

Heat oven to 400°. Mix all ingredients with pastry blender or hands. Dump onto a cookie sheet. Bake 12-15 minutes. Stir once or twice during baking to prevent edges from burning. Press hot crumbs into a (10x15-inch) jellyroll pan. Cool.

FILLING:

1 (8-ounce) package cream cheese (room temperature)
2 packages Dream Whip topping mix
1 cup powdered sugar
½ cup cold milk
1 can blueberry pie filling

Beat all except pie filling until creamy. Spread on top of cooled crumb crust. Top with blueberry pie filling or fruit filling of your choice.

Cooking with Daisy's Descendants (Illinois)

Lemon Lush

Great anytime, but especially in summer. Pistachio or chocolate pudding may be substituted.

FIRST LAYER:

¾ cup butter or margarine, softened
1½ cups all-purpose flour
1½ cups chopped nuts

Blend butter and flour well and add nuts. Spread in bottom of a 9x13x 2-inch pan. Bake at 350° for 20 minutes; cool and set aside.

SECOND LAYER:

1 cup confectioners' sugar
1 (8-ounce) package cream cheese, softened
1 cup whipped topping (use only 1 cup from 12-ounce container, reserve rest)

Mix all well; spread over cooled first layer.

THIRD LAYER:

2 (3¾-ounce) packages lemon-flavor instant pudding mix
3 cups milk
Chopped nuts

Beat pudding with milk for 2 minutes or until thickened. Pour over second layer and top with remaining whipped topping. Garnish with nuts and refrigerate. May be made a day ahead. Serves 10-12.

Connecticut Cooks III (New England)

Four-Layer Cherry Pie

Preheat oven to 350°. Spread the following layers in a 9x13-inch pan.

FIRST LAYER:

1 stick margarine, melted
1 cup flour
¾ cup nuts, finely chopped

Mix margarine and flour together. Use a spoon to press the mixture in the pan. Sprinkle nuts on top. Bake for 15 minutes. Chill well.

SECOND LAYER:

1 (8-ounce) package cream cheese, softened
1 cup confectioners' sugar
1 cup Cool Whip

Mix cream cheese and sugar well, then fold in 1 cup Cool Whip (from large container). Pour and spread over the first layer. Chill.

THIRD LAYER:

1 large can cherry pie filling

Pour and spread over second layer. Chill.

FOURTH LAYER:

Cool Whip (remainder of 16-ounce container)

Spread over third layer. Chill.

WYVE's Cookbook/Photo Album (Virginia)

Pistachio Delight

CRUST:

1 cup flour
1 stick margarine
2 tablespoons sugar
½ cup nuts

Cut in as pie crust and pat in 9x13-inch pan. Bake at 350° for 15 minutes. Cool.

CREAM:

⅔ cup sugar
1 (8-ounce) package soft cream cheese
1 (8-ounce) carton Cool Whip
2 small packages instant pistachio pudding
2½ cups cold milk

Cream sugar and cream cheese well and fold in ½ container of Cool Whip. Put on crust. Beat instant pudding and milk until thick; spread over cream cheese. Top with rest of Cool Whip. Sprinkle with nuts and cherries, if desired.

Seasoned with Love (Ohio)

Peanut Buster Dessert

CRUST:
1 cup flour
1 stick butter or oleo
⅔ cup chopped peanuts, dry roasted (unsalted)

Mix flour and butter like pie crust. Add peanuts and spread in 9x13-inch greased pan. Bake at 350° for 15-20 minutes until golden brown. Set aside until cool.

FIRST TOPPING:
⅓ cup creamy peanut butter
1 (8-ounce) package cream cheese
1 cup powdered sugar
2 cups Cool Whip

Cream first 3 ingredients, then blend in Cool Whip. Spread on top of cooled baked dough.

SECOND TOPPING:
1 small box French vanilla instant pudding
3 cups cold milk
1 small box chocolate instant pudding

Mix all together with mixer until thick. Spread on top of cream cheese topping.

THIRD TOPPING:
1 (8-ounce) container Cool Whip
Chopped peanuts
1 regular size Hershey Chocolate Bar, crushed

Spread Cool Whip on top of pudding mixture. Sprinkle with chopped peanuts and chopped chocolate bar. Refrigerate.

Note: You can use 1 small box instant vanilla pudding and 1 chocolate pudding. Use 1½ cups cold milk for each box. Spread 1 on top of the other.

Cooking GRACEfully (Ohio)

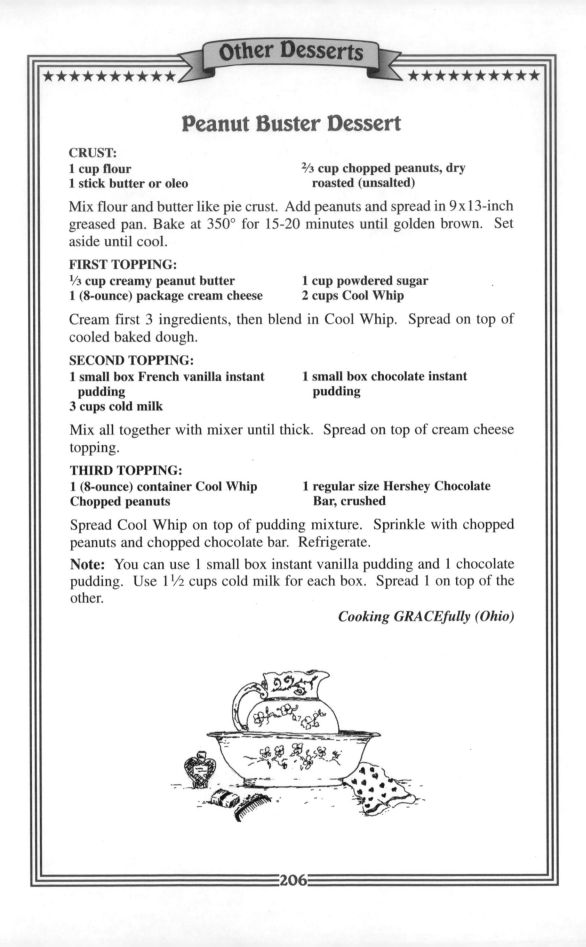

Chocolate Dumplings

SAUCE:

¾ cup brown sugar
¼ cup cocoa
1 tablespoon cornstarch
Dash of salt
2 cups water
2 tablespoons butter

Mix sauce in a large skillet and heat until it comes to a boil and thickens slightly. Remove from heat.

DUMPLINGS:

1 cup flour
½ cup sugar
2 teaspoons baking powder
1 teaspoon salt
2 tablespoons cocoa
1 egg, beaten
⅓ cup milk
3 tablespoons butter, softened
1 teaspoon vanilla

Stir dumpling batter in bowl and beat 1 minute. Return sauce skillet to stove and bring to a simmer. Drop dumplings by tablespoons into sauce. Cover and simmer gently about 20 minutes. Peek just once to make sure sauce is simmering. Serve hot with whipped cream. Yields 6 servings.

Franklin County Homemakers Extension Cookbook (Illinois)

Strawberry Pizza

CRUST:

1 stick margarine
1 cup flour
¼ cup powdered sugar

Melt margarine in pan; add flour and sugar. Mix; pat out on pizza pan. Bake at 350° for 10 minutes or until golden brown.

FILLING:

1 (8-ounce) package cream cheese
1 can Eagle Brand sweetened, condensed milk
⅓ cup lemon juice
1 teaspoon vanilla

Mix until smooth; spread on cooled crust.

TOPPING:

2 pints sweetened strawberries
4 tablespoons cornstarch
Cool Whip

Mix strawberries and cornstarch well and heat over low heat until thick. Spread on pizza and chill. Top with Cool Whip.

Cooking on the Road (Missouri)

Pretzel Dessert

CRUST:

2 cups crushed pretzels
¾ cup melted margarine
3 tablespoons sugar

Mix together and press into a 9x13-inch pan. Bake at 400° for 8 minutes. Cool.

FILLING:

1 (8-ounce) package cream cheese, softened
1 cup sugar
1 (8-ounce) carton Cool Whip

Cream together cream cheese and sugar. Fold in Cool Whip. Spread over crust.

TOPPING:

1 (6-ounce) box strawberry gelatin
2 cups boiling water
2 (10-ounce) packages frozen strawberries

Dissolve gelatin in boiling water. Fold in frozen strawberries. Let set about 8 minutes, allowing strawberries to thaw. Pour over cream cheese mixture. Refrigerate.

Favorite Recipes from the Heart of Amish Country (Ohio)

Moon Cake

1 cup water
½ cup butter or margarine
1 cup flour
4 eggs
1 (8-ounce) package cream cheese, softened
2 small boxes vanilla instant pudding, prepared
Cool Whip
Chocolate fudge ice cream topping
Chopped nuts

Bring water and butter to boil. Add flour all at once and stir rapidly until mixture forms a ball. Remove from heat and cool a little. Add eggs, one at a time, until shiny. Spread into ungreased 10x15-inch jellyroll pan. Bake at 400° for 30 minutes (watch!). Cool. Do not prick surface!

Beat cream cheese until creamy. Slowly blend pudding into beaten cream cheese. Spread on cooled crust and refrigerate for 20 minutes. Top with Cool Whip. Drizzle with chocolate fudge sauce (ice cream topping) and sprinkle with chopped nuts (slivered almonds are good).

Heavenly Delights (Great Plains)

Tornadoes

In this whimsical dessert, funnel clouds of pecan meringue touch down on dots of whipped cream and pools of brilliantly colored fruit sauce. It's not Oz, but it's close.

¾ cup pecan pieces
5 large egg whites
¼ teaspoon cream of tartar
1 cup sugar
1 teaspoon vanilla extract
2 cups fresh or frozen raspberries, blackberries, or strawberries
Sugar to taste
1 cup heavy cream, whipped

Preheat oven to 300°. Grind pecans to a fine paste in food processor. In a separate bowl, beat egg whites and cream of tartar until soft peaks form. Gradually beat in the sugar and vanilla extract until stiff peaks form. Fold in pecans. Fit a pastry bag with a #4 star tip and spoon in the meringue batter. Line 2 baking sheets with parchment paper. Pipe 24 (2-inch) mounds of meringue onto parchment to form inverted funnel shapes. Bake for about 10 minutes, then turn down the heat to 100° and leave the meringues to dry out for 1 - 2 hours, or until crisp. Store in airtight containers or serve immediately.

Purée the fruit in a food processor and add sugar to taste. Place 3 teaspoonfuls of whipped cream randomly on each dessert plate. Spoon about 3 tablespoons of fruit sauce around whipped cream. Place the pointed end of each meringue in a dot of whipped cream and serve. Makes 2 dozen (serves 6 - 8).

Pure Prairie (Great Plains)

Piña Colada Fruit Dip

1 (8-ounce) can crushed pineapple, undrained
¾ cup milk
1 (3½-ounce) package instant coconut pudding mix
½ cup dairy sour cream

Combine all in a food processor; process for 30 seconds. Pour into a plastic bowl with a lid. Refrigerate several hours or overnight to blend flavors. Serve dip in hollowed-out pineapple; either using the bottom half to form a cup, or cut lengthwise to form a boat. Serve with an assortment of fresh fruits.

Not Just Bacon & Eggs (Texas II)

Crêpes Suzette

CRÊPES:
1⅛ cups sifted flour
4 tablespoons sugar
Salt (pinch)
3 eggs, beaten
1½ cups milk
1 tablespoon melted butter
1 tablespoon Cognac
1 teaspoon butter

Sift together sifted flour, sugar and salt. Combine eggs and milk. Stir into dry ingredients until smooth. Stir in butter and Cognac. Let stand for 2 hours.

In a frying pan, heat sweet butter. Pour in 1 tablespoon of batter to cover bottom of pan with a thin layer. Rotate pan to spread batter evenly. Cook 1 minute on each side. Stack crêpes one on top of the other, separated by wax paper.

ORANGE SAUCE:
½ cup butter
½ cup powdered sugar
1 teaspoon orange rind, grated
Juice of 1 orange
¼ cup Grand Marnier or Cointreau
¼ cup brandy

Cream butter and powdered sugar and orange rind. Add orange juice and ¼ cup Grand Marnier or Cointreau. Spread on crêpes and fold or roll them up. Arrange on hot serving dish. Sprinkle with sugar and ¼ cup warmed brandy. Ignite and serve flaming. Serves 6.

Recipes and Remembrances of New Orleans I (Louisiana)

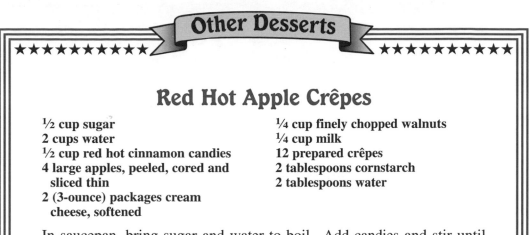

Red Hot Apple Crêpes

½ cup sugar
2 cups water
½ cup red hot cinnamon candies
4 large apples, peeled, cored and sliced thin
2 (3-ounce) packages cream cheese, softened
¼ cup finely chopped walnuts
¼ cup milk
12 prepared crêpes
2 tablespoons cornstarch
2 tablespoons water

In saucepan, bring sugar and water to boil. Add candies and stir until completely melted. Add apples. Cover and simmer for 5 -10 minutes or until tender. Let apples stand in syrup until deep pink, turning if necessary until uniform in color.

Meanwhile, mix cream cheese, walnuts, and milk until blended. Spread on crêpes. With slotted spoon, remove apples from syrup and lay apples over cream cheese mixture and roll up. Stir blended cornstarch and water into remaining syrup. Cook and stir until thickened and translucent. Return any leftover apple slices to syrup and spoon over crêpes. Serve warm or cold. Yields 12 servings.

Bon Appétit de Las Sandias (New Mexico)

★ **Editor's Extra**: Use marvelous crêpes recipe from Crêpes Suzette on previous page.

French Pears

8 fresh, ripe, large pears
1 (8-ounce) package cream cheese
½ - 1 cup chopped pecans
2 tablespoons to ¼ cup powdered sugar

Carefully peel pears. Slice each in half lengthwise and remove core. Do not break pear in the process. Set aside. Mix remaining ingredients according to taste. The mixture should have enough nuts to look pretty and provide enough crunch and enough powdered sugar to be slightly sweetened. Carefully stuff mixture into each pear half. Put stuffed pear halves together to form each whole pear again and wrap individually with plastic wrap. Store in covered container in refrigerator until serving time; preferably serve within 12 hours. To serve, place 1 pear in stemmed sherbet glass, pour warmed Chocolate Sauce over top, and sprinkle with crushed pecans, if desired.

CHOCOLATE SAUCE:
1 stick good margarine
4 squares semisweet baking chocolate
3 cups sugar
1 large can evaporated milk
1 teaspoon vanilla

In double boiler melt margarine and chocolate. Gradually add sugar. Stir constantly and blend well. Add canned milk. Blend well. Cook 10 minutes or until chocolate forms soft ball (has some body) when small amount is dropped in cup of cool water. Remove from heat. Stir in 1 teaspoon vanilla. Cool. Serve warm over pears. Store in refrigerator.

The Gulf Gourmet (Mississippi)

Triple-Dipped Strawberries

A showstopper when served in a pedestal dish on a dessert buffet.

3/4 pound white chocolate
1/2 pound milk chocolate
1/4 pound semisweet chocolate
2 tablespoons vegetable oil, divided
1 quart strawberries

In 3 separate double boilers or bowls over hot water, melt white chocolate and 1 tablespoon oil, milk chocolate and 2 teaspoons oil, and semisweet chocolate and 1 teaspoon oil, stirring until well blended.

Dip berries in white chocolate to coat 3/4 of the way up berry. Allow coating to harden, then dip into milk chocolate, about 1/2 of the way up berry, leaving a strip of white chocolate showing. Let harden, then dip tips of berries in semisweet chocolate. Store on a waxed paper-lined plate in refrigerator. Yields about 20-25 berries.

The Heritage Tradition (Ohio)

Chocolate Dipped Strawberries

Wonderfully easy—wonderfully delicious!

1 quart strawberries, washed and unstemmed

SAUCE:
2 tablespoons butter
1 (6-ounce) package semisweet chocolate morsels
1 teaspoon vanilla or orange extract (try it both ways!)
1 (14-ounce) can Eagle Brand sweetened condensed milk

Arrange strawberries on doilied plate. Place sauce ingredients in top of double boiler and stir until blended. Serve in bowl over hot water (or fondue pot) and let guests hand-dip the strawberries. If there is any sauce left over, freeze and re-use as fudge sauce for ice cream. Serves four.

Ship to Shore II (North Carolina)

The University of North Carolina at Chapel Hill was the first state university in the nation (1795).

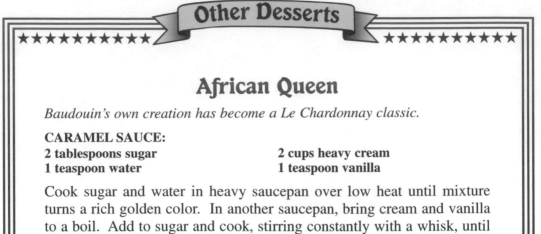

African Queen

Baudouin's own creation has become a Le Chardonnay classic.

CARAMEL SAUCE:
2 tablespoons sugar
1 teaspoon water
2 cups heavy cream
1 teaspoon vanilla

Cook sugar and water in heavy saucepan over low heat until mixture turns a rich golden color. In another saucepan, bring cream and vanilla to a boil. Add to sugar and cook, stirring constantly with a whisk, until smooth. Let cool.

2 bananas
16 sheets phyllo pastry
Melted butter
Sugar
4 large strawberries
20 orange wedges
4 mint leaves
4 scoops vanilla ice cream

Peel bananas and cut in half lengthwise. Brush one sheet phyllo with melted butter. Sprinkle with sugar. Repeat 3 times, stacking the sheets. Wrap one banana half in the pastry, refrigerate, and repeat with remaining banana halves. Bake wrapped bananas on sheet pan in preheated 375° oven until golden and crisp. To serve, place caramel sauce on half of each plate. Decorate the other half with fruit garnishes. Place cooked banana on sauce and top with ice cream. Serve immediately. Serves 4.

Note: Spray butter-flavor Pam on pastry sheets, and substitute evaporated skim milk and low-fat ice cream.

Le Chardonnay, Fort Worth
Fort Worth is Cooking! (Texas II)

Lemon Fluff

A delightful dessert.

1½ cups finely crushed graham cracker or vanilla wafer crumbs
⅓ cup chopped pecans
6 tablespoons butter

Combine vanilla wafer crumbs, pecans, and butter. Reserve ¼ cup crumb mixture and press remainder into 6x10x1½-inch baking dish. Chill.

FILLING:
2 (3-ounce) packages lemon gelatin
1¼ cups boiling water
½ cup whipping cream
1 (3¼-ounce) package instant lemon pudding mix
1 pint lemon sherbet
Pinch of salt

Dissolve gelatin in boiling water; cool to lukewarm. Whip cream until soft peaks form. Set aside. Add dry pudding mix to gelatin and mix. Add softened sherbet and beat at low speed on mixer until thick. Add pinch of salt. Fold in cream. Turn into baking dish and sprinkle remaining crumbs on top. Chill at least one hour. This dessert can be made a day ahead and it keeps nicely in the refrigerator.

Company Fare II (Oklahoma)

Ambrosia

1 cup grapefruit sections (each cut in half)
2 cups orange sections (each cut in half)
2 cups apples, cut in bite-size pieces
20 pitted cherries, sliced in half
2 cups sliced bananas
½ cup shredded coconut (use fresh, or coconut without sugar added)
80 small (mini) marshmallows
½ cup sour cream

Wash, peel, and section grapefruit and oranges. Put in large bowl. Wash, core, and cut apples. Add to above. Mix well. (This will prevent apples from getting dark). Wash, pit, and slice cherries and add to above mixture. Peel and slice bananas and add to above. Add coconut, marshmallows and sour cream. Mix all together. (If this recipe is prepared ahead, do not add marshmallows until ready to serve). Yields 16 servings.

Per serving: 81 calories; Exchange per serving = 1 fruit, ½ fat, ¼ bread; 14 grams carbohydrates, ½ gram protein, 2½ grams fat

Cooking for Love and Life (Louisiana)

Pistachio Pineapple Dessert

Good for St. Patrick's Day.

2 cups (about 14) shortbread cookie crumbs or vanilla wafer (about 50) crumbs
½ cup plus 3 tablespoons chopped pistachio nuts or pecans
¼ cup butter or margarine, melted
1 (8-ounce) package cream cheese, softened
1 (14-ounce) can sweetened condensed milk (not evaporated)
¼ cup lime juice from concentrate
1 (4-serving) package instant pistachio pudding and pie filling mix
1 (8-ounce) can crushed pineapple, undrained
1 cup (½ pint) whipping cream, whipped

Preheat oven to 350°. Combine cookie crumbs, 3 tablespoons nuts, and margarine; press firmly on bottom of 9-inch springform pan or 9x13-inch pan. Bake 8 -10 minutes. Cool. Meanwhile, in large bowl, beat cheese until fluffy. Gradually beat in condensed milk, then lime juice and pudding mix until smooth. Stir in remaining ½ cup nuts and pineapple. Fold in whipped cream. Pour in pan. Chill 6 hours. Garnish as desired.

Recipes & Remembrances II (Michigan)

List of Contributors

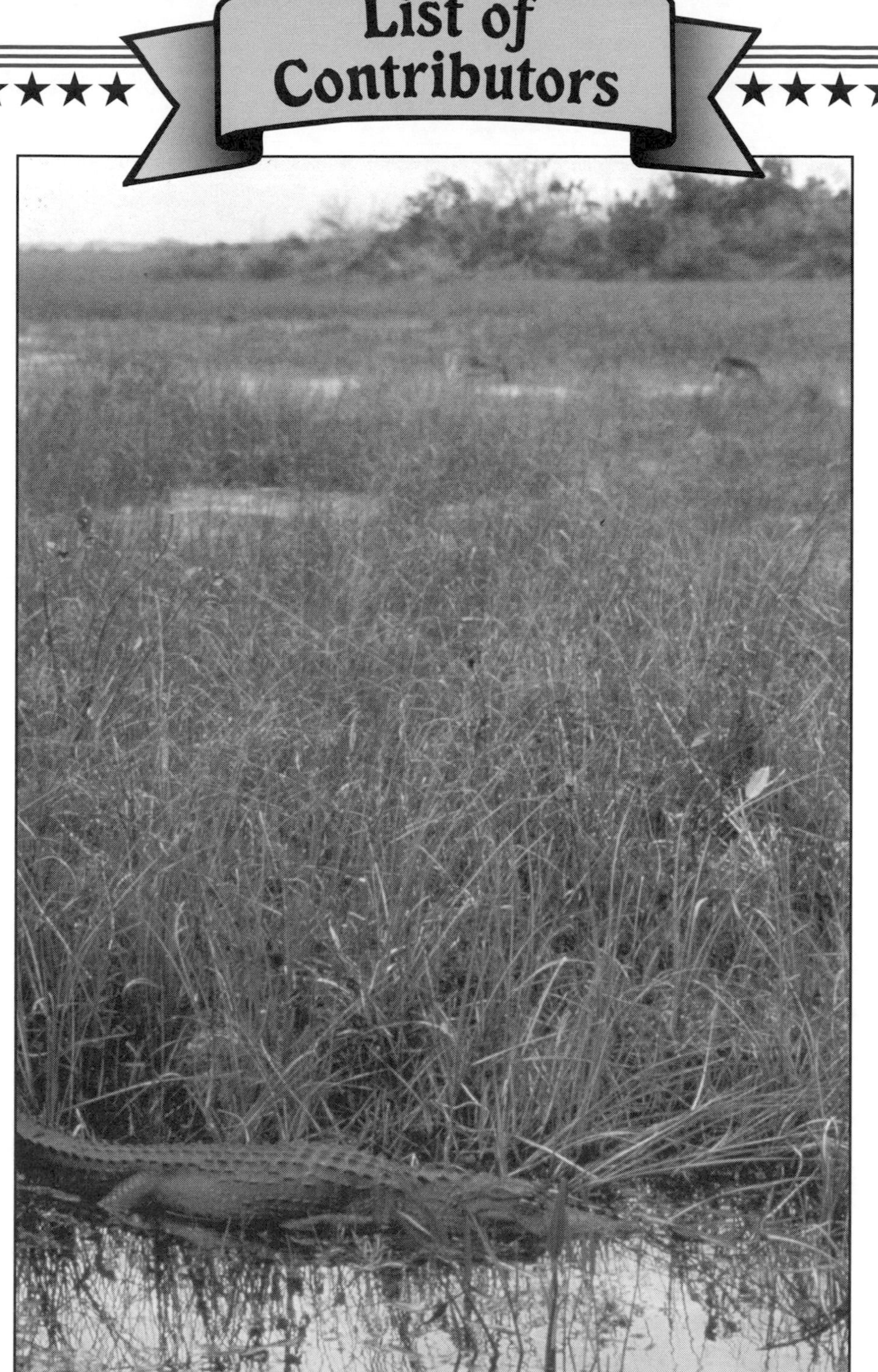

Everglades National Park, Florida, is the largest remaining sub-tropical wilderness in the continental U.S. Its abundant wildlife includes rare and colorful birds, and is the only place in the world where alligators and crocodiles exist side by side.

PHOTO COURTESY OF LOUISIANA OFFICE OF TOURISM

Contributors

Listed below are the cookbooks that have contributed recipes to *The Recipe Hall of Fame Dessert Cookbook,* along with copyright, author, publisher, city and state. The information in parentheses indicates the Best of the Best cookbook in which the recipe originally appeared.

...and Garnish with Memories ©1985 The Overmountain Press, by Patty Smithdeal Fulton, Johnson City, TN (Tennessee)

All-Maine Cooking ©1967 Courier-Gazette, Inc., by Down East Books, Camden, ME (New England)

Applause! ©1995 Oklahoma City Orchestra League, by Oklahoma City Orchestra League, Oklahoma City, OK (Oklahoma)

An Apple From the Teacher ©1993 Illinois Retired Teachers Assn., by Illinois Retired Teachers Association, Springfield, IL (Illinois)

The Apple Barn Cookbook ©1983 The Apple Barn and Cider Mill, by The Apple Barn, Sevierville, TN (Tennessee)

Apple Orchard Cookbook ©1992 Janet Christensen and Betty Bergman Levin, by Janet Christensen and Betty Bergman Levin, Stockbridge, MA (New England)

Appletizers ©1984 Johnny Appleseed Park District Friends, by Johnny Appleseed Metro Park District, Lima, OH (Ohio)

Aren't You Going to Taste It, Honey? ©1995 by the Toledo Blade Company, by Mary Alice Powell, The Blade Marketing Department, Toledo, OH (Ohio)

Asbury United Methodist Church Cook Book ©1990 Asbury United Methodist Church, by Asbury United Methodist Church, Magnolia, AR (Arkansas)

Atlanta Cooknotes ©1982 The Junior League of Atlanta Inc., by The Junior League of Atlanta, Atlanta, GA (Georgia)

Auburn Entertains ©1983, 1986 Auburn Entertains, by Helen Baggett, Jeanne Blackwell and Lucy Littleton, Rutledge Hill Press, Nashville, TN (Alabama)

Aunt Freddie's Pantry ©1984 Freddie Bailey, by Freddie Bailey, Natchez, MS (Mississippi)

The Bell Tower Cookbook ©1995 St. Andrew Catholic Church, by Catholic Community of St. Andrew Church, Rochester, MI (Michigan)

The Belle Grove Plantation Cookbook ©1986 by Belle Grove, Inc., by Belle Grove Inc., Middletown, VA (Virginia)

The Berns Family Cookbook, by The Berns Family, Waukon, IA (Iowa)

Best Made Better Recipes, Volume II, by Lincoln County 4-H Council, Stanford, KY (Kentucky)

Best Recipes of Berkshire Chefs ©1993 Miriam Jacobs, by Berkshire House Publishers, Stockbridge, MA (New England)

Bevelyn Blaire's Everyday Cakes ©2000 Blair of Columbus Inc., by Bevelyn Blair, Hill Street Press, Athens, GA (Georgia)

Beyond Loaves and Fishes, by St. Paul's Episcopal Churchwomen, Artesia, NM (New Mexico)

Blessed Be the Cook, by St. Anne's Altar Society, Camp Douglas, WI (Wisconsin)

Blissfield Preschool Cookbook, by Blissfield Preschool, Blissfield, MI (Michigan)

The Bloomin' Cookbook, by DuBoistown Garden Club, South Williamsport, PA (Pennsylvania)

Blue Willow's "Sweet Treasures," by CJ Gustafson, CT of IA., Inc, Harcourt, IA (Iowa)

The Blueberry Lover's Cookbook, by Muriel Pelham, Village Mills, TX (Texas II)

Bluegrass Winners ©1985 The Garden Club of Lexington, Inc., by The Garden Club of Lexington, Inc., Lexington, KY (Kentucky)

Bon Appetit de Las Sandias, by Woman's Club of West Mesa, Rio Rancho, NM (New Mexico)

The Bountiful Arbor ©1994 by the Junior League of Ann Arbor, by The Junior League of Ann Arbor, Ann Arbor, MI (Michigan)

Buffet on the Bayou ©1993 Houston Junior Forum, by Houston Junior Forum, Houston, TX (Texas II)

By Our Cookstove ©1983 Shekinah Christian School, by Shekinah Christian School Ladies Auxiliary, Plain City, OH (Ohio)

California Cookbook ©1994 Gulf Publishing Company, by Betty Evans, Gulf Publishing Company, Houston, TX (California)

Campbellsville College Women's Club Cookbook ©1987 Circulation Service, by Women's Alliance of Campbellsville University, Campbellsville, KY (Kentucky)

Cane River's Louisiana Living ©1994 The Service League of Natchitoches, Inc., by The Service League of Natchitoches, Natchitoches, LA (Louisiana II)

Canopy Roads ©1995 Canopy Roads, by Tallahassee Junior Woman's Club, Tallahassee, FL (Florida)

Carolina Cuisine ©1969 The Junior Assembly of Anderson, SC, Inc., by The Junior Assembly of Anderson, Anderson, SC (South Carolina)

Centennial Cookbook, by First Christian Church CWF, Seiling, OK (Oklahoma)

Centennial Cookbook, by St. Peter's Lutheran Church, New York Mills, MN (Minnesota)

Central Texas Style ©1988 Junior Service League of Killeen, Inc., by Junior Service League of Killeen, Inc., Killeen, TX (Texas II)

Charleston Receipts ©1950 The Junior League of Charleston, Inc., by The Junior League of Charleston, Inc., Charleston, SC (South Carolina)

Chattanooga Cook Book ©1970 Helen McDonald Exum, by Helen McDonald Exum, Chattanooga, TN (Tennessee)

Cherry Berries on a Cloud and More, by Trinity Pilgrim United Methodist Women, Brookfield, WI (Wisconsin)

Children's Party Book ©1984 The Junior League of Hampton Roads, Inc., by The Junior League of Hampton Roads, Inc., Hampton, VA (Virginia)

Christmas Memories Cookbook ©1985 Mystic Seaport Museum Stores, Inc., by Mystic Seaport Museum Stores, Mystic, CT (New England)

Christmas Thyme at Oak Hill Farm ©1994 Thyme Cookbooks, by Marge Clark, West Lebanon, IN (Indiana)

Collectibles III, by Mary Pittman, Van Alstyne, TX (Texas II)

A Collection of Recipes, by St. Joseph's Home and School Association, Stratford, WI (Wisconsin)

Colorado Cookie Collection ©1990 Georgia Patrick and Cynthia Ann Duncan, by C & G Publishing, Greeley, CO (Colorado)

Company Fare II, by Presbyterian Women First Presbyterian Church, Bartlesville, OK (Oklahoma)

Company's Coming ©1993 Junior League of Kansas City, by Junior League of Kansas City, Kansas City, MO (Missouri)

Connecticut Cooks ©1982 American Cancer Society, CT Division, by American Cancer Society, Connecticut Division, Wallingford, CT (New England)

Connecticut Cooks III ©1988 American Cancer Society, CT Division, by American Cancer Society, Connecticut Division, Wallingford, CT (New England)

Cook 'em Horns: The Quickbook ©1986 The Ex-Students' Association of The University of Texas, by The Ex-Students' Association of The University of Texas, Austin, TX (Texas II)

The Cook Book ©1979 National Council of Jewish Women, by National Council of Jewish Women, Shawnee, KS (Missouri)

Contributors

Cook Book, by Mary Martha Society of Redeemer Lutheran Church, Chico, CA (California)

Cook and Deal ©1982 D. J. Cook, by D. J. Cook, Vero Beach, FL (Florida)

Cook Book: Favorite Recipes from Our Best Cooks, by Central Illinois Tourism Council, Springfield, IL (Illinois)

Cookbook ©1981 The Women of the First Presbyterian Church, by First Presbyterian Church, Huntsville, AL (Alabama)

A Cookbook of Pinehurst Courses ©1980 Moore Regional Hospital Auxiliary, by Moore Regional Hospital Auxiliary, Pinehurst, NC (North Carolina)

Cookies and Bars ©1986 Dorothy Zehnder, by Dorothy Zehnder, Bavarian Inn Restaurant, Frankenmuth, MI (Michigan)

Cookin' in the Spa, by Hot Springs Junior Auxiliary, Hot Springs, AR (Arkansas)

The Cooking Book ©1978 Junior League Louisville, Inc., by Junior league of Louisville, Inc., Louisville, KY (Kentucky)

Cooking for Love and Life ©1979 Recipes for Life, Inc., by Recipes for Life, Inc., Lafayette, LA (Louisiana)

Cookin' for Miracles, by 310 Community Credit Union, Des Moines, IA (Iowa)

Cooking on the Road, by Montana Whitfield, Steele, MO (Missouri)

Cooking with Marilyn ©1988 Marilyn Harris, by Marilyn Harris, Pelican Publishing, Gretna, LA (Ohio)

Cooking Pure & Simple ©1988 Kincaid House Publishing, by June Hunter, Kincaid House Publishing, Newport Beach, CA (California)

Cooking with Morehouse Parish Sheriff Ladies' Auxiliary, by Morehouse Parish Sheriff Ladies' Auxiliary, Bastrop, LA (Louisiana II)

Cooking with Ms. Watermelon ©1990 Donna Presley, by Donna Presley, Hope, AR (Arkansas)

Cooking with Mr. "G" and Friends, by Kevin Grevemberg, Anacoco, LA (Louisiana II)

Cooking with Tradition ©1984 The Woodward Academy Parents Club, by Woodward Academy Parents Club, College Park, GA (Georgia)

Cooking with Daisy's Descendants ©1994 Elaine Gilbert Davis, by Elaine Gilbert Davis, Fairmount, IL (Illinois)

Cooking in Clover ©1977 Jewish Hospital Auxiliary, by Jewish Hospital Auxiliary, St. Louis, MO (Missouri)

Cooking With Grace, by St. Bernard Parish, Wauwatosa, WI (Wisconsin)

Cooking GRACEfully, by Grace Presbyterian Church, Martins Ferry, OH (Ohio)

Cotton Country Cooking ©1972 The Decatur Junior Service League, Inc., by Junior League of Morgan County, Decatur, AL (Alabama)

Country Classics II ©1997 Ginger Mitchell and Patsy Tompkins, by Ginger Mitchell and Patsy Tompkins, Karval, CO (Colorado)

The Country Gourmet ©1982 Mississippi Animal Rescue League, by Mississippi Animal Rescue League, Jackson, MS (Mississippi)

Covered Bridge Neighbors Cookbook ©1990 Circulation Service, Inc., by Covered Bridge Neighbors, St. Peters, MO (Missouri)

The Dallas Symphony Cookbook ©1983 Junior Group of the Dallas Symphony Orchestra League, by the Junior Group of the Dallas Symphony Orchestra League, Dallas, TX (Texas)

Dawn to Dusk ©1996 Holland Junior Welfare League, by Holland Junior Welfare League, Holland, MI (Michigan)

Decades of Mason County Cooking ©1992 Riata Service Organization, by Riata Service Organization, Mason, TX (Texas II)

Del Mar Fair's Fare, by Del Mar Fair, Del Mar, CA (California)

Didyaeverhaveaday? 1988 Pamela Weis, by Pamela Weis, Raspberry Patch Press, Quincy, CA (California)

Dining by Design ©1999 Junior League of Pasadena, Inc., by Junior League of Pasadena, Pasadena, CA (California)

Dining in Historic Ohio ©1987 Marty Godbey, by McClanahan Publishing House, Inc., Kuttawa, KY (Ohio)

Dining Door to Door in Naglee Park, ©1995 East Campus Commercial Organization, by The Campus Community Association, San Jose, CA (California)

Dining Under the Magnolia ©1984 Scott Wilson, by Scott Wilson, CEC, Grove Hill, AL (Alabama)

Dixie Cookbook IV ©1958 Women of the Church First Presbyterian Church, by First Presbyterian Church, Fort Smith, AR (Arkansas)

Dixie Delights ©1983 St. Francis Hospital Auxiliary, by St. Francis Hospital Auxiliary, Memphis, TN (Tennessee)

Dorthy Rickers Cookbook: Mixing & Musing, by Dorthy Rickers, The Cows' Outside, Worthington, MN (Minnesota)

Duluth Woman's Club 70th Anniversary Cookbook, by Duluth Woman's Club, Duluth, MN (Minnesota)

The Elsah Landing Restaurant Cookbook ©1981 The Elsah Landing Restaurant Inc., by Helen Crafton and Dorothy Lindgren, Elsah, IL (Illinois)

The Enlightened Gourmet ©1984 CGW Enterprises, by Ann Cotton, Henrietta Gaillard and Jo Anne Willis, CGW Enterprises, Charleston, SC (South Carolina)

Family Secrets ©1985 The William Henry Thomas Family, by Thomas Family Memorial Association, Tuscaloosa, AL (Alabama)

Fare by the Sea ©1983 The Junior League of Sarasota, Inc., by Junior League of Sarasota, Sarasota, FL (Florida)

Favorite Recipes from Quilters ©1992 Good Books, by Louise Stoltzfus, Good Books, Intercourse, PA (Pennsylvania)

Favorite Recipes, by St. Nicholas Orthodox Church, Barton, OH (Ohio)

Favorite Recipes from the Heart of Amish Country, by Rachel Miller, Sugarcreek, OH (Ohio)

The Fearrington House Cookbook ©1987 Jenny Fitch, by Jenny Fitch, Pittsboro, NC (North Carolina)

Feast of Goodness, by Gruver United Methodist Women, Gruver, TX (Texas II)

Feast of Goodness ©1994 Jennings Chapel Church, by Jennings Chapel Church, Marthaville, LA (Louisiana II)

Feeding the Faithful ©1983 The Women of Mauldin United Methodist Church, by United Methodist Women of Mauldin United Methodist Church, Mauldin, SC (South Carolina)

Ferndale Friends Cook Book, by Ferndale Friends, Ferndale, MI (Michigan)

Festival ©1983 Humphreys Academy Patrons, by Humphrey's Academy Patrons, Belzoni, MS (Mississippi)

Fiesta ©1987 Junior Woman's Club of Pensacola, by Pensacola Junior Woman's Club Inc., Pensacola, FL (Florida)

Fiftieth Anniversary Cookbook, by Northeast Louisiana Telephone Co., Inc., Collinston, LA (Louisiana II)

Fillies Flavours ©1984 The Fillies, Inc., by The Fillies, Inc., Louisville, KY (Kentucky)

The Fine Art of Holiday Cooking ©1992 University of Connecticut, by University of Connecticut, School of Fine Arts, Storrs, CT (New England)

First Christian Church Centennial Cookbook, by First Christian Church, Mason City, IA (Iowa)

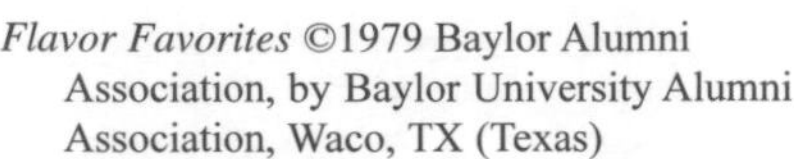

Flavor Favorites ©1979 Baylor Alumni Association, by Baylor University Alumni Association, Waco, TX (Texas)

The Flavor of Colorado ©1992 Colorado State Grange, by Colorado State Grange, Superior, CO (Colorado)

Flavors ©1978 The Junior League of San Antonio, Inc., by Junior League of San Antonio, San Antonio, TX (Texas)

Florence Cook Book, by Trinity Episcopal Churchwomen, Florence, AL (Alabama)

Foresters' Favorite Foods, by Pine Forest United Methodist Women's Organization, Dublin, GA (Georgia)

Four Generations of Johnson Family Favorites, by Ruth Johnson, Oklahoma City, OK (Oklahoma)

Four Square Meals a Day, by Women's Ministries, Lamar, CO (Colorado)

Fort Worth is Cooking! ©1993 Renie Steves, by Renie Steves, Fort Worth, TX (Texas II)

Franklin County Homemakers Extension Cookbook, by Franklin County Homemakers Extension, Benton, IL (Illinois)

Frederica Fare, by The Parents Association of Frederica Academy, St. Simons Island, GA (Georgia)

From a Louisiana Kitchen ©1996 Holly B. Clegg, Inc., by Holly B. Clegg, , New York, NY (Louisiana)

From Our Kitchens With Love, by St. Mark Orthodox Church, Rochester Hills, MI (Michigan)

Gardener's Delight, by The Ohio Association of Garden Clubs, Green Springs, OH (Ohio)

Generations of Good Cooking, by St. Mary's Parish, Oxford, IA (Iowa)

Georgia's Historic Restaurants ©1996 Dawn O'Brien and Jean Spaugh, by Jean Spaugh and Dawn O'Brien, John F. Blair, Publisher, Winston-Salem, NC (Georgia)

German Recipes ©1994 Penfield Press, by Penfield Press, Iowa City, IA (Iowa)

Giant Houseparty Cookbook ©1981 by Chamber of Commerce Philadelphia, MS, by Philadelphia-Neshoba County Chamber of Commerce, Philadelphia, MS (Mississippi)

Good Sam Celebrates 15 Years of Love, by Socorro Good Samaritan Village, Socorro, NM (New Mexico)

Good Food From Michigan ©1995 Laurie Woody, by Laurie Woody, Grawn, MI (Michigan)

Goodies and Guess-Whats ©1981 Helen Christiansen, by Helen Christiansen, Walsh, CO (Colorado)

Gourmet of the Delta ©1964 St. John's Women's Auxiliary, by St. Paul's Episcopal Churchwomen, Hollandale, MS (Mississippi)

Grade A Recipes ©1996 Prairie Vision Park, by Idalia Playground and Park Committee, Idalia, CO (Colorado)

Granny's Kitchen, by Theone L. Neel, Bastian, VA (Virginia)

Great Beginnings, Grand Finales ©1991 The Junior League of South Bend Inc., by Junior League of South Bend, South Bend, IN (Indiana)

Great Lakes Cookery ©1991 by Avery Color Studios, by Bea Smith, Avery Color Studios, Marquette, MI (Michigan)

The Guild Cookbook IV ©1993 Valparaiso University Guild, by Valparaiso Universtiy Guild, Valparaiso, IN (Indiana)

The Gulf Gourmet ©1978 The Gulf Gourmet, by Westminster Academy, Gulfport, MS (Mississippi)

Gulfshore Delights ©1984 The Junior Welfare League of Fort Myers, FL, Junior League of Fort Myers, Florida, Fort Myers, FL (Florida)

Have Fun Cooking With Me ©Lela J. Clarke, by Lela J. Clarke, Statesville, NC (North Carolina)

Heavenly Delights, by Sacred Heart Altar Society, Nelson, NE (Great Plains)

Heirloom Recipes and By Gone Days ©1993 Heirloom Enterprises, by Sherry Maurer, Zoar, OH (Ohio)

Contributors

The Heritage Tradition ©1987 Janet and Howard Melvin, by Janet Melvin, Heritage Restaurant, Cincinnati, OH (Ohio)

HERSHEY'S Fabulous Desserts © Hershey Foods Corporation, Hershey, PA (Pennsylvania)

High Fit - Low Fat ©1989 Regents of the University of Michigan, by The University of Michigan Medical Center, Ann Arbor, MI (Michigan)

Holiday Treats, by Theone L. Neel, Bastian, VA (Virginia)

Home Cookin', by NPS Denver Employees' Association, Denver, CO (Colorado)

Home Cookin': Almont Elementary PTA, by Almont Elementary PTA, Almont, MI (Michigan)

Honest to Goodness ©1990 Junior League of Springfield, by Junior League Publications, Springfield, IL (Illinois)

Hors D'Oeuvres Everybody Loves ©1983 Quail Ridge Press Inc., by Jo Barksdale and Mary Leigh Furrh, Quail Ridge Press, Brandon, MS (Mississippi)

Hospitality ©1983 Harvey Woman's Club, by Harvey Woman's Club, Palestine, TX (Texas)

Houston Fine Arts Cookbook ©1983 University of Texas Press, by Virginia Elverson, University of Texas Press, Austin, TX (Texas)

How to Make a Steamship Float ©1985 American Steamship Company, by Harbor House Publishers, Boyne City, MI (Michigan)

Hullabaloo in the Kitchen ©1983 Dallas A&M University Mother's Club, by Dallas A&M University Mother's Club, Dallas, TX (Texas)

I Promised A Cookbook, by Josephine Conner, Sioux Falls, SD (Mississippi)

Incredible Edibles, by Jai Baker, Auburn, CA (California)

Inn on the Rio's Favorite Recipes, by Julie Cahalane, Taos, NM (New Mexico)

Into the Second Century, ©1984 French Camp Academy, by French Camp Academy, French Camp, MS (Mississippi)

Iowa Granges: Celebrating 125 Years of Cooking, by Iowa State Grange, Cedar Rapids, IA (Iowa)

Island Events Cookbook ©1986 Island Events Cookbook, Edited by Jolie Donnell, Telluride, CO (South Carolina)

It's About Thyme ©1988 Marge Clark - Thyme Cookbooks, by Marge Clark, West Lebanon, IN (Indiana)

Jacksonville & Company ©1982 The Junior League of Jacksonville, FL, Inc., by Junior League of Jacksonville, Jacksonville, FL (Florida)

Jambalaya ©1983 Junior League of New Orleans, Inc., by Junior League of New Orleans, Inc., New Orleans, LA (Louisiana)

Joyce's Favorite Recipes ©1986 Robert and Joyce Breeding, Edited by Robert L. Breeding, Knoxville, TN (Tennessee)

The Junior Welfare League 50th Anniversary Cookbook, by Mayfield-Graves County Junior Welfare League, Mayfield, KY (Kentucky)

Just Inn Time for Breakfast ©1992 Tracy M. Winters and Phyllis Y. Winters, by Tracy and Phyllis Winters, Winters Publishing, Greensburg, IN (Michigan)

Just Desserts ©1988 The Shipley School, by Shipley School, Bryn Mawr, PA (Pennsylvania)

Kay Ewing's Cooking School Cookbook ©1994 Kay Ewing, by Kay Ewing, Baton Rouge, LA (Louisiana II)

The Kettle Cookbook, by The Soup Sisters of the Salvation Army, Cleveland, OH (Ohio)

Kids Cuisine ©Sparks Health System, by The Nancy Orr Family Center at Sparks Regional Medical Center, Fort Smith, AR (Arkansas)

Kitchen Keepsakes ©1983 Bonnie Welch and Deanna White, by Bonnie Welch and Deanna White, Kiowa, CO (Colorado)

Contributors

Kitchen Keepsakes by Request ©1983 Bonnie Welch and Deanna White, by Bonnie Welch and Deanna White, Kiowa, CO (Colorado)

The L.o.V.E. Chocolate Cookbook, by Jean Van Elsen Haney, Waterloo, IA (Iowa)

L'Heritage Du Bayou Lafourche © 1995 Lafourche FCE, by Lafourche Association for Family & Community Education, Lockport, LA (Louisiana II)

Le Bon Temps ©1982 Young Women's Christian Organization, by Young Women's Christian Organization, Baton Rouge, LA (Louisiana)

The Lite Switch ©1992 The Lite Switch, by June McLean Jeter, Arlington, TX (Texas II)

Loaves and Fishes ©2000 St. Paul's Episcopal Church, by St. Paul's Episcopal Church, Daphne, AL (Alabama)

Lone Star Legacy II ©1985 Austin Junior Forum Inc., by Austin Junior Forum Publications, Austin, TX (Texas II)

Look What's Cookin' at Wal-Mart, by Children's Miracle Network, Black River Falls, WI (Wisconsin)

Lost Tree Cook Book, by Lost Tree Chapel, North Palm Beach, FL (Florida)

Luncheon Favorites ©1991 Blue Owl Restaurant and Bakery, by The Blue Owl Restaurant & Bakery, Kimmswick, MO (Missouri)

Madison County Cookery ©1980 Madison County Chamber of Commerce, by Madison County Chamber of Commerce, Canton, MS (Mississippi)

Maine's Jubilee Cookbook ©1969 Courier-Gazette Inc., Edited by Loana Shibles and Annie Rogers, Camden, ME (New England)

Mammoth Really Cooks Book II, by Mammoth Hospital Auxiliary, Mammoth Lakes, CA (California)

Margaritaville Cookbook ©1984 VIPCO, by Ruth Perez and Brenda Vidal, Key West, FL (Florida)

Marketplace Recipes Volume II, by Action Advertiser, Fond du Lac, WI (Wisconsin)

A Matter of Taste, by Paulding County Republican Women, Paulding, OH (Ohio)

Mennonite Community Cookbook ©1950, 1957, 1978 Mary Emma Showalter, by Mary Emma Showalter, Herald Press, Scottdale, PA (Virginia)

Mennonite Country-Style Recipes ©1987 Herald Press, by Esther H. Shank, Herald Press, Scottdale, PA (Virginia)

Miss Daisy Entertains ©1980 Daisy King, by Daisy King and Marilyn Lehew, Rutledge Hill Press, Nashville, TN (Tennessee)

The Mississippi Cookbook ©1972 University Press of Mississippi, by The Home Economics Division of the Mississippi Cooperative Extension Service, University Press of Mississippi, Jackson, MS (Mississippi)

More Firehouse Favorites ©1998 San Diego Fireman's Relief Association, by San Diego Fireman's Relief Association, San Diego, CA (California)

More of the Four Ingredient Cookbook ©1994 Linda Coffee and Emily Cale, by Coffee and Cale, Kerrville, TX (Texas II)

Mushrooms, Turnip Greens and Pickled Eggs ©1971 Frances Carr Parker, by Frances Carr Parker, TarPar Ltd., Kinston, NC (North Carolina)

The Nashville Cookbook ©1976, 1977 Nashville Area Home Economics Assn., by Nashville Area Home Economics Association, Nashville, TN (Tennessee)

Natchez Notebook of Cooking ©1986 Trinity Episcopal Day School, by Trinity Episcopal Day School, Natchez, MS (Mississippi)

Nell Graydon's Cook Book ©1969 Nell S. Graydon, by Sandlapper Publishing Co., Inc., Orangeburg, SC (South Carolina)

Not Just Bacon & Eggs ©1991 Donna Duncan Jomaa, by Donna Duncan Jomaa, Straw Hat Productions, Houston, TX (Texas II)

The Octagon House Cookbook, by The Watertown Historical Society, Watertown, WI (Wisconsin)

Oma's (Grandma's) Family Secrets, by Linda F. Selzer, Homestead, IA (Iowa)

125 Years of Cookin' with the Lord, by Trinity Lutheran Church, Topeka, KS (Great Plains)

125 Years - Walking in Faith, by Women's Fellowship, First Congregational Church, Spencer, IA (Iowa)

Our Favorite Recipes II, by English Wesleyan Women's Missionary Society, English, IN (Indiana)

Out of Our League ©1978 Junior League of Greensboro, Inc., by The Junior League of Greensboro, Inc., Greensboro, NC (North Carolina)

Palates ©1995 MVA Colorado Springs Fine Arts Center, by Members' Volunteer Association Colorado Springs Fine Arts Center, Colorado Springs, CO (Colorado)

Palmetto Evenings, by American Cancer Society, Columbia, SC (South Carolina)

The Philadelphia Orchestra Cookbook ©1980 West Philadelphia Women's Committee for the Philadelphia Orchestra, by The West Philadelphia Committee for the Philadelphia Orchestra, Bryn Mawr, PA (Pennsylvania)

The Pick of the Crop ©1978 North Sunflower PTA, by North Sunflower PTA, Drew, MS (Mississippi)

A Pinch of Sunshine ©1982 Junior Service League of Brooksville, by Junior Service League of Brooksville, Brooksville, FL (Florida)

The Pioneer Chef ©1991 Telephone Pioneers of America, Oklahoma Chapter 41, by Oklahoma Pioneers of America, Bethany, OK (Oklahoma)

Potluck on the Pedernales ©1991 Community Garden Club of Johnson City, by Community Garden Club of Johnson City, Johnson City, TX (Texas II)

A Potpourri of Virginia Cooking, by American Cancer Society, Glen Allen, VA (Virginia)

Presentations ©1993 Friends of Lied, by Friends of Lied, Lied Center for Performing Arts, Lincoln, NE (Great Plains)

The Prima Diner ©1981 Sarasota Opera Society, by Sarasota Opera Society, Sarasota, FL (Florida)

The PTA Pantry ©1994 The Fairlawn Elementary School PTA, by Fairlawn Elementary School PTA, Akron, OH (Ohio)

Pure Prairie ©1995 Pig Out Pubications, by Judith Fertig, Pig Out Publications, Kansas City, MO (Great Plains)

Raleigh House Cookbook II ©1995 Raleigh House, by Martha R. Johnson, Kerrville, TX (Texas II)

Recipe Jubilee! ©1964 The Junior League of Mobile, Inc., by Junior League of Mobile, Mobile, AL (Alabama)

Recipes & Remembrances II, by Rockwood Area Historical Society, Rockwood, MI (Michigan)

Recipes from the Cotton Patch, by St. Luke's Episcopal Church, El Paso, TX (New Mexico)

Recipes and Reminiscences of New Orleans I ©1971 Parents Club of Ursuline Academy Inc., by, Ursuline Convent , Metairie, LA (Louisiana)

Recipes from Jan's Cake & Candy Crafts, by Janet Travis, Anderson, IN (Indiana)

Recipes Old and New, by St. Catherine of Alexandria Ladies Society, St. Louis, MO (Missouri)

Recipes and Memories, by Romeo Monday Club, Romeo, MI (Michigan)

Recipes from Our House, by Assistance League of Denver, Denver, CO (Colorado)

Recipes from the Heart, by Epsilon Omega Sorority, Dalton, NE (Great Plains)

Recipes and Remembrances ©1994 Marian Clark, Council Oak Books, Ltd, by Northfork Electric Cooperative, Sayre, OK (Oklahoma)

Regent Alumni Association Cookbook ©1995 Regent Alumni Association, by Regent Alumni Association, Regent, ND (Great Plains)

Return Engagement ©1989 The Junior Board of the Quad City Symphony Orchestra Assn., by Volunteers for Quad City Symphony Orchestra, Davenport, IA (Iowa)

Revel ©1980 Junior League of Shreveport, Inc., by Junior League of Shreveport, Shreveport, LA (Louisiana)

Ritzy Rhubarb Secrets Cookbook ©1992 Litchville Committee 2000 by Community Cookbooks, Litchville, ND (Great Plains)

Saint Mary Catholic Church Cookbook ©1994 St. Mary Catholic Church, by St. Mary Catholic Church, Garnavillo, IA (Iowa)

Salem Cook Book II, by Salem Lutheran Church Women, Montevideo, MN (Minnesota)

Sample West Kentucky ©1985 Paula Cunningham, Edited by Paula Cunningham, McClanahan Publishing House, Inc., Kuttawa, KY (Kentucky)

San Ramon's Secret Recipes ©1998 San Ramon Library Foundation, by San Ramon Library Foundation, San Ramon, CA (California)

Savannah Collection ©1986 Martha Giddens Nesbit, by Martha Giddens Nesbit, Savannah, GA (Georgia)

Seaboard to Sideboard ©1998 The Junior League of Wilmington, Inc., by The Junior League of Wilmington, Wilmington, NC (North Carolina)

Seasoned With Love, by Faith United Methodist Women, Woodward, OK (Oklahoma)

Seasoned With Love, by Reorganized Latter Day Saints Church, McLeansboro, IL (Illinois)

Seasoned with Love, by St. Joseph's Ladies Auxiliary, North Royalton, OH (Ohio)

Seasons in the Sun ©1976 Beaux Arts Inc., by The Lowe Art Museum, Coral Gables, FL (Florida)

Seems Like I Done It This A-Way II, ©1980 Cleo Stiles Bryan. by Cleo Stiles Bryan, Tahlequah, OK (Oklahoma)

Ship to Shore I ©1983 Ship to Shore, Inc., by Jan Robinson, Charlotte, NC (North Carolina)

Ship to Shore II ©1985 Ship to Shore, Inc., by Jan Robinson, Charlotte, NC (North Carolina)

A Shower of Roses ©1996 St. Therese Catholic Church, by St. Therese Catholic Church, Abbeville, LA (Louisiana II)

Simply Sensational, by Our Lady Queen of Apostles Parish, Hamtramck, MI (Michigan)

Simply Simpatico ©1981 The Junior League of Albuquerque, Inc., by The Junior League of Albuquerque, Albuquerque, NM (New Mexico)

Sisters Two II, by Nancy Barth and Sue Hergert, Ashland, KS (Great Plains)

The Smithfield Cookbook ©1978 Smithfield Junior Woman's Club, by The Junior Woman's Club of Smithfield, Smithfield, VA (Virginia)

Some Like It South! ©1984 The Junior League of Pensacola, Inc., by Junior League of Pensacola, Pensacola, FL (Florida)

Something Special Cookbook, by Areline Bolerjack, Enid, OK (Oklahoma)

Soupçon II ©1982 The Junior League of Chicago Inc., by The Junior League of Chicago, Inc., Chicago, IL (Illinois)

Southern Flavors' Little Chocolate Book ©1991 Southern Flavors, Inc., by Southern Flavors, Inc., Pine Bluff, AR (Arkansas)

Southwest Cookin', by Southwest Hospital Auxiliary, Little Rock, AR (Arkansas)

Contributors

A Sprinkling of Favorite Recipes, by Ronald McDonald House, Youngstown, OH (Ohio)

The Steinbeck House Cookbook ©The Valley Guild, by The Valley Guild, Salinas, CA (California)

Suncoast Seasons ©1984 Dunedin Youth Guild, Inc., by Dunedin Youth Guild, Inc., Dunedin, FL (Florida)

Sunny Side Up ©1980 The Junior League of Fort Lauderdale, Inc, by The Junior League of Fort Lauderdale, Fort Lauderdale, FL (Florida)

Symphony of Flavors, by Associates of the Redlands Bowl, Redlands, CA (California)

Taking Culinary Liberties, by Liberty High School Library, Library / Media Center, Colorado Springs, CO (Colorado)

Talk About Good II ©1979 The Junior League of Lafayette, Inc., by Junior League of Lafayette, Lafayette, LA (Louisiana)

A Taste of Salt Air & Island Kitchens, by Ladies Auxiliary of the Block Island Volunteer Fire Department, Block Island, RI (New England)

A Taste of Columbus Vol IV ©1991 Corban Productions, by Beth and David Chilcoat, Corban Productions, Worthington, OH (Ohio)

A Taste of Georgia ©1977 Newnan Junior Service League, by Newnan Junior Service League, Newnan, GA (Georgia)

Taste the Good Life! Nebraska Cookbook ©1991 Cookbooks by Morris Press, by Morris Press, Kearney, NE (Great Plains)

Tastes & Tales From Texas...With Love ©1984 Peg Hein, by Peg Hein, Heinco, Austin, TX (Texas)

Tasting Tea Treasures ©1984 Greenville Junior Woman's Club, by Greenville Junior Woman's Club, Greenville, MS (Mississippi)

A Tasting Tour Through Washington County ©1987 Springfield Woman's Club, by The Springfield Woman's Club, Springfield, MO (Kentucky)

Tea-Time at the Masters® ©1977 The Junior League of Augusta, GA Inc., by Junior League of Augusta, Inc., Augusta, GA (Georgia)

Texas Historic Inns Cookbook ©1985 Ann Ruff and Gail Drago, by Ann Ruff and Gail Drago, Texas Monthly Press, Austin, TX (Texas)

Thank Heaven for Home Made Cooks, by Dover Christian Women's Fellowship, Dover, OK (Oklahoma)

Thank Heaven for Home Made Cooks, by First Congregational U.C.C., Oconomowoc, WI (Wisconsin)

Think Healthy, by Fairfax County Department of Extension, Fairfax, VA (Virginia)

A Thyme For All Seasons ©1982 Junior League of Duluth, by Junior League of Duluth, Duluth, MN (Minnesota)

Trading Secrets, by Beaumont Heritage Society, Beaumont, TX (Texas)

Tradition in the Kitchen 2 ©1993 North Suburban Beth El Sisterhood, by North Suburban Beth El Sisterhood, Highland Park, IL (Illinois)

A Trim & Terrific Louisiana Kitchen ©1993 Holly Berkowitz Clegg, by Holly B. Clegg, Clarkson Potter, New York, NY (Louisiana II)

Trim & Terrific One-Dish Favorites ©1997 Holly Berkowitz Clegg, Inc., by Holly B. Clegg, Clarkson Potter, New York, NY (Louisiana II)

Trinity Lutheran Church Centennial Cookbook, by Trinity Lutheran Church, Mallard, IA (Iowa)

25th Anniversary Cookbook, by Lancaster Montessori School, Lancaster, OH (Ohio)

Twickenham Tables ©1988 The Twickenham Historical Preservation District Association, Inc., by Twickenham Historic Preservation District Association, Huntsville, AL (Alabama)

Up a Country Lane Cookbook ©1993 Evelyn Birkby, by University of Iowa Press, Iowa City, IA (Iowa)

Contributors

The Very Special Raspberry Cookbook ©1993 The Very Special Raspberry Cookbook Committee, by Carrie Tingley Hospital Foundation, Albuquerque, NM (New Mexico)

A Very Special Treat, by Arkansas Special Olympics, Little Rock, AR (Arkansas)

Vintage Vicksburg ©1985 Vicksburg Junior Woman's Club, by Vicksburg Junior Auxiliary, Vicksburg, MS (Mississippi)

Virginia Hospitality ©1975 The Junior League of Hampton Roads, Inc., by The Junior League of Hampton Roads, Inc., Hampton, VA (Virginia)

The Virginia Presidential Homes Cookbook ©1995 Historic Sherwood Forest Corporation, by Payne Bouknight Tyler, Charles City, VA (Virginia)

Watonga Cheese Festival Cookbook 17th Edition, by Watonga Cheese Festival, Watonga, OK (Oklahoma)

We're Cookin' in Cucamonga, by Betsy Neil, Rancho Cucamonga, CA (California)

Well Seasoned ©1982 Les Passees, Inc., by Les Passees Publications, Memphis, TN (Tennessee)

What Is It? What Do I Do With It? ©1978 Beth Tartan and Fran Parker, by Beth Tartan and Fran Parker, TarPar Ltd, Kinston, NC (North Carolina)

THE What In The World Are We Going To Have For Dinner? COOKBOOK ©1987 Sarah E. Drummond, by Sarah E. Drummond, Richmond, VA (Virginia)

What's Cookin' in Melon Country, by Rocky Ford Chamber of Commerce, Rocky Ford, CO (Colorado)

What's Cooking at Trinity, by Trinity Evangelical Lutheran Church, Wexford, PA (Pennsylvania)

When Dinnerbells Ring ©1978 Talladega Junior Welfare League, by Talladega Junior Welfare League, Talladega, AL (Alabama)

The Wild Wild West ©1991 The Junior League of Odessa, Inc., by The Junior League of Odessa, Odessa, TX (Texas II)

Woodbine Public Community Library Cookbook, by Woodbine Public Library, Woodbine, IA (Iowa)

Wyndmere Community Alumni Cookbook, by Wyndmere Community Center, Wyndmere, ND (Great Plains)

WYVE's Cookbook/Photo Album ©1990 WYVE Radio, by WYVE Radio Station, Wytheville, VA (Virginia)

Index

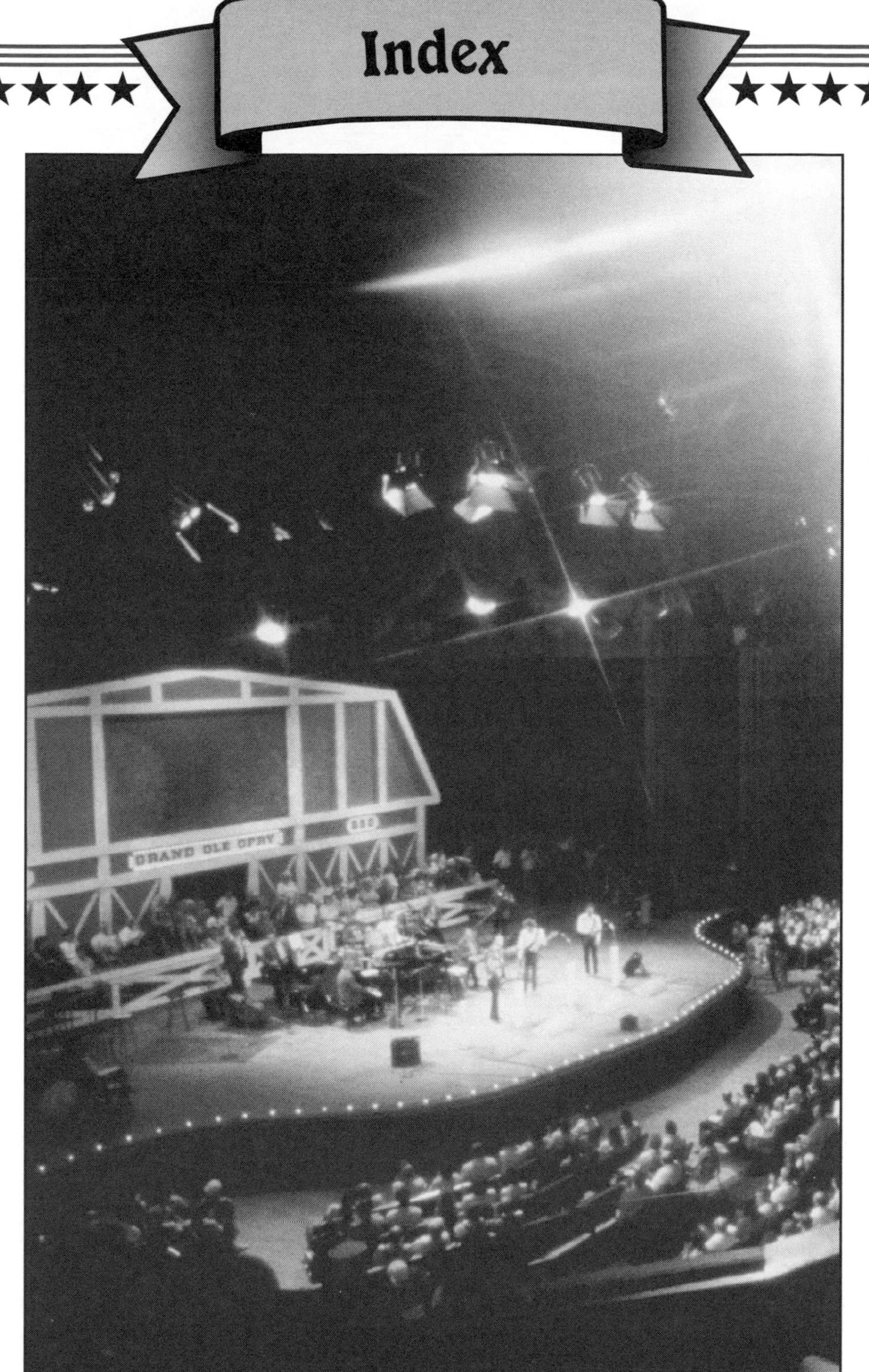

The Grand Ole Opry in Nashville, Tennessee, is the most respected institution in all of country music. Through the years, hundreds of artists have entertained on the Opry stage including such legends as Hank Williams, Sr., Patsy Cline and Elvis Presley.

PHOTO BY DONNIE BEAUCHAMP COURTESY OF GRAND OLE OPRY

Index

Index

Index

Index

Index

Q

R

S

BEST OF THE BEST STATE COOKBOOK SERIES

BEST of the BEST
from
ARIZONA
COOKBOOK
FAVORITE COOKBOOKS

Best of the Best
from
ARKANSAS
Cookbook
Selected Recipes from Arkansas'
FAVORITE COOKBOOKS

BEST of the BEST
from
California
COOKBOOK
Selected Recipes from California's
FAVORITE COOKBOOKS

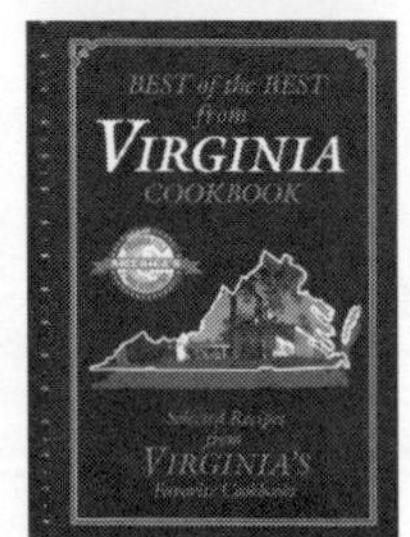

BEST OF THE BEST cookbooks shown above have been completed as of December 31, 2000.

BEST OF THE BEST STATE COOKBOOK SERIES

Cookbooks listed below have been completed as of December 31, 2000.

Best of the Best from
ALABAMA
288 pages

Best of the Best from
ARIZONA
288 pages

Best of the Best from
ARKANSAS
288 pages

Best of the Best from
CALIFORNIA
368 pages

Best of the Best from
COLORADO
288 pages

Best of the Best from
FLORIDA
288 pages

Best of the Best from
GEORGIA
336 pages

Best of the Best from the
GREAT PLAINS
288 pages

Best of the Best from
ILLINOIS
288 pages

Best of the Best from
INDIANA
288 pages

Best of the Best from
IOWA
288 pages

Best of the Best from
KENTUCKY
288 pages

Best of the Best from
LOUISIANA
288 pages

Best of the Best from
LOUISIANA II
288 pages

Best of the Best from
MICHIGAN
288 pages

Best of the Best from
MINNESOTA
288 pages

Best of the Best from
MISSISSIPPI
288 pages

Best of the Best from
MISSOURI
304 pages

Best of the Best from
NEW ENGLAND
368 pages

Best of the Best from
NEW MEXICO
288 pages

Best of the Best from
NORTH CAROLINA
288 pages

Best of the Best from
OHIO
352 pages

Best of the Best from
OKLAHOMA
288 pages

Best of the Best from
PENNSYLVANIA
320 pages

Best of the Best from
SOUTH CAROLINA
288 pages

Best of the Best from
TENNESSEE
288 pages

Best of the Best from
TEXAS
352 pages

Best of the Best from
TEXAS II
352 pages

Best of the Best from
VIRGINIA
320 pages

Best of the Best from
WISCONSIN
288 pages

Note: All cookbooks are ringbound except Arizona and California, which are paperbound.

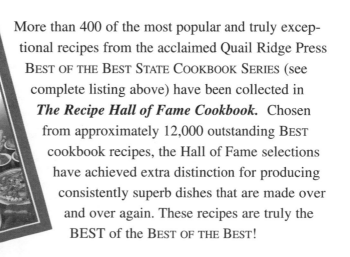

More than 400 of the most popular and truly exceptional recipes from the acclaimed Quail Ridge Press BEST OF THE BEST STATE COOKBOOK SERIES (see complete listing above) have been collected in ***The Recipe Hall of Fame Cookbook.*** Chosen from approximately 12,000 outstanding BEST cookbook recipes, the Hall of Fame selections have achieved extra distinction for producing consistently superb dishes that are made over and over again. These recipes are truly the BEST of the BEST OF THE BEST!

Recipe Hall of Fame Dessert Cookbook

An Entire Cookbook of Incredible Desserts!

What's for dessert? A strawberry shortcake! A flaky apple pastry! A light soufflé! How about cheesecake? Or let's just have some cookies and ice cream! No matter what dessert you choose, you'll find the BEST recipe for it in this book.

From old standards like Red Velvet Cake and Old-Fashioned Lemon Meringue Pie, to quick and easy favorites like Apple Spoon-Ups and Lazy Betty, to new and exciting creations like Pastry Tulip Cups and Mocha Polka Nut Torte, each of these incredibly delicious desserts will inspire a standing ovation.

Following the success of *The Recipe Hall of Fame Cookbook,* which sold over 200,000 copies in its first year, this newest book in the Recipe Hall of Fame Collection is sure to become a classic. Chosen from the more than 4,000 dessert recipes in the Best of the Best State Cookbook Series, each of which is already a chosen favorite from hundreds, these 318 recipes are the most popular, most requested, most memorable, knock-your-socks-off desserts ever!

Editors Gwen McKee and Barbara Moseley with winning recipes from Best of the Best State cookbooks.

Shown on the Cover: Holiday Chocolate Cake, Candy Counter Cookies, Toffee Crunch Trifle, Blueberry Cheesecake Macadamia, Margarita Pie, Amaretto Cream Puffs, Chocolate Truffles, White-Dipped Strawberries, Coconut Bonbons, Cherry Divinity, Piña Colada Rum Balls and Forgotten Kisses.

Cookbook / $16.95